# CONTENTS

AF235213

## PART 1  THE THAMES PATH 5

THE TIMELESS PATH  7
PRACTICALITIES 12
THE FIX 14
12 WONDERS OF THE THAMES PATH  15

## PART 2  THE CHALK STREAM 31

1. THAMES SOURCE TO HAILSTONE HILL ................................. 33
2. HAILSTONE HILL TO BYDEMILL BROOK ........................... 47
3. BYDEMILL BROOK TO RADCOT LOCK ............................. 63
4. RADCOT LOCK TO NEWBRIDGE ........................................ 79
5. NEWBRIDGE TO KING'S LOCK ........................................... 99
6. KING'S LOCK TO SANDFORD LOCK ...............................117
7. SANDFORD LOCK TO CLIFTON HAMPDEN BRIDGE .......137
8. CLIFTON HAMPDEN TO WALLINGFORD ....................... 155
9. WALLINGFORD TO WHITCHURCH ................................. 173
10. WHITCHURCH TO SHIPLAKE ......................................... 191
11. SHIPLAKE TO HURLEY ................................................... 213
12. HURLEY TO MAIDENHEAD BRIDGE ............................ 233
13. MAIDENHEAD BRIDGE TO OLD WINDSOR..................... 251
14. OLD WINDSOR TO SHEPPERTON LOCK ...................... 269
15. SHEPPERTON LOCK TO KINGSTON BRIDGE ................. 285
16. KINGSTON BRIDGE TO HAMMERSMITH BRIDGE ........ 301
17. HAMMERSMITH BRIDGE TO TOWER BRIDGE................. 325
18. TOWER BRIDGE TO WOOLWICH FOOT TUNNEL ........ 349

For Mum,
Our favourite river

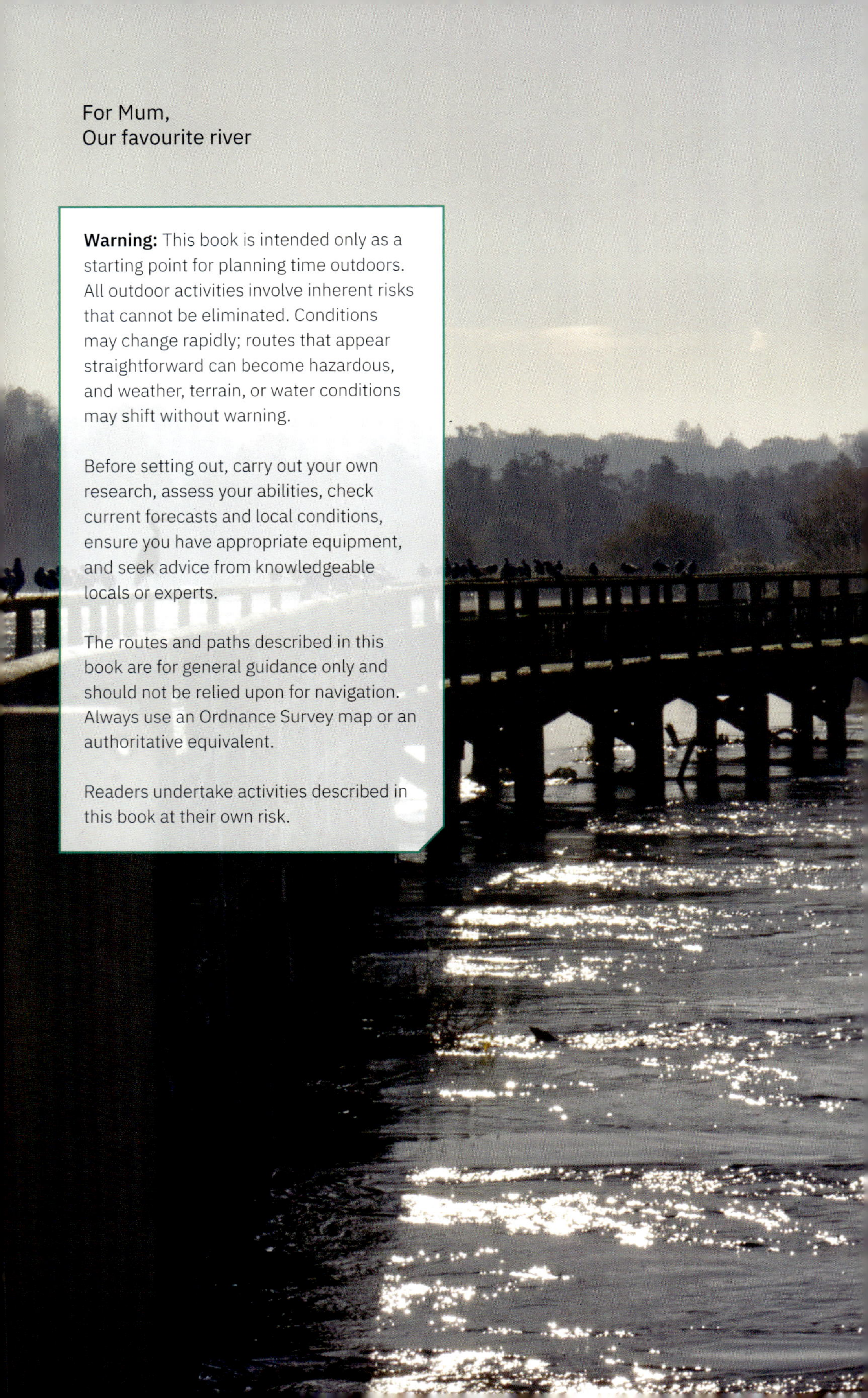

**Warning:** This book is intended only as a starting point for planning time outdoors. All outdoor activities involve inherent risks that cannot be eliminated. Conditions may change rapidly; routes that appear straightforward can become hazardous, and weather, terrain, or water conditions may shift without warning.

Before setting out, carry out your own research, assess your abilities, check current forecasts and local conditions, ensure you have appropriate equipment, and seek advice from knowledgeable locals or experts.

The routes and paths described in this book are for general guidance only and should not be relied upon for navigation. Always use an Ordnance Survey map or an authoritative equivalent.

Readers undertake activities described in this book at their own risk.

# STEPHEN NEALE

# THE
# THAMES
## PATH

## 1,000 mini adventures along England's only river-based National Trail

CONWAY

LONDON · OXFORD · NEW YORK · NEW DELHI · SYDNEY

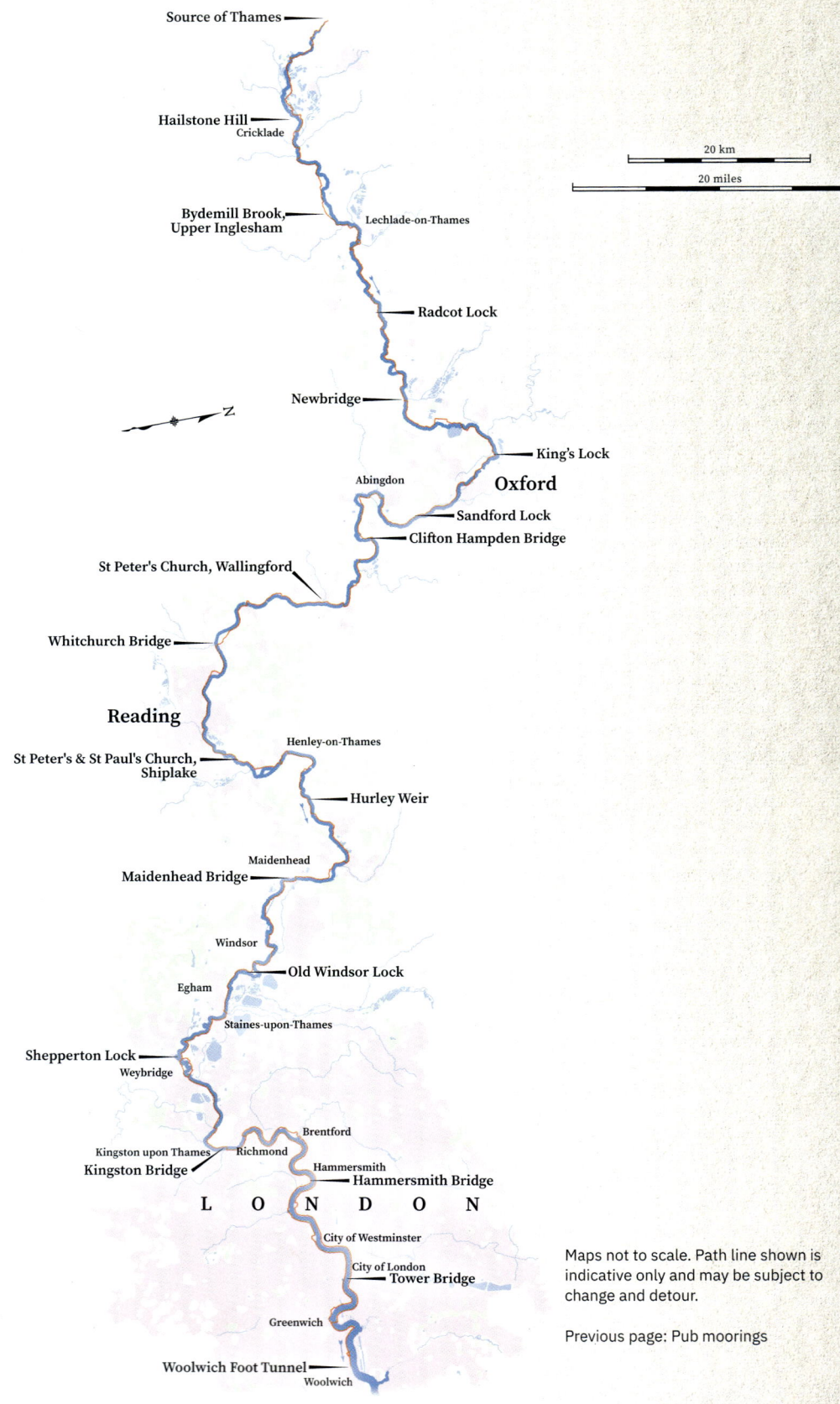

Source of Thames

Hailstone Hill
Cricklade

Bydemill Brook,
Upper Inglesham
Lechlade-on-Thames

Radcot Lock

Newbridge

King's Lock

Abingdon
**Oxford**

Sandford Lock
Clifton Hampden Bridge

N

St Peter's Church, Wallingford

Whitchurch Bridge

**Reading**

Henley-on-Thames

St Peter's & St Paul's Church,
Shiplake

Hurley Weir

Maidenhead
Maidenhead Bridge

Windsor

Old Windsor Lock

Egham

Staines-upon-Thames

Shepperton Lock
Weybridge

Brentford

Kingston upon Thames   Richmond
Kingston Bridge
Hammersmith
Hammersmith Bridge

**L O N D O N**

City of Westminster
City of London
**Tower Bridge**

Greenwich

Woolwich Foot Tunnel
Woolwich

20 km

20 miles

Maps not to scale. Path line shown is
indicative only and may be subject to
change and detour.

Previous page: Pub moorings

PART 1

# THE THAMES PATH

St Anne's Church, Limehouse

# THE TIMELESS PATH

The busy bee has no time for sorrow.
The hours of folly are measur'd by the clock;
but of wisdom,
No clock can measure...

—*from* The Marriage of Heaven and Hell *by William Blake*

Inside the grounds of a modest church in Limehouse, 300 yards from the Thames Docks, stands a grubby little pyramid made of Portland stone. It wasn't always grubby. When it was erected in 1727, it shone like a beacon – a gleaming pyramid of white chalk powder that had fallen through the narrow point of a long funnel. Today it looks out of place, as if a garden architect had mistakenly planted a palm tree in the grounds of a classic English garden.

Pyramids were iconic symbols of transformation in the ancient world – places where heaven and earth touched, where time stood still. This book is about that very transformation: how to cheat time. It's about your relationship with nature and how deepening that connection will help you beat the clock – and feel alive. More alive than the psychedelic rush you feel dancing in warm, shallow water at midnight with friends drinking nothing but warm breeze.

Most people, including you, don't interact with nature enough – because of time. That's an irony ancient people knew about... and secretly loved. The Thames is sometimes called Isis – the Egyptian goddess who defeated time. The Thames shows us how to cheat time.

This book will help you do that.

## DETOURS AND STEPPING STONES

Your journey is split into 18 sections from the source of the Thames to Woolwich. Each is represented by a stone: a rock, a stepping stone. But the stones in this book are not steps in time; they are steps into space – places to anticipate, to explore, to leave behind and to reflect on. The stepping stone is the first secret to cheating time. The second secret is detour.

Detours are attached to the 10 large stepping stones in each chapter. They are places within a short walk, paddle or cycle of the main path; anything from about 200 yards away. Detours are how you will lose yourself. You won't begin to know who, or where, you are until you are lost. They are places that invite you to step off the beaten track and follow your curiosity – to step away from the memory of where you were supposed to be going. These are steps into the unknown, like burning bushes of life that capture your attention, pulling you away from the order of your planned journey towards something more chaotic and unknown. Like sneaking off work for

Stepping Stones near the Thames

## CRONUS & ISIS

A 19th-century statue of Father Thames (Father Time) gazes over the water at St John's Lock, just east of Lechlade, in Gloucestershire. St John's is the furthest upstream lock on the Thames. It takes its name from a 13th-century priory that was there for a few hundred years – but it's long gone now. The lock was built of stone in 1790 and replaced in 1905. Nothing lasts forever. Time conquers all. St John's Lock lies 74 miles, as the crow flies, from the Greenwich's Prime Meridian – the timeline for the world's time zones. Isn't that wonderful? Thames, the home of time.

Cronus is the son of Mother Earth, Gaia, and father to the goddess Isis. He is often associated with a large dragon or crocodile, and of course, the Thames Serpent. His story goes like this: Cronos is the monster who devours his own children, until he is tricked by Isis into eating a giant (stepping) stone disguised as a baby, and then killed by his children. But he still plagues the earth, consuming as many in death as he can.

So we needed a fix – not a death fix but a time fix. Isis was the fix.

She wrapped her idea (baby) inside a single stone. She gave her baby a name: Horus – attention. We know it today in its loosest sense as meditation, but that is only a small part of

a guilty pleasure or finding time to meet a secret lover, detours make a short day feel much longer. They are ways of reconnecting with yourself, and with nature, as you blend chaos, order and danger. This involves taking risks – allowing detours to have your attention, before finding a way back.

Like the bridge in the song that creates tension – before the melody returns to verse or chorus.

## THE LIVING PATH

Nature will interact with you as you shift from walking the path, to leaving it, to becoming part of it. It will interact with you all the way. The slower you go, the more communication you'll feel between your frontal lobes and the wild – both inside and outside yourself. This connection releases the love and play hormone oxytocin. We don't need to get under the hood, any more than that.

Try to touch, taste, smell and listen as much as you can along the way. As you engage more with these four senses, your eyes will start to open. Touching Thames water is important – but even more important is getting your shoes and socks off and feeling grass under your feet. Discarding shoes is a universal sign of transformation – the second sign, after the pyramid. Walking barefoot on grass is superconductivity: the release of more energy from your body's cells, connecting to Earth's 7Hz 'timeless' frequency.

Touching nature on the Thames

what the ancient worship of Isis embodied.

If the first secret of cheating time is the stepping stone, and the second is detour, then the third and final secret is attention.

Like all goddesses and gods, Isis was the personification of that idea – the secret weapon that could defeat the monster. Her superpower was attention. But you cannot choose to be attentive.

It chooses you.

# HORUS

On the Thames north bank, almost opposite Embankment Tube station, stands a 20m (68ft) granite obelisk known as Cleopatra's Needle. Twice a month, during spring tides when the sun, earth, and moon align, the obelisk is splashed by sea spray. A plaque at the obelisk's base commemorates six men who were lost at sea delivering it from Cairo to London in 1877: William Askin, Michael Burns, James Gardiner, William Donald, Joseph Benton and William Patan. They were last seen trying to deliver Cleopatra's Needle on its voyage from Egypt to England.

The needle dates to 1450 BC and bears 12 hieroglyphic inscriptions carved into its four sides. Deciphered in 1926, these reveal the secret name of an Egyptian god: Horus.

Horus was the personification of paying attention, which is why he had a large eye. If these words have your attention, you are transcending time. If you're concentrating on them, they haven't captured you. Watching a baby smile at you might grab your attention. Maybe not. But you must start noticing what grabs your attention – because it's important.

Go touch Cleopatra's Needle and see if it gets your attention. It's breathtaking in scale and story. There are not enough pages here to do it justice. Touch the base and look up at the inscriptions. They are worn and alien, but according to the French philologist Jean-François Champollion, they read: 'Horus. King of the two countries. Who extends the south to the

Thames Time Dial at Tower Bridge

Great Sea. Son of the sun.'

The two 'countries' are Upper and Lower Egypt. These zones define where the Nile meets the tidal sea, and where the Nile is born from natural springs – just as we have Thames freshwater merging with Thames saltwater.

Stories are rarely what they seem; there are secrets to mixing freshwater and saltwater

Cleopatra's Needle

known to alchemists. You'll uncover those secrets as you explore the Thames. An alchemical experience.

This is because you'll be walking in one of the rarest habitats in the world. Not the Nile. But a living, breathing fossil of immense life: a chalk stream.

Loddon Lillies on a Thames chalk stream

# CHALK

Just south of Henley, the Thames becomes remarkable. It does something that no other river in the world can. Very briefly, it changes identity – it transforms. The freshwater river becomes a chalk stream, before returning to non-chalk water a little downstream.

Life originates with the mixing of two waters in the Babylonian creation myth – the oldest surviving creation story. The Babylonian god Tiamat, an incarnation of Isis in another time and culture, personified salt, or chalk water. The freshwater god was Apsu. The first life was born when those two waters mingled and merged.

# CHALK STREAMS

Chalk streams are rarer than glowworms in midday sun, but over the next five minutes we're going to give them some attention. There are only about 200 chalk streams in the world – and almost all are in southern England. Many of England's chalk streams link to the Thames, and six chalk streams empty directly into it.

Chalk streams are nature's most precious environments – incubators of new life. Atlantic salmon and trout spawn here, while rare plants including Loddon lilies, water crowfoot and starwort thrive along their banks. Mayflies, stoneflies, damselflies and dragonflies fly above the water's surface. Grayling, bullhead and minnows swim below. Kingfishers, bats, otters and water voles all depend on this habitat.

Chalk streams are not just quirky or mystical. They are scientifically remarkable for two special qualities: their temperature and nutrient content. While the temperatures of the world's seas and rivers are regulated by season and sunlight, chalk streams do something different. Their unique chemistry maintains a steady 10°C (50°F) year-round. That's important because it means they're cool in summer and warm in winter. Much like an English woodland, they act like an incubator for rare microbes and fauna.

This remarkable temperature regulation comes from rainwater percolating through chalk aquifers, absorbing a chemical cocktail of calcium and carbonate ions before it's forced back to the surface. The 'salt' that chemists refer to in chalk is a compound in fossil form that interacts with water. This compound is known as 'ionic', and its origin is the ionosphere. The ionosphere is literally 'out of this world' – it starts from about 30 miles above sea level, and it forms the inner edge of the Earth's magnetic sphere.

Ions affect our moods. You'll feel their impact before and after a storm: positive ions beforehand, negative ions afterwards. The presence of ions is strongest in wooded areas, where trees photosynthesise and give off oxygen.

# TREES

Where the river bends past Windsor Castle there is an island: Ankerwycke Island. Cross over from the other side of the riverbank, and you'll find the Ankerwycke Yew – a tree that is more than 2,000 years old. The mythical status of that tree transcends its age. It transcends time. So much so that it was chosen as the location for sealing and signing Magna Carta 800 years ago at Runnymede.

Wooded islands are another rare habitat – but not here on the Thames. From source to sea, the entire river forms an archipelago of more than 200 islands and islets. Almost all of them are wooded.

Willow dominates. English yews demand our attention. The oak enshrines English culture and lore. But it's the willow that will shape your Thames journey. Its shades and colours of yellow and green are more vivid and varied than anything else along the path – especially where they catch the glow of chalk light. Willow has been an important part of English life for

Ankerwycke Yew

Culham to Wallingford

thousands of years – crafted into ancient tools, woven into wicker baskets and carved into cricket bats. It holds a mysterious role in Celtic and Druidic rituals, most notably in the symbolic 'wicker man'. Even Christians in England embraced it as a substitute for palm branches on Palm Sunday during the Middle Ages.

In Egyptian mythology, the willow held special power as an aspirin-like pain reliever and death remedy. When they buried their god Osiris – Isis' brother, lover and husband – he was wrapped under and around a willow. The Thames is as much about myth and fairy tale as it is about art and artisan. It is as much Nile as England. The wind in the willows.

To walk with willow, yew and chalk stream is to lose memory of everything you've learnt since leaving childhood. It's time to forget – to find nature without the ticking of a clock, where you and the Thames can stretch backwards, forwards and outwards into the eternal moment of now.

To cheat time.

# PRACTICALITIES

Jubilee River

## BOOT, BIKE AND BOAT

There are three ways to move along the Thames (unless you're a bird or a ghost): by boot, by bike or by boat.

**The boot sections of this trail mostly follow the path.**
**The boat sections follow water.**
**Bikes are the third way.**

I love pushing my own bike. The bike is a multipurpose tool: either a wheelbarrow for gear (bags and packraft) or fast access to the many detours along the way that are too good to miss. Most of these are either bridleways, greenways or, best of all, boreens: those wonderful lost lanes that cars avoid at all costs because they're potholed, have no turning places and are narrower than an egg box.

I tramp with a £600 packraft, a £100 single-speed bike bought on eBay, and a £50 pair of boots or sandals. That's a lot of money – but it provides a lot of freedom, for a lot of years.

### Boots (or sandals)
Boots are worn or carried (on the bike).

### Boat: packraft
The packraft sits wrapped around my handlebars like a long airbag under the dashboard of a car. It's not self-inflating, so I carry two tiny battery inflaters that double up as phone chargers. The packraft paddle handles sit strapped to the crossbar and the paddles are packed inside a small pack that I carry on my back.

The packraft doubles up as a shelter from the rain, when used as a roof that is pegged down. On dry summer nights, it makes a great mattress to sleep on.

Backwaters are where the fun really happens. These are the places where boots and bikes can't get to. With punts, paddleboards, canoes and kayaks, Thames offers the best of England's waters.

Pangbourne Meadows

M4 Bridge

## Bike: Single Speed

The bike is pushed on the Thames Path, ridden along detours from the path, or carried inside the packraft when on water. It's simple, light, has a coaster brake, is single-speed, and can be left around without too much risk of being stolen.

## SHELTER

Shelter should always start with clothing. Carry a waterproof stuff bag of dry clothes in all weather: heatwave and blizzard.

There's not much need to ever go beyond this, unless weather warnings are out. Here's the kit:

**1.** a Merino wool base layer, upper and lower
**2.** a micro-thin fleece
**3.** a wool hat
**4.** cotton trousers that zip off into shorts
**5.** a combination of hard-shell jacket/bottoms and a soft-shell coat
**6.** a sleeping bag with a tog rating that matches the season, and a lightweight green bivvy.

# HOW MANY MILES?

Go at your own pace. The paths in this book have been explored at 10 miles a day, with the occasional detour. The world continues to change in 2026. Campsites, B&Bs and aires are unreliable, unsustainable and inconsistent as reliable options in my opinion. Treat them as bonuses rather than necessities. Start to learn how to wild camp, hide and how to have no impact.

Visiting the Thames for a one-day hike or paddle is as much fun as a six- or seven-day adventure. Mix and match. Bathe in cold water every morning or night, if you get the chance. It will keep you oiled.

# PUBLIC TRANSPORT

Nothing is quite as magnificent for public transport as the Thames Path. There are days when the rail or bus journey back to a car, campsite or hostel is as much fun as anything experienced all day.

There are one or two gaps in service at the furthest edges of Thames Path in the east, but it still has the best public transport network of any National Trail.

Tadpole Bridge to Bablock Hythe

# THE FIX

You have in your hands a rough guide to connecting with nature along the Chalk Path

This book aims to help you find the time to do that and to fuel your energy levels across a series of mini-adventures throughout a day. Your slow journey is about inhaling Thames air, earth and water, to stoke a fire that makes you feel alive and grabs your attention.

If you make it back home, share your stories. Storytelling is the final fix.

## KEY TO SYMBOLS

These symbols appear alongside location titles as a guide to the habitat, geology or theme of a place:

Wild Water

Woodland

Mother Nature

Good for Dark Skies

Accomodation

Restaurant or Café

Sacred

Historic

Boat Facilities

Bridges

Detour by Foot

Cycling

Packrafting

Stepping Stones

### KEY TO ABBREVIATIONS

This is a guide to the directional abbreviations used within the location texts:

N – north
S – south
W – west
E – east
R – right
L – left
FP – footpath

BW – bridleway
Rd – road
Ln – lane
PRoW – public right of way
ECP – England Coast Path
TP – Thames Path
FB – footbridge

# 12 WONDERS OF THE THAMES PATH

## Best for

### AIR
1. MABON: AUTUMN EQUINOX
2. ART
3. MAGIC

### WATER
4. WINTER SOLSTICE
5. CHALK STREAMS
6. KAYAKS AND PADDLEBOARDS

### EARTH
7. OSTARA: SPRING EQUINOX
8. WILD WOODS
9. MOTHER NATURE

### FIRE
10. SUMMER SOLSTICE
11. SUNSETS AND HILL VIEWS
12. STAR WATCHING

Pub moorings

Runnymede

# AIR

## 1. Best for...

### MABON: AUTUMN EQUINOX

The end of English summer might be the best Thames time. It's full of wild food, sunflower-edged fields and dazzling trees reflected in water.

The first signs of autumn are fruit: grain fields ripen, blackberries fatten and apples fall. By late September beech trees are heavy with nuts, and the paths and wooded edges ferment with rotting fruit and the sweet smell of death.

The September equinox occurs 21–24 September, when the sun crosses the celestial equator and rises directly in the east, setting directly in the west. Before this date the sun rises and sets farther north, and after the equinox it rises and sets more to the south. Around the equinox, the sun dips lower in the sky, making this the best time to explore the Thames' wooded shores; where beams of sunlight creep beneath the green leaf canopy onto the forest floor.

Look for dewy dawns and mist-filled mornings. This is the best time to explore chalk streams. Look for fungi each morning around damp edges before feet, paws or mice nibble them away.

Late October and November are best for exploring the wooded river valleys that glow in sunshine and dappled reds that seem to have the ability to hang forever. It's also the season when geese and migrant waders return.

After the blaze of colour, nuts and fruit are the next treasures: chestnuts, hazelnuts and early sloes after an early frost.

For all the beauty of autumn, don't underestimate how much food you would need to find if really trying to stay alive. Pay attention to how squirrels forage. See how much, and how fast, they eat. They need to eat seeds from 100 spruce cones just to survive a day.

Mill Bank, Henley

Each location listed in these boxes is numbered to match the 10-mile section of the Thames Path in which it appears – so 4. means you'll find the location in the fourth stretch from the source.

**4. Rushey Lock** – Once a famous campsite for decades. These days, you shouldn't rely on it unless you're truly in need of rest.

**4. Tenfoot Bridge** – Watch kids jump and dive from the bridge, even as warning signs say danger.

**5. Pinkhill Weir Crossways** – One of the most beautiful locks on the Thames.

**9. Berkshire Towpath** – It may seem a shame to leave the river for an inland detour – but this one's worth it.

**9. St Bartholomew's Church** – A flint and stone church built in the late 13th century. Jethro Tull is buried here.

**9. Basildon Park** – Landscaped by Lancelot 'Capability' Brown. It is one of many proofs that he has left of excellence in his art.

**10. Brunel Bridge** – A wooden bridge built by Brunel alongside the Great Western Railway bridge.

**12. Grosvenor Island** – Best viewed from Richmond.

**13. Bray Lock** – Rebuilt in 1885 after Charles Dickens described the previous structure as 'rotten and dangerous'.

**17. Battersea Bridge Gardens** – Touch the James McNeill Whistler Statue under the green canopy of poplar trees.

Demon with Bowl statue

# 2. Best for...

## ART

The Thames is where you'll fall in love with England, and then London. The Thames, the tide, the smoke. So much of the beauty is connected to reflections in the water, not in what is real.

Art is in the willowy landscapes and meadows where water runs between banks of reeds, grasses and chalky plants. The mysterious, opaline glow that falls over the Thames at dawn and dusk. Artists tried to catch that long before Monet, Turner and Gainsborough – the luminescence of chalk, water and yew, blurred in an invisible spray of mist and ions. White and green.

At midday in spring the narrow paths east of Oxford are bright purple tunnels of sweet-smelling Himalayan balsam; bushes wider than a tennis court of roses, and sweeter too. Invasive and beautiful, just like you. The willows bend in the breeze like feathers. Poplars turn silver on the merest breath of wind, shimmering like water running over a stoney bank. You feel past, present and future converge in all these slow encounters of beauty. Touching new things, new ideas and nature in a timeless song, borrowed by blackbirds.

J.M.W. Turner, William Blake, Dante Gabriel Rossetti, William Hogarth and William Morris. They loved this place so much they chose to live here, on the Thames. Non-Brits lived here too: Claude Monet, James Whistler and Vincent van Gogh. New York and Paris are the art centres of the world. But nothing compares with the Thames from village to city centre, as the influencer of culture, history and art. That has almost nothing to do with us, and everything to do with the unique nature of Thames air.

Shiplake

## 3. Best for...
### MAGIC
Magic is an energy force that is beyond our knowledge. It's a faith. But we are learning. Thames air is full of three things: energy, frequency and vibration.

We know enough to understand that we live inside a kind of battery – a world that is charged both negatively and positively. It's why we feel static when things fall a little out of balance. We don't need to know too much, but it helps us to know some basics. Our bodies are made up of trillions of tiny battery cells, powered by energy generators known as mitochondria. Mitochondria need three things to function and give us energy:

**3. Kelmscott Manor House** – The Cotswold home of William Morris.

**8. Joseph Tubb** – See the Poem Tree, a 300-year-old beech carved with Tubb's– 20-line poem in 1844–45.

**11. Shiplake Lock** – George Orwell and his friends fished here.

**11. Henley Bridge** – Look for the sculptures of Isis and Tamesis by Anne Seymour on the bridge that spans the river.

**14. Chertsey Bridge** – The Tate holds a pencil sketch of Chertsey Bridge by the artist J.M.W. Turner.

**15. Garrick Island Path** – Learn the story of David Garrick, who most famously brought Shakespeare to contemporary audiences. He was painted by Thomas Gainsborough.

**16. Alexander Pope's Villa and Grotto** – Pope dug a tunnel beneath the Rd, and, decorating it with spars, it became 'the grotto'.

**16. Gainsborough's Tomb** – Find the grave of William Gainsborough in the local churchyard.

**16. Hogarth's Tomb** – the famous painter and engraver was buried here in 1764.

**16. The William Morris Society** – Based at Kelmscott House in Hammersmith; a magical memorial to Morris' legacy.

Cleopatra's Needle

air, water and earth. The earth takes the form of calcium – or chalk. Together these three elements produce fire, or energy.

The most important hormone linked to survival and success of our children is oxytocin. They need two things to maintain that: to be social and to be in nature. Walking, running or climbing trees outdoors is a brilliant way to be in nature and to make friends.

So connect with the magic of nature. Spend more time around the Thames' calcium-rich environment of chalk streams, green leaf and woodland.

**12. Marlow Lock Island** – There's a marvellous music about Marlow Weir. It's wondrously soothing and indescribably comforting to smoke a lazy pipe and listen to its lingering lullaby, a soothful song,

**12. Picnic Island** – The clue is in the name.

**13. St Michael's Church, Bray** – Its sculptures include a damaged Sheela na Gig.

**13. Summerleaze Footbridge** – A gravel conveyor belt in disguise, taking gravel from the construction of the new Eton College.

**15. The Coronation Stone, Kingston upon Thames** – thought to be the site where Anglo-Saxon kings were crowned.

**16. The National Archives** – Millions of documents tell the stories of the nation.

**17. Waterloo Bridge** – At dawn under mist in September, it glows under a Monet moon.

**17. Cleopatra's Needle** – The Egyptian obelisk from Alexandria sits vertical on the river-stairs of the Victoria Thames Embankment opposite Adelphi Terrace.

**18. Greenwich Reach** – The Royal Naval College buildings were once used by the Royal Hospital School in Greenwich, before becoming part of the National Maritime Museum in 1934.

**18. St Anne's Church, Limehouse** – A pyramid-topped tower, designed by Hawksmoor. The land is medicine. Trees are medicine and magic.

# WATER

## 4. Best for...
### WINTER SOLSTICE

The River Thames is not at its best in winter. But... it is full of water. And that's enough. It's a reason to come.

There's something surreal about wading in lakes of shallow floodwater in proper wellies, or floating in a punt over meadow and earth – moving over water and land that is powder dry and flowering in summer. It feels alchemical, in the way that a tide coming in and out is magic.

The tidal Thames ebbs and flows on the moon, twice a day. The freshwater Thames does the same with the seasons.

The best place to see the flooded Thames is between its source and Lechlade. It's a lake, either side. Inevitably flood means danger. There are many risks around weirs and fast-moving water, so avoid these areas or take advice.

Look for dippers east of Oxford. They are rare on the Thames, but they sometimes feed around stoney parts near the Cotswolds. Dippers are incredible because they can hunt under the ice.

We often miss the magic of winter, tied up in thoughts of grumbling, dark days and the chaos of Christmas.

Solstice – from the Latin sol (sun) and sistere (to stand still) – occurs a few days before Christmas, usually on 21 December, the shortest day. It's a literal reference to the sun dying or appearing to stand still, its daily movement resting at its most northerly point before reversing its direction and moving south. Much like a giant tanker on a sea that can't turn so quickly in the heavenly void, the sun appears motionless for a few days before it picks up the pace again. It's a unique time in nature that sadly mostly passes us by today.

We revel in eclipses with our children but choose to stay indoors with TV and hot dinners at solstice. Our ancient ancestors were wiser than that. They saw things a bit differently. Instead of mourning the changing seasons and the end of summer, they celebrated.

The 'deathly hallows' we experience were a celebration of nature, represented by the iconic motifs of holly, mistletoe and sloes for those who were trapped indoors.

Look for the geometric patterns of ice on grass where mist has been frozen.

Get out there. Stay out all day and gasp when midday winter sun bursts through momentarily like a solar eclipse.

**5. King's Lock** – Spend several hours walking the lock.
**6. Osney Lock** – Look for otters at dawn or dusk around one of the prettiest locks on the Thames.
**16. Teddington Lock** – Explore every nook, bridge and walkway. Get your bearings.
**16. Isleworth Ait (South)** – You must visit at low tide; there are enormous trees.
**17. 118 and 119 Cheyne Walk** – Where J.M.W. Turner spent his final years and died in 1851.
**17. Memorial to Dante Gabriel Rossetti** – Drink stories from the non-functioning water fountain dedicated to the Pre-Raphaelite painter and poet.
**18. Brunel Museum** – A quirky museum on the history of the world's first underwater tunnel.

# 5. Best for...
## CHALK STREAMS

Discover where nature becomes chemist – or alchemist. Calcium chalk is the yang to water's yin: where nature breathes life into nature, and into you. It's where your mitochondrial cells dance to the song of hydra and dust. Calcium and $H_2O$. Alchemy. Memory.

Chalk gives birth to life in a marriage of two worlds coming together. No wonder, then, that chalk wells, streams and waterfalls are associated with the eternal.

Stonehenge and Canterbury are the 'modern' manifestations of that realisation – places marked as shrines so we wouldn't forget or lose the knowledge. But we did both. Isn't that heartbreaking? That we've allowed the sewage farm under the cover of darkness to pollute the most precious font in nature.

Chalk streams epitomise the conjunction of love, marriage and birth – the coming together of two worlds. They do this better than estuaries because while estuaries are a meeting of freshwater and saltwater, of calcium and sodium, chalk streams are an alchemy – a mild,

Culham to Wallingford

Loddon Lily

**3. River Cole** – Densely packed in reeds, mud and birds. A landscape that feels alchemical.

**3. River Coln** – The most beautiful, fast-flowing trout stream on the Thames.

**5. Hagley Pool** – The chalk stream looks plain from the bridge, but it's important.

**10. River Pang** – Find the small chalk stream where it enters the Thames.

**10. Kennet and Avon Canal** – Explore 87 miles of navigable river and canal.

**10. St Patrick Bridge** – Here you can find one of the hidden chalk streams that feeds the river.

**11. Marsh Stream** – Look for the chalk stream opposite Phillimore's Island on the south bank.

**11. River Loddon Chalk Stream** – In the evening the banks in the lanes are bright with numerous glowworms.

**12. River Wye, Bourne End, Buckinghamshire** – Listen to nightingales where the River Wye empties into the Thames close to Bourne End.

**17. River Wandle** – A chalk stream that was once home to William Morris's mill, where he produced wallpaper and fabrics.

mineral-rich alkaline soup of nitrate, phosphate, potassium and silicate that breathes energy and life into cells like a mother's milk.

The Thames is a chalk stream. Don't let anyone tell you otherwise. It's where salmon and trout once bred. There's a salmon ladder, I think, on almost every lock from Teddington to St John's.

The last salmon seen in the Thames was 1972. When I was a child that would've made me cry. Now I've become almost immune. A hypocrite. Look what we've allowed ourselves to become.

Our chalk streams are not dead. They're just polluted – when it rains a lot, when we build over them. Trapped inside human-made ditches we call 'cuts'; like caged canaries inside pipes we foul and choose to look away.

I was going to say: it's not all bad. But it is – because it rains a lot in the UK. The very thing that makes our nation beautiful, rainwater, is the very thing that makes us defile our greatest natural resource. Our sewage system isn't fit for a species that calls itself civilised – let alone for the wild.

A solution is to write to your MP. Tell people. Do something. Anything.

Inhale the chalk air. Touch chalk water and pay attention.

# 6. Best for...
## KAYAKS AND PADDLEBOARDS

Punts, packrafts and paddleboards open up all your options on the Thames. There's nowhere else in the world that can match the Thames for boating. A sliding river to navigate, intersected with unlimited back channels to explore: creeks, canals, riverlets and chalk streams.

The possibilities to camp and explore the undergrowth are multiplied thousands of times with low-beamed, small boats and punts. You now have access to places almost no one else can reach.

Thames navigation is a right enshrined in law. It's been tested in the court, and British justice is remarkably sensible when it comes

Teddington Weir

to the commercial and mindful benefits of UK navigation. If only that extended to sleeping.

This book is largely about the accessible Thames and where it's legal to go. But there are vast sections of riverbank that are inaccessible to the walker. Sometimes these places are among the most beautiful.

There are other times when the lack of access is down to a selfish or shortsighted landowner, past and present. Kayaks, canoes and punts solve that. They combine two magical rights: the public right of way and the right of navigation.

Fishing and kayaking on the tidal Thames are not rights limited by daylight or, more importantly, by time. That's a crucial distinction, because most of our domesticated world outside the four walls of our homes is controlled by time. Things close: libraries, shops, the gym, pubs, parking spaces, school and workplaces.

The same cannot be said for the freshwater Thames. You must either find a legitimate place to wild camp with permission, like a lock campsite managed by the Environmental Agency (if any ever reopen in 2027) or speak to a lock keeper and ask for permission.

Lock keepers are overworked, overstressed and probably, by the time you've approached them, out of love with anyone looking for a pitch for the night. They are, though, the most knowledgeable people on the Thames and will often solve genuine problems for boaters with sleep and mooring concerns.

If in doubt, and in a canoe or punt, use the tried and tested rule: camp late, leave early, leave no mess.

Phillimore's Island, Shiplake

Halfpenny Bridge

## FOR SAFETY

- Check tide times if on the tidal Thames.
- Do not kayak alone.
- Always carry warm clothing and spare sets.
- Always let other people know where you are going.
- Carry a radio or, at the very least, a well-charged phone with spare batteries.

## COMMON SENSE WILD CAMPING ON THE THAMES

- Do it alone.
- Leave no trace.
- Take all rubbish home.
- Stay below the high-tide mark (foreshore).
- Pitch after dusk and pack down before dawn.
- Keep fires well below the high-tide mark.

**3. Halfpenny Bridge** – The official start mark of the navigable Thames.

**3. Cheese Wharf** – A tiny stone beach where kayaks stop over.

**9. Old Papist Way Slipway, Ferry Lane** – A rare treasure. A slipway and parking.

**11. Hurley Lock** – A paradise for onlookers and boaters who come to ride the current.

**12. Marlow Slipway, St Peter's St** – Suck in the river views and Quarry Wood hills.

**12. Boulter's Lock** – Popular for whitewater freestyle kayaking.

**15. Felix Road Recreation Ground** – An old common, with a slip down from the steps.

**16. Richmond Lock** – The lock includes slipways for small boats, which allow kayaks and rowing boats to bypass the sluices.

**16. Grand Union Canal** – The principal navigable waterway between London and the Midlands.

**16. Duke Meadows** – A stone beach and canoe ramp.

# EARTH

## 7. Best for...
### OSTARA: SPRING EQUINOX

Wood anemones, crocuses and snowdrops against wet sunshine and grass are a pleasure beyond words.

The March equinox has a dramatic effect on the Thames as the subsolar point leaves the southern hemisphere and crosses the celestial equator. The moon's pull drags back Thames tides to their absolute lowest in the days following the equinox, making this an incredible time to feel good.

Look for the summer migrant birds returning to nest along the Thames. Storks are back, and starlings are increasing again after a decline.

The Thames Path warms quickly from mid-March, but not too far past an average of 18°C (64°F).

Everything is starting to breed, reproduce and mate. Frogs spawn around ditches and pools by late February. Bees and butterflies are about from March.

White blackthorn blossoms are followed quickly by cherry flowers and hazel catkins.

The bluebells that carpet ancient woodlands in March start to die back by late April, as the air fills with the scents of wild garlic and hawthorn blossom. It's a wonderful moment when this equinox combines with warm weather and low-pressure breezes.

Translucent beech leaves unfurl towards the end of April, later than most others trees. They are refreshing eaten on the move.

This is the best time to wild camp, with the sun setting after 8.30pm and rising with the dawn chorus just before 5am.

Look to hide under hedgerows and water edges by early May when the trees are all full of leaf.

---

**6. The Trout Weir Pool** – A small pebble beach and island beneath the bridge.
**13. The Brocas** – Beech, oak and maple leaves glow with spring sunshine.
**17. Adelphi Terrace** – The home of Dr Thomas Monro, sponsor of J.M.W. Turner. Thomas Girton and others learnt their trade as artists here.
**6. Wolvercote Common** – Listen to skylarks behind the gravel beaches where locals swim.
**12. Battlemead Common** – Wet marshland good for birdwatching
**13. Dorney Lake** – Listen to terns where river meets lake.
**14. Staines Bridge** – The deep water here makes it a popular spot for fishing.
**16. Eel Pie Island** – Watch sand martins and bats flitting over the river and island.
**16. Leg O'Mutton Reservoir** – Look for non-native, escaped pet turtles basking in the sun on the banks.

---

## 8. Best for...
### WILD WOODS

So much of the Thames is enchanted wood.

Trees fall down to the riverbank where pixies play and fairies furl for fun.

The Celts and their predecessors loved the wooded places: the islets, the groves, the chalk hangers and cliffs.

Trees are the most prolific brushstrokes along

Staines Railway Bridge

Source of the Thames

the path and its islets. Nothing quite captures the glory of cool air around the wooded riverbank.

The towering beech hangers of woodland shrink the width of the river in an illusion that is almost garden-like.

You must touch Thames trees as you go. They will touch you back.

Trees are relatively recent in Britain after the long Ice Age. They returned just before we did. Pine, birch and yew first. Their seeds came blown in on the southerly winds or carried by birds.

We're deeply connected to trees. Pay them some attention and touch.

Invaders have been severing indigenous people from their woodland since before the Romans. The English did it in Scotland with the clearances. To walk in these woods and riverside

glades is a freedom that is difficult to measure.

I've never experienced as deep a connection between trees and water as around the Thames. The southern section of the Wye Valley is a rare exception, but it lasts less than 30–40 miles.

Wild English wood is one of the most precious natural habitats we have. Through a combination of good luck, hard work and negotiation, we have remnants of what our ancestors shared and valued most in nature – clean air, water and woodland.

**3. White Poplars** – Listen to poplars make poetry.
**5. Wytham Great Wood** – You can see Oxford from the high ground.
**9. Gatehampton Eyot** – Large wooded islands on the south bank, formed by the breakaway of a naze (headland).
**9. Hartswood Reach** – Inhale the scent of woodland on both sides of the path.
**10. Holme Park Wood** – Listen for owls.
**12. Quarry Wood** – A vast hillside of beech and bluebells.
**12. Grass Eyot** – Home to some of the tallest poplars to be seen on any Thames island.
**13. Monkey Island Riverbank** – Known for its walnut trees, among other things.
**14. Magna Carta Island** – Not a wood, but home to one of England's oldest trees, the Ankerwycke Yew, which dates back to the time of Magna Carta.
**17. Wandsworth Park** – An avenue of 77 limes line the main northern footpath.

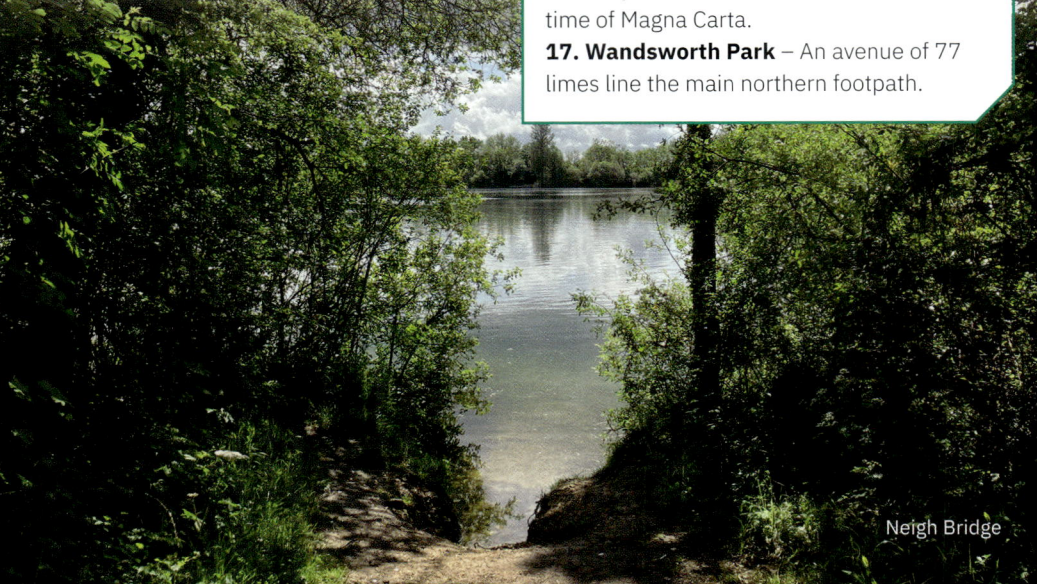

Neigh Bridge

## 9. Best for...
### MOTHER NATURE

England is one of the most important places in the world for nature, thanks in part to its damp climate. Nature revels in hydration.

The Thames Valley is home to some of the greatest fungi systems in the world, unique tidal marsh and estuarine salt systems that attract the largest collection of migratory birds in the world.

The oldest trees in the world are here too: pollards and yews.

Otters have returned to almost all English rivers after the DDT pesticide was banned in 1984. Now beavers are soon to be reintroduced following successful, albeit unofficial, trials around Oxford.

Sand martins, house martins, swallows and swifts fill the space between walker, water and riverbank. They are playful, filling the places they nest along riverbanks, locks and barns.

Grafton Lock

Hartswood

**3. Grafton Lock** – Dancing house martins by day, shooting stars at night. Possibly the highlight of the day. Nature loves this place.

**8. Clifton Hampden Riverbank** – A cliff of sandstone clothed in luxuriant trees on the bed of the river.

**9. Runsford Hole** – The best place on the river to see kingfishers.

**10. Pangbourne Lock** – Large pike fish gather here because of the great depth of the pools.

**10. Mill Pool** – One of the prettiest spots on the Thames.

**10. Charvil Lakes** – Flooded gravel pits within 1 mile of the Thames. Listen for blackcaps in summer.

**12. Cook Marsh** – Rare marshland combined with chalk slopes.

**16. The Isleworth Parish Church (All Saints)** – Watch tidal bats over the river, while standing in the graveyard at dusk.

**16. Kew Bridge** – The largest area of intertidal mud habitats in the upper Thames, which is incredibly rich in flatworms, freshwater shrimp and six species of leech.

**18. Deptford Creek** – Find shellfish on the foreshore at low tide. One of the best places to access the shore.

# FIRE

## 10. Best for...
### SUMMER SOLSTICE

Sit beside the Thames. There is nothing more beautiful than listening to birdsong on this river under willow shade.

If winter was the time to wade through Thames floods, summer is the time to inhale the arial pools of pure $H_2O$ created by trees on the breeze. Moisture in the air. A single Thames tree will evaporate 300 litres of water on a warm day.

Look for wild cherries. They are the first summer fruit. Starlings and blackbirds strip a tree in a single sitting.

Many flowers have started to die back; the hawthorn and blackthorn blossoms have gone. But field poppies are best in June. Other than the longer days, they are the second sign of mid-summer. You're most likely to see them around the edges of grain fields, green and red against the straw grass.

Yellow iris and water lilies are full. Dragonflies fuel themselves on energy.

Nowhere in the world enjoys such a perfectly temperate climate for walking, climbing, exploring and camping. Neither too hot, nor too cold. The chalk air steams and the water stays cool as the shaded hangers. Cold to touch, even in August.

English summers are famously wet, but it's a reputation rather than a reality. An unimaginative cliché of washed-out holidays that don't match the yearly average of four hours of sunshine per day and an average maximum temperature of 13°C (55°F).

Temple Island

For all that, gnats breed in the shadows and can be a pain riverside. Summer rain is the best way to beat them. A walk through tree cover and warm showers might be more fun than jumping from a lock into a weir pool.

Deer rut in July, so look out for them when they are preoccupied. They can be seen anywhere from Cricklade to Windsor.

If guaranteed sunbathing dawn to dusk is your idea of a perfect holiday, then the Thames in summer is a coin toss. But if packrafting, cycling and exploring on foot, with sunshine breaks and detours between, is more your thing, then there's nowhere better.

**1. Swill Brook** – The first named tributary to enter the Thames.
**3. Bydemill Brook** – Hide inside a mass of green canopy and blanket.
**4. Duxford Ford** – Listen to fish feeding and jumping on the water, an explosion in the silence.
**8. Little Wittenham Road** – Lost Ln. Cycle across the neck of the peninsula.
**11. Temple Island** – Possibly the most beautiful folly in England.
**12. Jubilee Creek** – Look for oyster mushroom between dead trees and wet dawn.
**15. Platt's Eyot** – An island that grew from osier beds.
**15. Hampton Court Gardens** – Designed by Sir Christopher Wren, opened to the public by Queen Victoria in 1838.
**16. Kew Gardens** – Somewhere to learn.
**16. Duke's Meadow** – Japanese Knotweed mixes with flowers.

Windsor

Hartslock Wood

on warm, high-pressure days with flying ants.

It's OK to carry a camera phone up onto these hills to look down, or into the shallows to look up at the sun. To inhale and remember the view. But it's never the same. For all the genius of AI lenses and megapixel magic, I wish I could remember how to sketch. To draw like we did when we were small children. How did we do that?

I clean primary school classrooms in the late afternoons. Children paint and draw almost every day, and leave their work out on tables that I see after they've gone. I've never seen a bad painting.

The younger the children, 5 or 6 years old, the closer their work is to psychedelic and geometric patterns in nature. The closer they are to nature. Like stars hallucinating over the Thames.

## 11. Best for...

### SUNSETS AND HILL VIEWS

Thames shallows and wooded cliffs are where you'll find the rarest, most mottled views and shapes. If the Chalk Cliffs at Beachy Head and the Valley of Rocks of Devon embody bold, breezy drama, the Thames is the opposite: a calming, meditative fire of reflections in water and still air.

Trees arch over meanders and reaches, their branches touching the slow-running waters. These silent hiding places contrast with the beacons of salt path that shine from each headland like lighthouses over rocky caves.

Sunrises and sunsets are the preludes and finales to the golden hours along the wooded valleys of Goring and Whitchurch hills.

Nature celebrates: more trout feed on the surface; swifts and swallows fly higher and higher

**7. The Global Retreat Centre** – Forest Bathing. Come down anytime.
**8. Shillingford** – Probably the best view on the Thames... all the better if you can arrive by packraft.
**9. Hartswood** – Summit of Hart's Wood with views. Best in autumn.
**11. Henley Bridge** – Iconic place to take in the river and its views.
**12. Moor Cliff** – Between yew and beech. You must climb to follow a waterfall of chalk, yew and beech.
**13. Maidenhead Bridge** – View of the heart-cheering turrets of Windsor Castle occasionally come in sight.
**13. Deadwater Ait** – One of the best views on the Thames, dominated by two wonders: Windsor Castle and Brunel's handsome bridge.
**14. Old Windsor Lock** – The magnificent trees of Windsor Castle, and the towers rising above them.
**16. Richmond Hill** – The best view of the Thames and Glover Island.
**17. Tate Modern** – Much like Westminster, the most emotional art is not contained within these walls but in the views.

Embankment to Tower Hill

Allow your eyes to adjust to the changing phases, either way. It's a powerful experience being in nature, watching the light change. Everything changes around it. The sky, the things moving in the air, the water, the light. They all combine to create unique reflections, something like the paintings by those primary school kids.

Auras, green flashes, rainbows and strange cloud formations are common. Nature begins to do something different. You start to see and hear things that are not entirely in keeping with the daylight norm. It can be unnerving, but it's good to walk into the darkness. Once your eyes have adjusted, look skywards for the North Star – the anchor around which it's possible to start exploring the celestial map on a regular basis. On a clear night anywhere will do, but some of the best places on the Thames are where the land rises east of Goring into the Chilterns.

## 12. Best for...
### STAR WATCHING

The Thames at night is a comforting place. It doesn't have the menace of coastal ghosts. I've no idea why. Mostly unaffected by light pollution, so much of the Thames lies outside of resort towns and cities.

Wait for a clear night and choose a rural location. It doesn't matter whether you're at a lock or at the end of a dead end, like Ferry Lane. Give yourself time. Arrive an hour or two before sunset or sunrise, and walk or packraft a little. You don't need to move far.

**1. Manorbrook Lake** – Watch stars over the top of the lake.
**4. Chimney Lagoon** – See fish feed here on the surface in summer.
**8. Benson Lock** – Cross the lock footbridge with some of the best views on the river.
**11. Aston Ferry Lane** – Children and adults often swim here.
**11. Magpie Eyot** – One of the Thames' most enchanted islands.
**12. Cliveden Deep** – Where Thames meets Cliveden. It's emotional.
**13. Pigeonhill Eyot** – Small and tree-covered. Bronze Age artefacts have been found here.
**17. Westminster Bridge** – The art is in the sky, at night.
**17. Public views terrace** – Come here at night. It's an iconic skyline.
**18. Rotherhithe Beach** – Sit in the sand at sunset and imagine anything you want.

Thames Meadows

PART **2**

# THE CHALK STREAM

**Coates**

Trewsbury Farm

Thames Source

A433

Thames Head House

A429

**KEMBLE**

**Kemble**

**Ewen**

*River Thames / River Isis*

Poole Keynes

Upper Mill Farm

Old Mill Farm

*Flagham Brook*

*Somerford Lakes*

**Somerford Keynes**

Neigh Bridge

*Lake 32*

Lower Moor Farm

*Netherwood Lakes*

*Mallard Lake*

**Lower Mill Estate**

*Mill Lake*

*Lake 65*

*Lake 30*

*Swillbrook Lakes*

*Somerford Lagoon*

*Farmhouse Lake*

*Lake 92*

*Lake 29*

*Freeth Mere*

*Lake 40*

**North End**

*Swill Brook*

**Ashton Keynes**

*Lake 69*

B4696

*Lake 75*

B4696

*Lake 83*

*Lake 82*

*Wickwater Lake*

Leigh Farm

*Waterhay Lake*

**Waterhay**

*Manorbrook Lake*

*Lake 72*

*River Churn*

*Hailstone Hill*
Hailstone Farm

A419

B4040

**Cricklade**

1 km

1 mile

# 1. THAMES SOURCE TO HAILSTONE HILL

Thames Meadows

## BIRDSONG

The Thames starts life as an underground spring, but if you arrive in summer you'll struggle to find its pulse. Within less than a mile water has cracked the earth open; and within another the skeletal bones of willow and Cotswold stone are vibrating with its heartbeat.

Bats wheel on the marl lake breeze, owls shuffle in pollards and skylarks flit over meadows. The Thames' birds sing with the confidence of a choir, as the river breathes into everything it touches, including you – the traveller.

## 10 STEPPING STONES

Thames Lakes
Ewen Canal
Old Mill Farm
Mill Lake
Freeth's Wood
Holy Cross Church
Ashton Keynes Lake
Brook Farm Wood
Manorbrook Lake Wood
Hailstone Hill

Source of the Thames

## Source of the Thames, Nr Coates

Feel around a pile of stones. Beneath your hand is a 15m (50ft) radius of sunken ground where the earth gives birth to water. The stones are surrounded by a grove, of sorts. A large ash to the E, and then a circle of oak, maple and willow, as well as lots of nettles, buttercups and grasses. There's a mediative silence here, too, until a train passes. The Thames head stone? It probably won't outlive you or the grove of trees. It's a trinket, not to the river but to us, so we remember we saw something special.

51.694561, -2.029594

## → DETOUR – WALKING ¾ MILE

## Thames and Severn Way, Coates

From the source of the Thames, consider moving N for ⅓ mile to Trewsbury House Fort, a prehistoric hillfort. There's no public access, but it can be seen from the path through the trees. This path joins up with the Thames and Severn Way.

51.699019, -2.031659

## Trewsbury Mead, Coates

You are currently 90m (300ft) above sea level. Start downhill towards London along an avenue of gnarled ash trees, between buttercups and soft grass. This walk is through some of the richest and greenest meadow you'll see in 180 miles.

51.692450, -2.028283

### Fosse Way, Nr Kemble

Cross the Rd, which dates back before the Iron Age but is now the A433. This is the Fosse Way, which the Romans adopted and upgraded as a Rd and frontier marker when they invaded in 43 AD. It links Exeter, in S Devon, with Lincoln, in the Midlands, via Bath, Cirencester and Leicester.

51.689398, -2.023618

### Thames Stone, Nr Kemble

Sitting among the willows this is the first glimpse of wide water, and trees line the riverbank. Old herbalists would chew willow leaves like aspirin for toothache or use them as a gargle for colds. The catkins were mashed for food, the flowers eaten as a pick-me-up. The best views are after winter flooding when the fields look like shallow blue lakes over green baize.

51.689259, -2.022155

### Thames Head, Nr Kemble

Thames Head is on your L just after you cross the A433, or Fosse Way. It can be a wide pool or a dry bowl depending on how the springs are running. This place is also known as Lyd Well. It's not somewhere to rush through, even though there are many miles ahead. It has a peaceful air.

51.689190, -2.022800

### Thames Meadow, Nr Kemble

Patches of wildflowers puncture this meadow. The earth feels more solid where the path moves from the river, and you can smell the mineral freshness in the air.

51.684539, -2.017749

Thames Meadows

Well Wood

### Well Wood, Nr Kemble

Find a way into the woodland. This is a lovely place to find shade.

51.685223, -2.016197

### THAMES OLD WALL, LYDWELL

Touch the stones around the riverbed, which are framed by a beautiful stone wall. A large, still pond forms here in winter and spring, but it runs almost dry in summer.

51.684765, -2.016570

### Thames Lakes, Kemble

Smell the wells and springs that gurgle to the surface. It's waterlogged in winter, and there's a sense of soggy resignation if you haven't come in waders. Moss carpets the trunk of almost every tree in a patchwork of brown and green camo. The TP is part of the Thames and Severn Way here.

51.683800, -2.016043

### Dismantled railway/Rd, Nr Kemble

Rough, uneven surfaces underfoot are a change from the grasses and soft spring ground. Look for the faded tracks that might lead to something unexpected or interesting.

51.679962, -2.015105

 **→ DETOUR – WALKING ½ MILE**

### Kemble Station, Kemble

Kemble Station is ½ mile from the TP, where it crosses the A429; 2 miles from the source of the Thames; 8 miles from Cricklade and 14 miles (by train) from Swindon.

**➤ Find** the FP that joins the TP (51.680156, -2.015197) and follow W.

51.676570, -2.022941

 ### Clayfurlong Bank, Nr Kemble

Elder and ash hang over the path as the river starts to take shape. Notice how the thinnest willow branches that bend in the breeze almost flow with the river. The meadow edges are lined in tree arches and giant hogweed flowers.

51.679225, -2.012474

 ### Kemble Bank, Kemble

Inhale the scent of oxeye daisies in spring. They weave like a stream through feral barley.

51.679447, -2.012631

 ### Kemble Wood, Kemble

This beautiful little ash, hazel and maple wood is the first of hundreds along the path. Forage in between taking shade – the TP is a snack-larder of fruits, nuts and fungi 365 days a year.

51.678080, -2.010187

 ### Parker's Bank, Ewen

Paddle in the rocky Thames. There are stoney banks everywhere – even in winter. These are good places to stay cool or to rest.

51.677674, -2.008013

 ### Parker's Bridge, Ewen

The Thames is still a stream where the Rd cuts through. The path is bordered by elder, maple and parked cars that take up too much space.

51.675251, -2.007056

 ### Parker's Wood, Ewen

A tiny hazel woodland beside the Rd and an easy place to get down into the river for shade.

51.675476, -2.003483

## Poulton Well, Ewen

The old well (now part of a house) lies around 90m (300ft) W of the bus stop.

51.675476, -2.003483

## The Brook Bridge, Ewen

Sit on the lichen-covered stone overlooking grazing meadows. The river is dry here much of the year – more like a desert of cleft hoofprints, mud and rock than a sparkling stream. Maple and ash trees provide some shelter from the sun.

51.674320, -1.995335

## EWEN CANAL, EWEN

This isn't actually a canal, but it looks and feels like one as it runs along the back gardens of houses in Ewen. Beautifully straight, watered and lined with a dry-stone wall. It has an elegant beauty about it – perhaps because it's engineered and old. To walk here in the summer rain without coat or umbrella is one of the day's highlights.

51.674410, -1.995264

## Ewen Woods, Ewen

Inhale the scents of willow and herbs. Old folk buried their dead under willow trees to symbolise rebirth. There are occasional spikes of water lily, yellow iris and watercress between the haphazard mix of mud and stone riverbed.

51.674892, -1.991055

Ewen Canal

 ### Ewen Springs, Ewen

Listen for warblers where garden fences mix with ferns and soft moss. The air is crisp and fresh here, and more alive with nature than almost anywhere else on this first section of river. Barbed wire often blocks access, which is a shame. Look for the first flash of blue of kingfishers.

51.674290, -1.989104

 ### Old Covert Woods, Herts/Bucks border

Lots of green in spring: young shoots of bramble and dandelion, the soft green heads of dock, and nettles. Smell the scent of spring-laden oak woodland. There is a gate across a shallow Thames foot crossing, but it's usually locked, and access is likely private.

51.673434, -1.987054

 ### Upper Mill Farm, Nr Somerford Keynes

A beautiful little woodland dell, perfect for shade and shelter. Horse chestnut and ash set against a picture-postcard riverside farm. Upper Mill Farm was once a water mill.

51.665348, -1.983025

# ③ OLD MILL FARM FP, POOL KEYNES

Go barefoot through the grass, worn down by years of boots. You'll run the gauntlet of thorns, bees and other nasties, but... the stepping stones might be steady enough to cross to the other bank. The mill runs right beside the shallow river. Incredible to think that such a meagre current of water had enough energy to power industry. The stonework of All Saints' Church in Somerford Keynes stands in the distance. The church FP is just S of the mill.

51.659462, -1.983660

## Manor House Path, Somerford Keynes

The path here is lined with hazelnut, dead wood fungi and brambles. It's best in late autumn.

51.657170, -1.982399

## → DETOUR – WALKING ⅓ MILE

### All Saints' Church, Somerford Keynes

One of the oldest stone-built churches in Gloucestershire lies just ⅓ mile from the path. Dating back to 695 AD, the first Christians here were baptised in the River Thames. The N doorway is thought to be the oldest part of the building.

➤ **Find** the FP that joins the TP (51.656522, -1.982299) and walk E.

51.658495, -1.977572

## Kemble Mill Bridge, Kemble

Cross the wooded bridge over Thames bridge. There is a FP out onto Somerford Lakes Reserve. The boreen (Rd) skirts the lake S, or N back to Ewen, and is part of a network of Lns and BWs that make much of this first 10 miles navigable by bike from Cotswold Water Park to the source of the Thames. The Ln NW of Ewen is another alternative to the TP if you are on a bike.

51.652657, -1.980227

## Neigh Bridge Country Park

Listen to the cackle and whistles of the breeding snipe, curlew and golden plover around Neigh Bridge Country Park. The Cotswold Lakes, which the park is a part of, are the most extensive marl lake system in Britain. The lakes were carved from more than 140 gravel pits. The lakes span 42 sq miles and attract over 20,000 waterfowl each year, and they include 40 different species.

➤ **Find** Neigh Bridge County Car Park (51.650658, -1.974605).

51.651994, -1.976247

Neigh Bridge

### Minety Lakes, Somerford Keynes

Look out for Daubenton's bats skimming over the lake, particularly just before dusk. Pochard and smew also feed here.

51.647146, -1.964748

### 4 MILL LAKE, SOMERFORD KEYNES

These lakes originated as manmade gravel pits, but time is a healer. The entire water zone now hums with the industry of nature.

51.650547, -1.970329

### Wooded Lake, Somerford Keynes

Three colours dominate this stretch: white, green and yellow. The chalk path and wildflowers are often white. The willow woodland is green and full of magic – the poet Robert Graves suggested the words 'witch' and 'Wicca' derived from willow. The grassy dells are dappled with yellow dandelions.

51.647063, -1.962709

### 5 FREETH'S WOOD, NR ASHTON KEYNES

Like all waterside woods, these trees are especially hardy: maple, horse chestnut, hawthorne and oak. Dog roses are easy to miss between the chorus of birdsong. Soprano bats hunt over the still water at dusk.

51.645191, -1.954819

### → DETOUR – WALKING ½ MILE

## Swill Brook, Somerford Keynes

Walk alongside the first named tributary that empties into the River Thames. It's a wonderful FP that follows the sometimes-dry river W along the SW edge of the wooded Cotswold Park. This is the first of more than 100 named and unnamed rivers, creeks and brooks that enter the Thames. The Thames is as much about these waters as anything else. Swill Brook ends at Swillbrook Bridge, Rigsby Ln, a beautiful three-arched stone crossing. The 1-mile Ln is a boreen, which can be followed N back to Neigh Bridge Country Park Car Park (51.650979, -1.975710).

➤ **Find** the FP that joins the TP (51.645144, -1.955015), just before Freeth's Wood and walk S.

51.637563, -1.952571

## Lake 92, Somerford Keynes

Wander along the wide riverside, woodland and lakeland path. The shallow river is lined with ivy-banked sides and hornbeam.

51.645997, -1.948758

### → DETOUR – WALKING ½ MILE

## Furze Brake Lake, Ashton Keynes

There is an island of ash trees on Furze Brake Lake, a ½-mile detour from the TP, which raptors favour for fishing. Marsh harriers are most common.

➤ **Find** the FP that joins the TP (51.645975, -1.948979) and walk N.

51.650066, -1.951458

## The Wooded Spine, Somerford Keynes

Smell the scent of wet wood along one of the most unusual strips of woodland along this path: a FP that dissects two of the deepest gravel pits in Cotswold Lake. This is a good place to find shelter from sunshine or rain.

➤ **Find** the FP that tracks E of Furze Brake Lake path (51.648076, -1.953320).

51.650479, -1.957922

## Lake 64 Woods, Ashton Keynes

A FB dell. A natural crossing with the opportunity to get down into the river in summer over chalk stone and lime.

51.645863, -1.944752

Ashton Keynes

## Manor House Bridge/Rd, Ashton Keynes

Smell the alder, ash and maple. The B4696 bridge is the boundary introduction to Ashton Keynes. The town divides the E and W sections of Cotswold Lakes. Walk N on this Rd to find Holy Cross Church (see below).

51.646066, -1.941963

## Green Ln, Church Walk, Ashton Keynes

Move slowly or sit on the bench and savour one of the best views along this stretch. A classic Cotswold scene – a stone riverbank, bridge and houses surrounded in spring by yellow daffodils, rape and white blossom. Weeping willows frame the scene.

51.646549, -1.937756

## → DETOUR – WALKING ¼ MILE

## 6 HOLY CROSS CHURCH, ASHTON KEYNES

A quarter of a mile N of the TP is Holy Cross Church. Look around the graveyard for the Commonwealth graves. The stained glass is impressive. The nave was built in the 12th century, but sadly the door is often locked. Two western arches with round columns and responds and circular abaci also date to around the 12th century, while the oak pulpit is 19th century. There are several monuments and wall tablets with detailed inscriptions.
➤ **Find** the lost Ln that joins the TP (51.646667, -1.937288) and walk NW.

51.648301, -1.941083

## 7 ASHTON KEYNES LAKE FP, ASHTON KEYNES

Look for hobbies. The raptors hunt large insects but are quick and missable. There are 13 species of dragonfly and damselfly around these lakes.

51.649574, -1.927767

Manorbrook Lake

### Lake 82/83 FP, Ashton Keynes

Move among water lilies and listen to the sound of waterfowl. This is the re-entry point into the waterpark.

➤ **Find** Waterhay Car Park (51.638706, -1.914364).

51.642963, -1.921114

### ➔ DETOUR – CYCLING ½ – 6 MILES

### Rixon Farm BW, Ashton Keynes

Find the wooded elbow that marks more than 6 miles of BWs and country Lns around the entire waterpark. The BW E follows the TP for more than 3 miles into Cricklade. The N track, away from Cricklade, moves away from the TP towards S Cerney and the River Churn, a tributary of the River Thames, via Fridays Ham Ln, and includes 2 miles of BWs.

51.640343, -1.913963

### BROOK FARM BW AND WOOD, ASHTON KEYNES

Listen to the birds. It's not a chore, it's an attention fix. Nightingale, warblers – some are unrecognisable and like nothing else you'll ever hear. Spring birdsong defines this section of the path more than anything else.

51.640816, -1.908895

### Brook Farm River Bridge, Ashton Keynes

Find the Thames 180m (590ft) S of the path. It's a minor detour, but it's important to keep in touch with the river. This might be the first time since entering the Cotswold Lakes at Neigh Bridge Country Park that you've seen it.

51.639436, -1.907741

### Manorbrook Lake, Ashton Keynes

Watch the stars over the top of the lake. The water here is a strange, bright turquoise blue. Notice how the water colour changes from lake to lake.

51.644165, -1.907118

### MANORBROOK LAKE WOOD NW, ASHTON KEYNES

Migrant winter birds arrive here from around November. Breeding season is usually done by the end of July. Listen for marsh harriers. There is a bird-watching hut and hours of lake and woodland walks. The path becomes a BW that runs S of the Cleveland Lakes Nature Reserve.

51.644165, -1.907118

 ### Manorbrook Lake Wood NE, Ashton Keynes

Listen to the breeze in the black poplars – the small leaves rattle like a shoal at low water. These are rare trees. Unusually large birches stand either side of them, trunks as thick as oak.

51.646369, -1.899556

 ### Lake 72 Woods N, Ashton Keynes

In spring, sit on the riverside between common hogweed and cleaver. The path leaves the river to follow the wooded trails but it's OK to explore the river-edge dells, which are set back from the BW.

51.647213, -1.890176

 ### HAILSTONE HILL (SE DETOUR)

Feel the climb up Hailstone Hill. Swallows dip and feed at the Thames FB in summer. Stones Ln starts here before it climbs 100m (330ft) to the summit of Hailstone Farm. This hill is a minor shortcut into Cricklade; one of four paths that run parallel to the NW into town, each path like a string on the body of a bass guitar. Stones Ln is the E-string: simple, direct. The disused railway is the A. The BW, the D. The FP over N Meadow, the G, fiddly and sometimes broken by flood. Here you must decide whether to find a B&B in Cricklade or keep walking on to find a wild camp: the rattle and hum of two perfect choices.

51.651258, -1.889289

Hailstone Hill

Hailstone Hill ▲

Hailstone Farm

B4040

River Churn

Latton

Cricklade
North
Meadow

A419

Wharf Farm

Cricklade

B4553

N

Ampney Brook

Calcutt

Eysey

Water Eaton
House

River Thames / River Isis

Blackburr Farm

Castle Eaton

Kempsford

Manor Farm

Hannington
Wick

Hannington Bridge

Bridge Farm

Bydemill Brook

Sterts
Farm

1 km

1 mile

Bydemill Brook at
Upper Inglesham

Upper
Inglesham

A361

# 2. HAILSTONE HILL TO **BYDEMILL BROOK**

## MEADOW

Cricklade hosts two events in its hay meadows each year. In late spring, more than 500,000 snake's head fritillary fill the N Meadow, while in winter the same meadow floods with rainwater. You can arrive here in spring with a camera and a sense of wonder at being in the company of 80 per cent of Britain's fritillaries, and some other visitors. Or you can arrive in winter with a packraft and a sense of humour to glide across flooded fields, and you will be alone.

## 10 STEPPING STONES

Andoversford Line BW
N Meadows
Cricklade NW
Hatchetts Ford
Eysey Manor FB
N Farm Dew Ponds
Castle Eaton Entry FB
Blackford Ln
Hannington Wick Bridge
Bydemill Brook

### Hailstone Hill (NW), Nr Cricklade

A late start is OK to explore the first hay meadow of the day, where you can smell borage among the wildflowers. The path crosses onto a dismantled railway. Remarkable how often sites associated with redundant industry or human abandonment are most alive with nature. As if nature makes more of an effort once a rival has left. You'll notice that all the way along the Thames.

51.648380, -1.882343

### ANDOVERSFORD LINE BW, ANDOVERSFORD

Look for hazel flowers and yellow catkins in January and February. This 3-mile dismantled railway is a wooded arch between S Cerney and Cricklade, and a mix of hard gravel, soft green edges and horse dung. Victorian children would make dens from thin stems of rooted hazel. They would bend and tie the trees horizontally, before wrapping them in bracken, canvas or blankets.

51.652713, -1.886308

### → DETOUR – CYCLING ½ MILE

### Cotswold Water Park, Andoversford Line BW N, Cerney Wick

Touch an avenue of pine by the Rd bridge. The trees include a large Mexican white pine. Lns from this crossroads lead either to Cerney Wick or back towards Ashton Keynes.

➤ **Find** the BW that joins the TP (51.652714, -1.886308) and move NW.

51.657322, -1.896425

### S Cerney Water Park, S Cerney

Inhale carbon-low air along 2 miles of tree-lined BW. The dismantled railway runs in and out of S Cerney Water Park.

➤ **Cycle** 2 miles off Rd from Andoversford Line BW (see above).

51.667899, -1.912940

### River Andoversford Line BW S, Nr Cricklade

Cross the FB where the TP rejoins the river. Depending on the time of year, the PRoW follows the Thames intermittently until it gets past Cricklade. Take time now to get down to the water around the shallow stone riverbed.

51.651192, -1.881834

Path to North Meadow

###  → DETOUR – CYCLING 1 MILE

## Horsey Down, Andoversford Line BW N, Nr Cricklade

Avoid on sunny weekends, but otherwise this is a lovely wooded Ln into Cricklade.

➤ **Find** the BW that joins the TP (51.651326, -1.881967) and move SE.

51.650047, -1.878930

## Disused Canal, Nr Cricklade

Just ⅓ mile on from the disused railway line, you stand over a flood meadow.

➤ **Find** and follow the N path along the old, disused canal to 'The Basin', where it meets the River Churn.

51.651485, -1.875025

Millennium Wood

 **→ DETOUR – WALKING ½ MILE**

### Weymoor Bridge, Latton

Feel the energy around a redundant water junction that once linked two canals. Boats laden with cargo would leave the Thames and Severn Canal here to join up with the Wilts and Berks Canal from 1819. The canal eventually joined the Kennet and Avon at Semington near Melksham. This is where the River Churn met the Thames and Severn Canal.

➤ **Find** the FP that joins the TP (51.651453, -1.875008) and walk NW for ½ mile.

51.657314, -1.874356

 ### ② N MEADOWS BW, CRICKLADE

Smell meadow foxtail and great burnet beside one of the best lowland hay meadows in England.

➤ **Find** where the BW meets the TP (51.651430, -1.874974).

51.648235, -1.871691

 ### N Meadow (N) National Nature Reserve (NNR), Cricklade

More than 500,000 snake's-head fritillaries bloom in the N Meadow NNR some years. The purple-coloured flowers get their name from the snakeskin pattern on their petals. These meadows were once common all over England.

51.650425, -1.872227

## N Meadow (Mid), Cricklade

In winter, the grass here floods and you can packraft across one of the most beautiful flood meadows in England. By late spring, the water has evaporated and the meadow has become a flowering carpet of grass and rare blooms. You can see St Sampson's Church in Cricklade from the meadow.

51.648658, -1.867408

### → DETOUR – WALKING 275M (900FT)

## N Meadow (E), Cricklade

A short 275m (900ft) detour takes you to the eastern section of the N Meadow. Common sorrel, meadow vetchling and red fescue grow here. 'Strewing herbs' like meadowsweet are fun to sit around and smell.

➤ **Find** the FP that joins the TP (51.646721, -1.865176), which lies close to the weir, and walk NE.

51.647511, -1.863889

## ③ NW CRICKLADE, CRICKLADE

Cricklade was once an important Celtic centre and was a seat of learning before Oxford took over in the 11th century. For some reason all the books and knowledge were moved there. Cricklade even had its own mint, and the coins are a collector's item today. Some can still be found in the meadows.

51.646324, -1.864546

## Cricklade Town Wall, Cricklade

Explore the layout of the old town. A monastery was built by the Knights Hospitallers close to the river. Parts of the original preceptory were used to build Cricklade Priory.

51.644965, -1.859969

St Sampson's Church

## Cricklade

The first town on the Thames is the most intact example of a late Saxon new town in Britain.

➤ **Walk** the back streets that run parallel with the High Street. The original layout of the old town remains, even though houses have been rebuilt several times.

51.641319, -1.854938

## St Sampson's Church, Cricklade

Cricklade was once home to a wise collective of monks. The church is dedicated to the 5th-century Welsh saint Samson of Dol – one of only five in the UK dedicated to the saint. Two crosses linked to the churchyard are considered rare.

51.640763, -1.858102

## Cricklade High Bridge, Cricklade

Cross the bridge that marks the river/town boundary.

51.644504, -1.854910

## ➔ DETOUR – PACKRAFT 180M (590FT)

### River Churn, Cricklade

Waterway without foot access. Paddle or packraft to where the River Churn empties into the Thames, less than 90m (295ft) from Cricklade High Bridge (see above). This is where the River Thames starts to widen and pick up speed. The River Churn rises at Seven Springs in Gloucestershire and flows S for more than 23 miles to Cricklade, emptying into the Thames from the NE. The Churn is greater in length than the Thames at this point, but it is the Churn that gives up its name to the Thames, rather than vice versa.

➤ **Paddle** by packraft or kayak from Hatchetts Ford. Alternatively, find the riverbank just before the bridge beside the TP (51.644408, -1.855094) and paddle E.

51.644924, -1.853291

## ④ HATCHETTS FORD, CRICKLADE

Step into the water at this famous ford – a place to cool hot feet or launch a boat. In the late 19th century this was a stop for watering cattle, too. It later became a place where local Baptists held their baptisms. The congregation would watch from the banks, at Hatchett Bridge.

51.642693, -1.851002

### Cricklade Museum, Cricklade
Like a Tardis. Tiny museum packed with more than 12,000 items – mostly local stuff from the 19th and 20th centuries.

51.641148, -1.851369

### River Key, Cricklade
Look for the launching site for small boats just beside the river bridge. The River Key runs around the perimeter of Cricklade's old town wall before entering the Thames. The river rises at Braydon Forest near Purton.

51.642400, -1.846100

### Manor Farm FB, Cricklade
The Thames gets faster and wilder after Cricklade – partly because the rivers Churn and Ray add to the volume of water. There's a BW and bridge here. The BW leads back to the A419.

51.642784, -1.845173

### Ampney Brook, Cricklade
Ampney Brook empties into the river 45m (150ft) W of Manor Farm FB.

51.645253, -1.839370

### EYSEY MANOR FB, EYSEY
Watch swifts flying and feeding in late summer. The BW zigzags around the broadleaf woods N towards Eysey Manor.

51.645130, -1.838292

Water Eaton

### River Ray, Latton

Sit underneath the old hawthorn bush that marks the place where the River Ray meets the River Thames. The tight meanders either side are lined in dock leaves, purple teasel and bees.

➤ **Find** where the river enters the Thames 137m (450ft) W of Water Eaton House Bridge (see below), on the opposite bank to the TP.

51.644402, -1.825097

### Water Eaton House Bridge, Water Eaton

Listen to the warblers and watch the fish that flit and feed beneath the branches. There's lots of shelter and places to hide along this section. Common reeds fill the space beneath the bridge and water.

51.644101, -1.822497

### Eaton Chalk Stream, Water Eaton

In the spring, smell the elder flowers – it's overwhelmingly subtle, but nice.

51.650024, -1.813779

### Water Eaton Wood, Water Eaton

Where the river meets the trees is a tangle of fresh green nettles for foraging. The riverbank is thick with maple and willow trees.

51.653372, -1.811535

### N FARM DEW PONDS, NR WATER EATON

Listen for the murmur of fat birds on the wing. Thousands of wood pigeons fly over the stubble and flooded meadow here, searching for food. The sky is full of them, a mass of motion.

51.657288, -1.811448

 ### Round House Riverbank, Nr Water Eaton

A willow woodland. The N bank is particularly good for large trees, just S of the flooded gravel pits.

51.663174, -1.805041

 ### Round House Naze, Nr Castle Eaton

It's not quite a collective of islands, but a mass of plant life, likely fed by springs and immoveable minerals, which helped create the tight bend in the river. Lots of willow for shelter. In summer, you'll hear people splashing about in the river close to the neighbouring private jetty on the opposite bank.

51.662936, -1.801815

 ### Castle Eaton W, Castle Eaton

You will need walking sticks here from spring. So much of this path is overgrown. There are lots of nettles that will soak your trousers. It can also be hard going in the high grass.

51.660748, -1.797158

Castle Eaton West

##  Castle Eaton Path End W, Castle Eaton

The river is navigable from here for 2 miles, and it is possible to launch your packraft from this point. Overhanging branches from fallen trees may require a small saw to avoid snagging your boat.

51.660471, -1.794571

##  → DETOUR PACKRAFTING ⅓ – 2 MILES

### St Mary the Virgin Church Riverbank, Castle Eaton

The riverbank was once accessible from the churchyard but sadly, no more – so enter the river further W from the TP and paddle up to the church (see p57). Nettles and loosestrife grow in spring and summer.

➤ **Find** the riverbank beside the TP before Castle Eaton (51.660600, -1.795242) and paddle E for ⅓–2 miles.

51.662556, -1.790465

##  7 CASTLE EATON ENTRY FB, CASTLE EATON

Cross the second of three FBs into Castle Eaton. The Street is full of old buildings made of local stone and rooted in Cotswold culture. Houses date from 1650 to 1850. The village is friendly.

51.659663, -1.793977

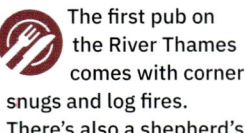

**THE RED LION**

The first pub on the River Thames comes with corner snugs and log fires. There's also a shepherd's hut for overnight hire.

The St, Castle Eaton, SN6 6JZ

www.theredlioncastle
eaton.co.uk

01285 706533

## St Mary the Virgin Church, Castle Eaton

River views – but detached from the river itself. The nearby meadows of the 12th-century church were mentioned in the Anglo Saxon Chronicles. Hemp-nettle and yellow cress grow along the riverbank in a mass of greens.

51.662457, -1.789729

## Castle Eaton E, Castle Eaton

Walking out of Castle Eaton you enter a wormhole of green brush and boreen. Blackford Ln is one of the day's highlights.

51.660709, -1.786554

## BLACKFORD LN, CASTLE EATON

Boreens are like cosmic wormholes. Mostly carless, they are full of the sound of grasshoppers and birdsong.

51.661743, -1.777482

🚴 → DETOUR – CYCLING  1 MILE

## Yew Tree Farm BW, Nr Castle Eaton

If you have a bike, this is a fast route to the fabulous Hannington Bridge, a picturesque three-arched bridge built in 1841. A 1-mile detour, it will take you along a lost Ln once associated with yews.

➤ **Find** the lost Ln/BW that joins the TP at Blackford Farm (51.660805, -1.767972) and follow N and then E.

51.660806, -1.767972

## Castle Eaton Path End E, Nr Kempsford

A large, wooded pond marks the point at which you can enter the Thames by packraft.

51.662548, -1.766446

Hannington Bridge

## THE GEORGE

The only pub in the village, but good for fish and chips, steak and kidney pies, and roasts.

High St, Kempsford, GL7 4EQ

www.thegeorgekempsford.co.uk

01285 810236

## → DETOUR ½ – 1 MILE

### Kempsford Riverbank, Kempsford

Explore Kempsford – the site of a Royal Palace in Saxon times – by boat.

➤ **Find** where the riverbank joins the TP (51.662548, -1.766446) and packraft NW for ½–1 mile.

51.667934, -1.767979

### Church of St Mary the Virgin Riverbank, Kempsford

Nothing of the royal palace that stood here remains, apart from a single wall with a large, mullioned window. The terrace, which has been converted into a green walk, is believed to be haunted by a 'Lady of the Mist'. She was named by villagers because she usually appears floating above the river in pale moonshine.

51.666973, -1.768308

### Kempsford Riverbank, Kempsford

Huge fish feed here around deep pools.

51.668053, -1.770694

### The Ford, Kempsford

The village of Kempsford was originally known as Kynemeresford, which meant 'the ford of the great marsh' – 'kyne' referring to 'great', 'mere' referring to the marsh, and 'ford' a reference to the ancient ford that stood here.

51.669195, -1.776446

### Church of St Mary the Virgin, Kempsford

Look for tombs, stained glass and ancestral headstones.

51.666975, -1.768308

### Yew Tree Farm River Exit, Nr Kempsford

From the N bank, look out for roe deer. The males are black backed, the females fawn. The best way to see them is usually from the water. The river opens up in places, pooling in deep lagoons at the bends. Sit still and you might see perch feeding on the surface.

➤ **Enter** the water. It's a mile's paddle to Hannington Bridge, but there is also almost 3 miles of pathless river, so take an hour or two to explore.

51.662234, -1.762083

Boreen to Hannington Wick

 ## HANNINGTON WICK BRIDGE, HANNINGTON WICK

From here, look down over the river. There can be a strong current, even rapids at times, and there's a causeway either side with flood arches. No path runs along the river, but E and W of this bridge is considered to be some of the most fertile meadow in England.

51.663204, -1.749151

 ### → DETOUR – PACKRAFTING 1 MILE E

### Brazen Church Riverbank, Nr Hannington Wick

Paddle E from Hannington Wick Bridge for around 1 mile to find a wooded riverbank for shelter and fish watching. The woodland is almost 1-mile long and is private, but this area is one of the most secluded places on the Thames. The banks are high; the riverbed sometimes shallow and shingly.

➤ **The** River Thames crosses the 76m (250ft) contour a mile above Castle Eaton. St John's Lock is 68m (223ft) above sea level. So, there's a drop of 8m (27ft) in the 8 miles between the 76m (250ft) contour and the last lock.

51.665458, -1.741919

### Fingers Island, Nr Hannington Wick

There's an island of willow and oak trees in the centre of the river. Much of the S bank backwater is overgrown, but the N bank is often navigable.

51.666072, -1.741064

### Hand Island, Nr Hannington Wick

Much of the original backwater here is overgrown.

51.666934, -1.740165

### Foot Island, Nr Hannington Wick

Look for glowworms after dark during the summer months.

51.667662, -1.735248

### Hannington Wick Bridge, Hannington Wick

This bridge is an access superpoint and is also at the centre of an off-road cycling network, which runs along the ancient Rd to Highworth Church in the S, 4 miles away and back to Kempsford.

51.663204, -1.749151

## → DETOUR – CYCLING 3 MILES

### Little Crouch Plantation

Little Crouch Plantation is a pine plantation 1 mile from the river along a boreen and then FP.
➤ **Find** the lost Ln that joins the TP (51.659826, -1.747009) and follow to the SE.

51.653835, -1.730030

### Highworth via Crouch Hill, Highworth

N of the market town of Highworth is Highworth Church.

51.631236, -1.710393

## → DETOUR – CYCLING 1 MILE

### Kempsford Bridge, Kempsford

Cycle back to Kempsford from Hannington Bridge along the Thames and Severn Way. This detour is about 1 mile.
➤ **Find** the Rd that joins the TP (51.662553, -1.748723) and follow NW to Kempsford.

51.668014, -1.768035

###  Bridge Farm Lost Ln BW, Hannington Wick

The Lns around Sterts House are lined with maple and willow trees. The Rd gives way to the BW from Sterts Farm. Follow the 2-mile track to Upper Inglesham. Look for green leaves and flowers by May; taste the hazelnuts in autumn and the magic of mushrooms by November.

51.660444, -1.744594

###  Willow Tree BW, Hannington Wick

Walk along a 4-mile BW from Castle Eaton to Upper Inglesham. There's really nowhere to go after that unless you've parked a car at either end. In which case, it's an impressive ride along the valley of no access.

51.659924, -1.742304

###  Sterts Farm Wood W, Hannington Wick

These woodlands offer somewhere to shelter from sunshine or bad weather. The smell of pine trees is best after summer rain.

51.661701, -1.733050

###  BYDEMILL BROOK, NR UPPER INGLESHAM

Look for dragonflies around Bydemill Brook. Emperor and brown hawker dragonflies feed here.

➤ **Bydemill** Brook rises N of Stratton St Margaret, flowing N past Stratton and to the W of Highworth. It joins the River Thames at the same place as the trail, 300m (985ft) NE.

51.667342, -1.718915

Bydemill Brook

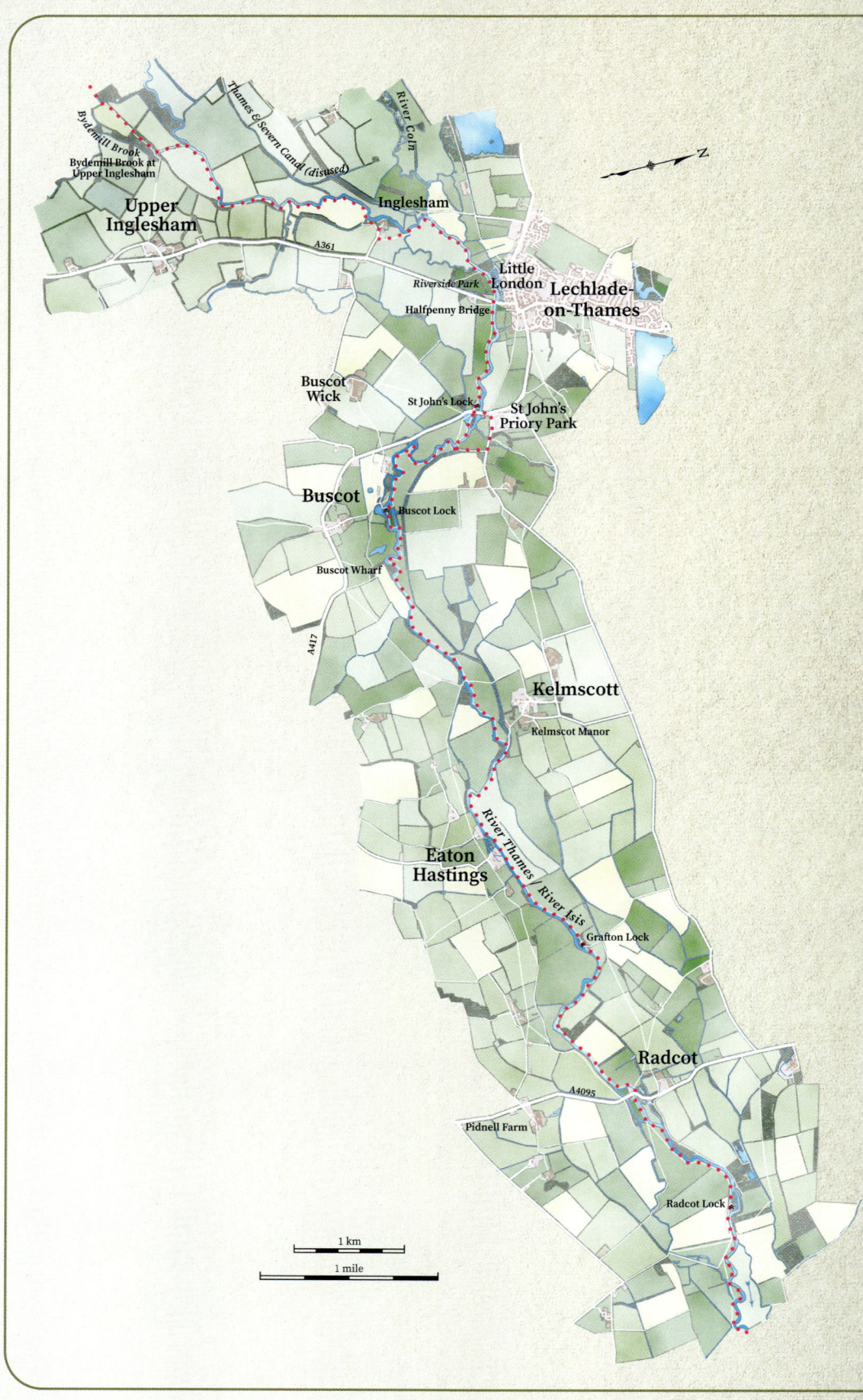

# 3. BYDEMILL BROOK TO RADCOT LOCK

Halfpenny Bridge

## WILLIAM MORRIS

William Morris was a writer, designer and socialist. He lived at Kelmscott Manor in Kelmscott, not far from the River Thames, until his death in 1896. Morris chose to spend his last years reading poetry. The Celtic word for poetry is 'el al' – moving water. There's not a single settlement for 30 miles along this section of the riverbank. If you only ever walk one section of the TP, make it this one.

## 10 STEPPING STONES

Sterts Farm Riverbank
St John the Baptist Church, Inglesham
Roundhouse Bridge
Halfpenny Bridge
Old Father Thames, St John's Lock
Bloomers Hole FB
Buscot Lock
Kelmscott Manor House
Grafton Lock
Radcot Bridge

## Bydemill Brook, Nr Upper Inglesham

Follow the brook to the fork in the path: one fork heads SE towards the BW to Upper Inglesham, the other heads NE, following the riverbank towards the Thames. Lots of invasive purple loosestrife – an anti-inflammatory herb – can be found here.

51.667342, -1.718915

## STERTS FARM RIVERBANK, NR UPPER INGLESHAM

Packraft over the shallows in summer. Sometimes there's only a few inches of water over the gravel and white chalk. The reeds are thick and dense for long stretches.

51.669895, -1.718795

## → DETOUR – PACKRAFTING 1 MILE W

## Bydemill Brook, Nr Upper Inglesham

Hide inside a mass of green canopy and blanket where the brook enters the Thames.

51.669816, -1.719302

## Enclosure Bend, Hannington

Lots of willow and poplar trees overhang the bend in the river.
➤ **Find** the riverbank where the TP meets the Thames (51.669815, -1.719302), and paddle W.

51.668696, -1.721155

## Enclosure Naze, Hannington

Steep, sandy banks on the N side are where the sand martins nest. The river is narrow here and often clogged with fallen willow.

51.669638, -1.721958

## Mairéad Lagoon, Nr Hannington

A lagoon where fish feed on the still water. The wide water coincides with a break in the willow plantations on either side – a halfway break along one of the most beautiful parts of that walkers can't access. A chance to reflect on nature, alone or in good company.

51.667133, -1.727668

## Brazen Island, Hannington

Collapsed riverbanks and rush islands combine to make a bottleneck of poplar and willow trees. It's eerily quiet here, and a nice place to watch fish feeding on the surface.

51.667571, -1.730920

### Inglesham Lagoon, Inglesham

A water inlet of reed and willow that is sometimes used as a mooring. A nice place to sit and have a break.

51.671466, -1.711406

### Upper Inglesham Wood, Upper Inglesham

Riverside woodland in which to hide between poplar, maple and arches of perennial ivy. Less than 275m (900ft) of canopy but good shelter from the sunshine.

51.671638, -1.710764

### Gobnait Ait, Inglesham

A collapsed riverbank that falls between being a wooded island and a platform, depending on how much silt is in the backwater. It lies on the opposite side of the riverbank to the path, so a packraft is needed to explore.

51.676346, -1.709520

### River Cole, Inglesham

There are many places to launch a packraft here. Cross the southern fork of the River Cole just S of Inglesham. There is a small FB across the River Cole next to a bend in the Thames. The river mouth is densely packed with reeds, mud and birds. Much of the grassy riverbanks appear to have collapsed. The sunken banks act as a windbreak or place to sit over the river and reeds.

51.677430, -1.709941

### Willow Benches, Inglesham

Look for natural benches of fallen waterside willows.

51.680049, -1.709508

### Inglesham Island, Inglesham

Forage for hawthorn leaves and blossom in April and May. You will need to force your way under the brush and it's extremely muddy, even in summer. There is a sunken island on the facing riverbank that floods in winter.

51.680795, -1.709509

### Inglesham Lagoons, Inglesham

Two adjoining lagoons form chicanes that swing upstream of Inglesham. It's a good place to fish watch on a hot, still day. The wire fence around the edge of the lagoons keeps cows out and stops the riverbank collapsing under them.

51.683395, -1.707082 & 51.683196, -1.706459

## → DETOUR – PACKRAFTING 365M (1,200FT) E

### Inglesham Island, Inglesham

A wooded islet that can only be explored from the river. The path detours away from the riverbank at the Inglesham lagoons, which makes this part of the river especially quiet in summer.
➤ **Find** the riverbank where it leaves the TP (51.683424, -1.705987), and paddle E.

51.684077, -1.705737

### Old Weir, Inglesham

Find the deepwater pool that was once the old Inglesham Weir. Pike feed here because of its depth and cool temperatures.

51.684734, -1.705887

### Inglesham Ford, Inglesham

Kayak or paddle the old ford that was used as a crossing by villagers with their farm animals. There was once a Ln down to the ford, but it is now overgrown and lost.

51.685467, -1.705241

## ST JOHN THE BAPTIST CHURCH, INGLESHAM

Explore one of the rarest churches in England, which was gifted by King John to the Cistercian monks of Beaulieu Abbey in the New Forest in 1205. William Morris, who lived at Kelmscott, a few miles upriver, famously campaigned to restore St John's in the 1880s, because he knew it was an important place to protect. His main interest was the fading wall art that celebrates nature, and he raised cash for repairs to the church through his artwork and also his association with the Pre-Raphaelite Brotherhood. The unusual church bells are set inside a 13th-century bellcote.

51.684444, -1.705036

### The Cross, St John the Baptist Church, Inglesham

Touch the 15th-century cross in the churchyard. The rare cross has no crossbar – just a crested capping. Some of the earliest Christian crosses, particularly from the Byzantine period, were vertical pillars.

51.684444, -1.705036

Inglesham

### Anglo Saxon Carving, St John the Baptist Church, Inglesham

Look for the Anglo-Saxon carving of the Mother and Child on the internal S wall of the church. The carving was used as an outdoor sundial until 1910, and you can still see the incised meridian lines and the hole for the scratch dial.

51.684444, -1.705036

### Inglesham Old Village, Inglesham

You won't see it, but you might feel the spirit of a ghost village around here. Nothing remains apart from mounds and sunken Lns either side of the A361, and, of course, the church.

51.684119, -1.703019

### The Thames and Severn Canal, Inglesham

The Thames and Severn Canal, which ran for 29 miles, was completed in 1789 and linked England's two largest rivers, the River Thames and the River Severn. The last boats to travel this section of the canal left in 1927, with the rest of the canal being abandoned in 1933.

51.6881, -1.7052

Roundhouse Bridge

### Inglesham Round House, Inglesham

Sit in the shade of Lombardy poplars. The Round House was once known as the lock-house, and it guarded the entrance to the Thames and Severn Canal from trespassers. You can still find remnants of the old canal at Kempsford in the form of a sunken trench that runs across the High Street (51.668810, -1.768881).

51.687504, -1.705476

### ROUNDHOUSE BRIDGE, LECHDALE

Watch swallows feed their young in the nests that they build under the bridge. The bend in the river is where the River Coln meets the River Thames. This is the start of where the Thames begins to broaden out and become navigable for powered craft.

51.688223, -1.704507

### → DETOUR – CYCLING 3 MILES W

### Cotswold Lakes Crossroads, Lechdale

A lost Ln that is good to explore on bike.
➤ **The** FP and lost Ln join the Thames FB beside the TP (51.688242, -1.704638). Follow this N.

51.691911, -1.704287

### Lechlade W – Cotswold Lakes, Lechdale

A lost Ln and FP along the Thames and Severn Way.

51.690935, -1.717678

### Fairford E – Cotswold Lakes, Lechdale

Look for dog rose rosehips around the water's edge. They have more vitamin C than oranges.

51.686242, -1.732389

### Whelford N – Cotswold Lakes, Fairford

There are dead-nettles all along here from April onwards. With their white and purple flowers, they look similar to stinging nettles, although they are not closely related and don't sting. They come from the mint family, even if they don't taste minty.

51.692711, -1.751710

### River Coln Riverbank, Lechdale

Sit under ash and alder trees at the mouth of what some have said is the most beautiful, fast-flowing trout stream on the River Thames. The River Coln slides into the River Thames at Inglesham Round House. For hundreds of years, it has been praised by artists and poets for its beauty.

➤ **There's** direct access to the mouth of the River Coln from the Thames FB (51.688213, -1.704613).

51.688201, -1.704661

## → DETOUR – PACKRAFTING ½ MILE W

### River Coln, Lechdale

There is good shelter here under thickets of elder and willow. It's almost impossible to navigate in summer, but the green dies back in winter.

➤ **Find** the riverbank where it meets the TP (51.688107, -1.704863) and paddle W into the mouth of the River Coln on the opposite bank.

51.688087, -1.705534

### River Coln, Lechdale

Look for greater burdock upstream. The ancients considered the roots a delicacy.

51.688269, -1.707687

## BRIDGE HOUSE CAMPSITE

 A family-run touring site for motorhomes, caravans and tents. Dogs must be kept on a lead. Disabled toilets and baby changing facilities.

Thames St, Lechlade, GL7 3AG

www.bridgehousecamp site.co.uk

01367 252348

## THE RIVERSIDE

 A pub with rooms and a garden overlooking the River Thames.

Lechlade-on-Thames, GL7 3AQ

www.riverside-lechlade. com

01367 252534

## THE TEA CHEST

 A café for sandwiches and cuppas close to the river.

The Riverside Park End Wharf, Lechlade, GL7 3AQ

www.facebook. com/100063605738804

01367 253015

## Lechlade Marina, Lechdale

Moorings, boatramp and parking.

51.692262, -1.696468

## Bell Ln, Lechdale

Bring a pack lunch to sit beside the slipway. There is a bench at the end of the Ln under the trees.

51.692898, -1.693488

## ④ HALFPENNY BRIDGE, LECHDALE

Good views and somewhere to get in the water. This is the official starting mark of the navigable River Thames – even though many boats do carry on for another few minutes to the Roundhouse Bridge (see p68). Kayaks and punts navigate to Cricklade, and beyond. The Ha'penny Bridge is the first of 106 navigable bridges between Lechlade and London. It was erected in 1792 to replace a ferry. Tolls were once charged to cross the bridge, and a toll house is all that now remains after a local rebellion resulted in the toll being scrapped in 1839.

51.692154, -1.692841

## St Lawrence Church, Lechlade

Touch the stone of the 15th-century church. The church has a fabulous eight-sided spire. Inside is a 13th-century piscina and carvings.

51.693842, -1.690403

## Lechlade

Put on your sunglasses – Lechlade's streets glow with the colour of Cotswold stone in summer.

51.692154, -1.692841

## River Meanders, Lechlade

Walk the grass meanders between two of England's most beautiful bridges. There is an army hut on the opposite shore – one of 60 placed along the River Thames in 1943 to keep out invaders. Bushes of purple Himalayan balsam are everywhere. The seeds can be eaten raw in late summer and taste like nuts. Leaves were used by the ancients to treat burns. Because the plant is considered invasive it's an offence to carry or disperse the seeds.

51.691001, -1.684486

## River Leach, Lechlade

Paddle to the mouth of the river that gives Lechlade its name.

51.6891, -1.6772

St John's Lock

###  River Cole, Wiltshire & Oxfordshire

Cross the boundary between Wiltshire and Oxfordshire: a hard stone and wooden FB across the River Cole. The river empties into the Thames around a bushy mouth.

51.6887, -1.6772

###  Saint John's Island, Lechlade

Stand on the first proper island on the River Thames – Saint John's Island – a beautiful, manicured space of trees, flowerbeds and cut grass. Inevitably, St John's is the highest island on the river – a heady 76m (250ft) above sea level. It's also home to the first lock on the Thames, St John's Lock (see below).

51.688971, -1.677552

###  St John's Lock, Lechlade

Move around and explore the first lock on the river. Six of the 45 non-tidal locks on the river are between Lechlade and Newbridge. These locks are the most remote and beautiful in England, so worth some time to explore or even a stopover. Layered in a sense of timeless beauty, it's easy to feel like an intruder who needs to move on. Don't, unless you want to. This is the first of three locks in this section. Notice how things are a bit more manicured; the path is mown, which is beautiful, the river a bit wider.

51.688971, -1.677552

## TROUT INN

Pub with a riverside garden by the weir pool to St John's Lock. Family-run inn serving real ales, ciders, wines and spirits, as well as daily blackboard specials. Before becoming a pub, the inn was a workhouse.

St John's Bridge, Faringdon Rd, Lechlade, GL7 3HA

www.thetroutinn.com

01367 252313

## ⑤ OLD FATHER THAMES, ST JOHN'S LOCK

Touch the statue of Old Father Thames by Raffaelle Monti, which stands outside the lock house. It has been here since 1974 when it was relocated from the source of the Thames. You've gone from wading through nettles and knee-high grass to exploring an engineered garden of high culture and storytelling.

51.688971, -1.677552

## St John's Bridge, Lechdale

The original wooden bridge was built by Lechlade Priory in 1229 across the old ford, because of constant winter flooding.

51.689676, -1.678873

## Church FP, Lechdale

A lost Ln and FP back to St John's Church.

51.690304, -1.678420

## The Trout Inn Slipway, Lechdale

A slipway by St John's Bridge for launching boats. The launch pre-dates the pub as it is natural.

51.689507, -1.677698

## ⑥ BLOOMERS HOLE FB, NR BUSCOT

Walk across one of the most fabulous pedestrian bridge arches on the Thames: Bloomers Hole FB. The crossing was lifted in to place by a Chinook helicopter from nearby RAF Brize Norton in 2000. It is made from two 27m (89ft), 8-tonne steel beams, which have been wrapped in wood, and it looks like a willow arch that defies geometry.

51.687594, -1.675502

## White Poplars, Nr Buscot

Listen to the poetry of the poplars. The merest breeze moves their leaves into a shimmer of trickling water. They are strangely popular with the tuneless, cawing magpies.

51.687553, -1.674888

## St John's Bridge E Ditch FB, Nr Buscot

In spring, listen for cuckoos – you will hear one or two every day in May.

51.688747, -1.677456

### Cheese Wharf, Nr Buscot

A tiny stone beach for kayak stopovers. Look for blackhead gulls and cormorants. Always interesting to see seabirds so far upstream.

51.683774, -1.676507

### Cheese Wharf Naze, Nr Buscot

Ghosts are a theme all along the Thames and here you can walk the serpentine loops of the part of the river that is said to be the home of the headless boatman. The story goes that in the late 1500s a boatman was accused by a farmer of stealing sheep. The farmer caught the alleged thief and beheaded him on this riverbank naze (headland).

51.684009, -1.675940

### Buscot Old Parsonage, Buscot

An 18th-century riverside site owned by the National Trust. It is periodically closed for building works.

51.681749, -1.674244

South Path into Kelmscott

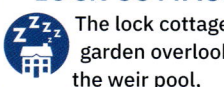
 ## ⑦ BUSCOT LOCK, BUSCOT

Look for otters around the smallest lock on the River Thames. The neighbouring Buscot Park, once owned by Robert Tertius Campbell, had a sugar-beet distilling factory. It closed in 1879.

51.681478, -1.668913

 ## Brandy Island and Buscot Lock Island, Buscot

The streams that divide the lock's islands are good places to watch bats. The Buscot estate was left to the National Trust in 1956.

51.681213, -1.667647

 ## St Mary the Virgin, Buscot

Look for the Pre-Raphaelite stained glass windows on this church, which were designed by Sir Edward Burne-Jones, a close friend of William Morris, in 1921. The 13th-century building is next to Buscot Old Parsonage, a few metres from the River Thames. The river floods towards the back garden in winter.

➤ **The** church is on the other side of the bank from the TP, so requires a ⅓-mile detour via Buscot Lock.

51.681574, -1.673346

 ## Buscot Naze, Buscot

A thicket of Himalayan balsam and reeds.

51.680578, -1.661778

 ## Fiveways, Phillips Farm FB, Nr Kelmscott

A crossroads of five parts. The FB serves five exits and was built in 1936 on the site of the last flash lock (an early lock design) on the river. It was known as Hart's Weir.

51.685213, -1.644671

 ## ⑧ KELMSCOTT MANOR HOUSE, KELMSCOTT

The rented home of William Morris is surrounded by old limestone and the scent of a Cotswold village. The garden retains many of the old trees that Morris loved, including his favourite black mulberry. Morris was a revolutionary textile designer and socialist activist, and he lived here with his wife, Jane, and daughters, May and Jenny, until his death in 1896. His wife bought the house in 1913, but after her death in 1914 it was passed on to Morris' daughter, May. When she died in 1938, she bequeathed the house to Oxford University, who subsequently passed both the house and land on to the Society of Antiquaries of London in 1962.

51.688217, -1.637849

Kelmscott

### THE PLOUGH INN

 Pub classics or snacks for sharing. Bedrooms upstairs in the 17th-century stone building. A 5-minute walk across the fields from the TP.

Kelmscott, Lechlade, GL7 3HG

www. theploughinnkelmscott. com

01367 253543

## St George's Church, Kelmscott

Visit where William Morris and his family are buried. Lots of medieval wall art, stained glass and love.

➤ **Walk** about a ⅓ mile from the riverbank and Kelmscott Manor House. Morris was buried in a tomb designed by his friend Philip Webb.

51.692413, -1.640941

## Eaton Hastings Naze, Eaton Hastings

Green naze of more than 50 herbs and wildflowers. A good place to learn about plants by taking photos in April and May.

51.684181, -1.63001

## St Michael and All Angels Church, Eaton Hastings

Pure William Morris – the window art is a Morris gallery. Look for the W window, where his stained glass shows archangels Michael, Raphael and Gabriel. There are also stained-glass windows by Sir Edward Burne-Jones and Ford Madox Brown.

51.684871, -1.620935

### Lower Farm Bank, Nr Eaton Hastings

The riverbank becomes especially beautiful after Lechlade. The Thames opens into wide lagoons where trout feed on still days.

51.684181, -1.630011

### GRAFTON LOCK, NR RADCOT

You will love this place, so stay a while. Otters, house martins and lock keeper gossip. The nesting house martins are the stars in summer – outperforming four species of bat at night. Otters feed on crayfish – you might see the shells.

51.691284, -1.608823

### Grafton Lock Meadow, Nr Radcot

Paddle across to one of the rarest meadows in England. This place is a remarkable contrast: full of flood in winter; wildflowers and hay meadows in summer. Meadow-rue, yellow rattle and 18 species of wild grass can be found here.

51.689894, -1.607967

### Radcot Wood, Radcot

Look for garlic mustard around the woodland's edges. Large white flowers and hairless, heart-shaped leaves. The crushed leaves smell a bit like garlic.

51.693523, -1.589493

## RADCOT BRIDGE, RADCOT

The oldest bridge on the River Thames has three Gothic stone arches that span the river like a cathedral roof. The old bridge, built around 1200, was only saved from demolition when boat traffic was diverted along the Thames' other channel. Over the central arch is the sunken socket of a cross, which, it is said, babies were baptised in until the end of the 19th century.

51.693645, -1.588662

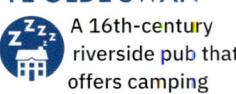

### YE OLDE SWAN

A 16th-century riverside pub that offers camping and glamping facilities, including bell tents and wooden cabins and 40 grass pitches.

Radcot, OX18 2SX

www.yeoldeswan.cc.uk

01367 810220

Radcot

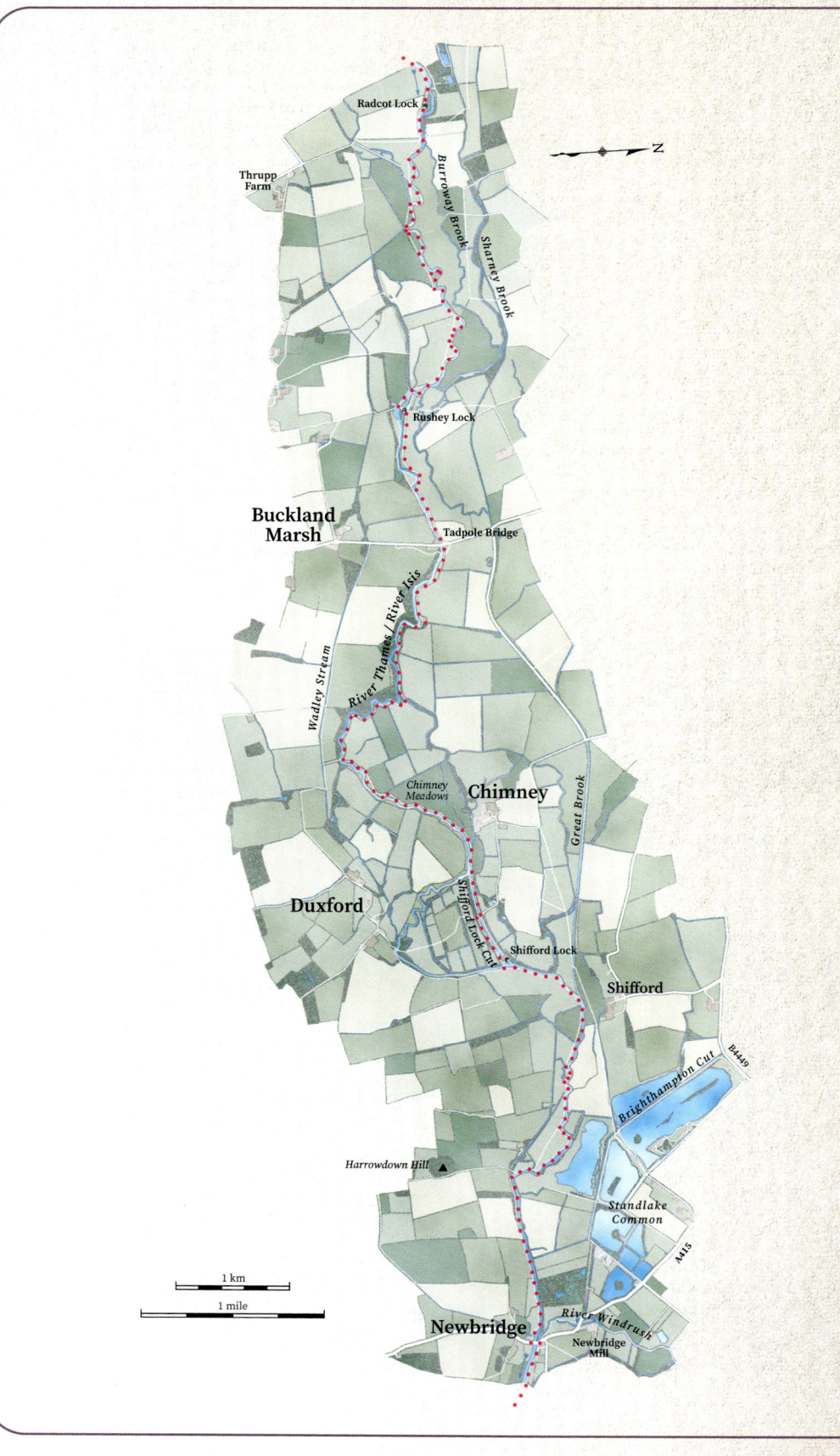

Newbridge

# 4. RADCOT LOCK TO NEWBRIDGE

## HIDE

The best of this river is 'cut' from the TP. The crossing at Duxford is a curling meander that took too long for barges to navigate, so was bypassed by the Shifford Cut. You can find your way down into this old backwater by boat or on foot. Isis is more serpent-like here.

## 10 STEPPING STONES

Radcot Weir
Old Man's Bridge
Rushey Lock
Tadpole Bridge
Tenfoot Bridge
Duxford Ford
Shifford Lock Cut
Shifford Lock
Samson's Island
Newbridge

## Radcot Lock, Radcot

Smell the flowers. Like so many lock gardens, this place is always full of colour and flowers in spring and summer. There is a combined fish and canoe pass – the only one of its kind on the River Thames.

51.699591, -1.572369

## Radcot Lock Island, Radcot

Look for the large lagoon at the N of Lock Island.

51.699900, -1.572511

## RADCOT WEIR, RADCOT

Full of moving water, noise and drama. It is interesting how often people prefer picnic spots around weirs over calmer millponds.

51.699900, -1.572511

## OLD MAN'S BRIDGE, RADCOT

Touch the water. They used to call this place the Harper Weir Bridge, High Bridge and Old Man's Weir. The bridge spans what can seem more like a pool than a river. This has been a local bathing place for centuries, although getting out of the river from the steep riverbank is never easy.

51.699596, -1.568152

Old Man's Bridge

East of Old Man's Bridge

 **→ DETOUR  – CYCLING 2 MILES NE & NW**

## Clanfield

The Knights Hospitaller built a moated preceptor here. The moated site is now occupied by Friars Court, a family home that opens its gardens for private tours and weddings, but the preceptory buildings are gone. There are also two caravan sites and a holiday cottage.

**➤ Find** the FP that joins the TP (51.699688, -1.568167) and head NE towards the BW and lost Ln. This 2-mile detour will take you to Clanfield.

51.716282, -1.588453

## Saint Stephen Church, Clanfield

Find the lancet windows that date to the 12th century. Deserted village earthworks are in the field to the SW.

51.717425, -1.591057

## Ghost Pubs, Radcot

Look for signs. There used to be inns either side of Old Man's Bridge, one may have been The Spotted Cow, the other, The Trout. Historian Fred Thacker wrote in 1909 that both inns were 'a scene of much gambling, cock fighting, and other shady proceedings'.

➤ **For** a detour, walk the path N towards the Spotted Cow Cottages. The path is perhaps all that's left of those days.

51.699596, -1.568152

## Burroway Brook, Clanfield

Look for shade or cover in the trees where the brook meets the Thames. Old willow branches sometimes grow out in an 'L' shape and make a natural seat or shelter.

51.699852, -1.567351

## Hide, Clanfield

Houseboats line the riverbanks between bare hawthorn patches. Thickets between these mobile homes are places to rest, fish and hide.

51.699880, -1.567373

## Old Nan's Weir, Nr Radcot

This small weir and flash lock was called Old Nan's Weir. A 1790 survey decided the site was unsuitable for a pound lock, so Rushey Lock was constructed and 'Nan' was put out of work. A hut once sat here, next to the still visible pool and willows by the FB.

51.698711, -1.560181

## Burrow Brook Loop, Nr Radcot

Blue-banded demoiselles follow walkers all along this section. It's easy to become distracted by their short lives rather than their moment in the sun – caught between admiration for their beauty and the uncomfortable knowledge that their time is so short. The males have only one thing on their minds – they're looking for green females.

51.698447, -1.556438

## Burroway Brook, Nr Buckland Marsh

Cup a yarrow leaf in your hand and breathe in its scent. The smell of yarrow flowers rises from ankle high. It's considered a weed in the city, but around here it thrives – white, pink, mauve and sometimes yellow flowers, as if the plant can't quite decide.

51.702328, -1.541357

### Rushey Weir, Nr Buckland Marsh

Walk around the oldest-surviving paddle and rymer weir in the country. A beautiful little island and weir, crowned with a lock keeper's house that has a pyramidal roof. The house was built in 1894. The gardens are well kept, and there are picnic tables about, which is thoughtful.

51.698293, -1.533936

### RUSHEY LOCK, NR BUCKLAND MARSH

The N bank weir pool is deep, surrounded by large trees and drowning flies that fall victim to trout. There has been a campsite here for decades, but don't rely on it anymore. Just like the lock, it'll be gone eventually.

51.698730, -1.533931

### Sharney Brook Chalk, Buckland Marsh

There is a hawthorn planted where the brook enters the Thames. Hawthorn was often planted close to springs and wells, and it is common to see them along the Thames close to a lush bowl of grass, without obvious signs of water.

51.699543, -1.534086

### Tree Bend, Buckland Marsh

Hide here. The FP leaves the river with the potential to detour into vast thickets of trees and bushes. Even dogs get lost in this blanket of willows and pink flowers. Pushing into the undergrowth is worthy of the strange plant smells alone. They are beyond the reach of any perfume.

51.698706, -1.526865

Rushey Lock

Tadpole Bridge

## THE TROUT AT TADPOLE BRIDGE

Possibly the best pub on the freshwater Thames. Outstanding service, food and location. The food focus is fish and seafood, but there are also steaks and Sunday roasts. It has a riverside garden and each bedroom is named after a fishing fly. Explore the remote bridge too.

Buckland Rd, Buckland Marsh, SN7 8RF

www.butcombe.com/the-trout-at-tadpole-bridge-oxfordshire

01367 870382

### ④ TADPOLE BRIDGE, BUCKLAND MARSH

The bridge is a gateway to almost 10 miles of lost Ln and boreen. The BWs and Lns cross to Buckland (to the E) and Carswell marshes (to the W). An easy ride E on the BW to either Tenfoot Bridge over the Thames, 2 miles away or 3 miles via Duxford's lost Lns to Duxford Ford. Hinton Waldrist and its church are worthy too. Tadpole Bridge was built in the late 18th century and has a single arch.

➤ **Find** where the FP meets Tadpole Bridge and walk or cycle S to the BW E (51.695697, -1.517388).

51.695713, -1.517251

###  Pylon, Buckland Marsh

Hide in the everglades. There's lots of mooring, but big boats can't get into the undergrowth like you can by shallow punt or packraft. The entire 1½ miles from Tadpole Bridge to Tenfoot Bridge has been replanted with trees. It's best in winter but come in a wetsuit and 5mm booties.

51.699773, -1.512544

### Tadpole Wood Naze, Buckland

A wooded plantation meanders along the riverbank. Explore by boat to find shelter and warblers.

51.699584, -1.507365

###  Tadpole Wood Straight, Buckland

Look for giant dock and plantain. Some of these leaves are bigger than horse saddles. Good for wrapping food in.

51.698166, -1.502004

###  Chimney FP, Chimney

Chimney thickets are as wild as the grazed meadows are tame. Take some time to explore the denseness of it all. Avoid the cows and bullocks wherever possible.

51.698849, -1.497359

###  Chimney Lagoon, Chimney

Fish feed here on the surface in summer. The best view of the lagoon is about 27m (89ft) before the World War II shelter, looking N. Otherwise get onto the water.

51.698257, -1.496888

###  TENFOOT BRIDGE, CHIMNEY

Watch kids jump and dive from Tenfoot Bridge – immortal superheroes falling through air, their enjoyment a blur of reckless joy. Tenfoot Bridge is all that remains of a flash weir, which was removed in 1869. Locals demanded a 'right of way' was retained and a wooden bridge was built, which has since been reclaimed by kids. Signs tell them not to jump...

➤ **The** bridge connects a BW back to Tadpole Bridge or SW to the back Lns of Hinton Waldrist and church, 2 miles away. The BW also loops to Shifford Weir.

51.693714, -1.489828

Tadpole Bridge to Chimney Meadows

**→ DETOUR – CYCLING 2 MILES S**

## St Mary the Virgin Church, Buckland

A late 12th-century Crusader chest is kept in this 12th-century church. The heart-burial of William Holcott of Barcote Manor (1575) is also in the chancel in a special triangular locker.
➤ **Find** the FP on the S bank of Tenfoot Bridge (51.693878, -1.489843) and walk S onto the BW.

51.681451, -1.505828

## Duxford Lost Ln

Two miles of lost Ln and boreen to Duxford Ford (see p88) and the village of Hinton Waldrist, where the MP Airey Neave is buried in the churchyard.

51.696444, -1.473180

 ## Chimney Meadows (N bank), Chimney

Wildflowers, wading birds and wildfowl. Yellow cowslips in April and May are among the many common plants that thrive across these 250ha of floodplain, meadows and wet woodland.

51.704319, -1.478025

 ## Chimney Bird Hide, Chimney

An ostentatious little hut mostly surrounded by blue sky, marsh and a deficit of birds. Open the hide window in August for a Nirvana-like shock of cool marsh air.

51.700714, -1.483818

 ## Chimney Hole, Chimney

Smell hawthorn flowers and reeds around the collapsed or cut riverbank. Chew on hawthorn buds... good for heart and blood flow.

51.701878, -1.482236

 ## Serpent (N bank), Chimney

The Serpent lies on the opposite bank to the FP. A snake-like stream to Duxford Ford by boat. If you have no boat, there's a bridge and BW to the ford, about 275m (900ft) E of here.

51.704236, -1.476763

Chimney Meadows

→ DETOUR BOX – PACKRAFTING
275M (900FT) – 1 MILE S

## The Thames Serpent, Chimney

The original Thames. The Isis is more serpent-like here than perhaps anywhere else on the entire river. The river wants to connect E. It tries eight times before the thick, packed gravel ground yields. Humans don't have that sort of patience, which is why water always finds a way to win. Thickly grown with reeds and waterlilies.

➤ **Find** the riverbank where it meets the TP (51.704210, -1.476916) and paddle S.

51.702529, -1.475322

## N Bank Creek, Chimney

Paddling across Duxford Ford is the highlight of this stretch, subject to river flow and anything else that conspires to change your course.

51.703956, -1.476794

Shifford Lock Bridge

## → DETOUR – CYCLING ⅔ – 4 MILES

### Chimney Farm, Chimney

**Find the lost Ln line of ash and willow trees.**
➤ **Find** the BW that joins the TP (51.705030, -1.470846) at the FB and follow NW.

51.706135, -1.482199

### Great Brook, Chimney

Look for shoals of fish-fry on Great Brook in late spring. The water is clear on both sides by the willow and reeds. A lost Ln follows the brook all the way back to the Tadpole Bridge Rd (Buckland Ln).

51.713045, -1.492711

### St James' Church, Aston

A lost Ln takes you to Aston and its church. The church is modern; the yews are ancient.

51.724907, -1.505965

### Cold Harbour Cottages Lost Ln, N, Shifford

Find the lost Ln that once connected Chimney to Shifford via the Thames crossing. The track is unkept but has remained a PRoW for more than 800 years. You'll need a packraft to cross Great Brook and the Thames. When the water level is low, it's possible to cross the ford across the brook at the FP (51.712452, -1.464191), which runs from Chimney across the Shifford ghost village to Standlake.

51.715102, -1.465924

### Shifford Church Ln, Shifford

A lost Ln to the church and lost village via Cote.

51.715298, -1.463231

### St Mary's churchyard, Shifford

Explore the church, the only remaining relic of a village on these water meadows N of the Thames. The Gothic Revival-style church, which was built in 1863 by Joseph Clarke, replaced a 13th-century chapel. The stonework of the ford across the Thames was recorded in 958.

51.715143, -1.463173

### Preaching Cross, St Mary's Church, Shifford

Touch the base and broken shaft of a 15th-century preaching cross in St Mary's churchyard. There is a similar shaft at Isleworth church, albeit that one is still intact.

51.715143, -1.463173

### → DETOUR – WALKING 2 MILES

### Old Shifford Ford, Shifford

The last remaining ford access to Old Shifford. Use it or lose it in summer if the brook runs dry – otherwise packraft across.
➤ **Find** the BW that joins the TP (51.705030, -1.470846) at the FB and follow NW and then E on the FP.

51.712415, -1.464282

Shifford exit

## Old Shifford Village, Shifford

A ghost village, with Rds and access that have been removed from history. Walk the old village meadows.

➤ **Find** the ford (above) and continue walking towards Standlake, via Standlake commons and pits.

51.713463, -1.460067

## Shifford Lock Wood FB, Shifford

Cross the FB onto the S side of the Thames, which is surrounded by hawthorns. Locals would collect leaves and haws here for salad, jam or to use them as a poultice to draw out splinters.

51.704748, -1.470510

## → DETOUR BOX – WALKING ⅔ MILE S

## Duxford Ford, Duxford

Listen to the fish feeding and jumping out of the water. There used to be a ferry here. The path S from Shifford Cut FB leads to Duxford Ford over the old weir stream. The ford is a popular spot for otters, which hunt crayfish.

➤ **Find** the BW that joins the TP (51.705030, -1.470846) at the S end of the FB and follow S.

51.698544, -1.466112

Shifford Ox-eye daisies

Rambling rector

### Ford Wood, Duxford

Explore the thick brush and woodland of this flood marsh. Beware adders.

51.698919, -1.466904

### Duxford Towpath, Duxford

Look for white lilies, which grow along the water's edge in summer.

➤ **This** towpath circles back to the TP and Shifford Lock and is an alternative to walking the Shifford Cut, albeit the trees are not as beautiful.

51.702114, -1.462837

 ### Shifford Wood Walk, Shifford

Touch the giant poplars. They tower over the wooded path like a scene from Swift's Gulliver's Travels. These monsters are one of this stretch's many highlights.

51.705343, -1.468279

 ### Shifford Wood Cut, Shifford

Hide around the riverbank of Shifford Wood Cut.

51.706040, -1.467024

 ### Shifford Weir, Shifford

The weir replaced the flash lock at Tenfoot Bridge. Shifford was a major town more than 1,000 years ago.

51.706978, -1.464197

 ### SHIFFORD LOCK, SHIFFORD

A lock between the villages of Shifford, Duxford and Chimney. It replaced the flash lock at Tenfoot Bridge, about ¾ mile downstream.

51.706850, -1.465626

## Old Thames Loop, Shifford

An alternative detour path to Duxford Ford if you missed the BW from Shifford Bridge.

➤ **Find** the loop ⅓ mile back along the TP.

51.707023, -1.464172

## Shifford Brook, Shifford

It is virtually impassable in spring and summer, but a Thames waterway nonetheless, brimming with plants and wildlife. The entrance to the brook opens up into a deep, wide pool.

51.707829, -1.464536

## Shifford Exit, Shifford

Planted willow avenues and fences, with deep, thick banks. It is all a bit too managed, with lots of information signs.

51.710079, -1.463124

## Great Brook, Shifford

Watch herons feed in the rushes and trees, where the brook joins the river.

51.712839, -1.459997

## → DETOUR – PACKRAFTING ⅓ MILE NW

### Great Brook, Shifford

Explore the mouth of the brook and find the FP bridge.

➤ **Find** the riverbank where it meets the TP (51.712767, -1.460084) and paddle W across the river.

51.712792, -1.461003

### Cold Harbour Cottages Lost Ln, Shifford

Find the lost Ln from Chimney to Shifford. The track is unkept but has remained a PRoW for more than 800 years. You'll need a packraft to cross Great Brook and the Thames. When the water level is low, it's possible to cross the ford across the brook at the FP (51.712452, -1.464191), which runs from Chimney across the Shifford ghost village to Standlake.

51.712650, -1.466325

### St Mary's Ford and Path

The original track from the church to the river has been lost to time. Chimney tenants would travel to St Mary's Church by boat, paddling along the Thames, and were granted free passes when the lock was put in at Shifford in 1896, as the church ministers insisted that it was the right thing to do. Perhaps the old church path and ford can be reinstated soon as someone has identified the exact location of the PRoW.

51.712830, -1.461124

## Shifford

A ghost hamlet mysteriously severed from the Thames. The village had a ford and was a 'stone's throw' from the river's N bank. More than 1,000 years ago, this was one of the most important historic sites in England, and the place where King Alfred the Great held one of his earliest parliaments. Records show the village had dwindled to less than 20 houses in the 17th century. By 1881 the population had risen again to almost 100, but it dwindled again in the mid-20th century until it vanished entirely. The village, the old ford, the old Rds, all gone (see St Mary's Church and churchyard, p91).

51.715069, -1.463137

### Riverbank, Shifford

Marvel in the colour of the Thames: white daisy and bindweed flowers merging against the lime-green willows and grasses. Follow the serpentine bends. The daisies are so thick in summer that it's almost like paddling through streams of white flowers. Best to do so in bare feet, but beware bees.

51.712067, -1.450946

### Shifford Water, Shifford

Take shelter under the willows at Shifford Water – a wide section of the Thames that is almost lagoon-like.

51.712483, -1.448868

### Thameside Gravel Beach, Nr Shifford

An oasis of shallows and narrow gravel beach lined with wildflowers. The river bend forms a natural bowl that swallows fly and dip into for insects in late summer.

51.711521, -1.444097

### Quarry Wood, Nr Shifford

Packraft under the mass of willows for shelter on the N bank.

51.712203, -1.442606

### Samson's Ford, Nr Shifford

Listen to the fish around the old crossing at the head of an island. A hawthorn marks the spot, a sign of a spring or well?

51.711643, -1.441078

### SAMSON'S ISLAND, NR SHIFFORD

A woodland of poplars surrounded by water and birdlife.

51.711375, -1.440360

## Former Limbre's Weir, Nr Newbridge

In 1909, Fred Thacker described finding the remains of the weir's old stonework against the first slopes of Harrowdown Hill: 'The surviving stonework so hidden behind festoons of creeper and bramble and the tall reeds that you would not notice it unless specially searching.'

51.708568, -1.431360

## → DETOUR – WALKING ½ – 1½ MILES

### Harrowdown Hill FP, Nr Longworth

The woodland on the S bank is ash. Patchworks of peppermint moss and ivy trace the trunks. Look for King Alfred's Cakes, fungi that the ancients used as firelighters, and which often grow on ash trees.

➤ **Harrowdown** Hill is a ½-mile detour. Wooded and 100m (325ft) high. The walk is worthy of the 2-mile round trip into Newbridge, via the lost Ln BW of Common Ln. Find the FP that joins the TP (51.707719, -1.438266) and follow it W and then N.

51.702497, -1.437965

### Common Ln BW, Longworth

Lost Ln to Newbridge and/or Southmoor.

51.697293, -1.435668

### Brighthampton Cut, Newbridge

Explore the thick willow canopy around the artificial land drain, which was dug in the 19th century.

51.709529, -1.427783

## Newbridge Pool, Newbridge

Water pool on the approach to Newbridge and the River Windrush. Much of the ambience is people enjoying the Maybush Pub's garden, which looks across the water. There is a small, private launch for customer-use.

51.709833, -1.418027

## River Windrush, Newbridge

Mudlark around the River Windrush shallows after a long, hot summer's day. The Windrush takes its name from its power; a huge volume of water is emptied into the Thames. For all its energy, though, the weed and willow are more prolific here than along almost any other Thames backwater. For that reason alone, it's very special. The Thames gets a lot deeper and wider after the River Windrush.

51.710172, -1.417563

**→ DETOUR – WALKING ⅓ – 1½ MILES N AND W**

## Windrush Bridge, Newbridge

Mud, willow and hogweed.
**➤ Find** the FP that joins the TP (51.710214, -1.417394) by Newbridge and walk NE.

51.711477, -1.420192

## Windrush Naze, Newbridge

Smell the meadowsweet from June onwards. These frothy flowers were used as a strewing herb by the ancients. It was also used as a flavouring in soups and teas.

51.712937, -1.419860

## Standlake Lakes, Standlake

Look for terns over the flooded quarries. There is a BW NE towards Standlake town.

51.715928, -1.443798

 **→ DETOUR – PACKRAFTING ½ MILE N**

## Windrush Bank, Newbridge

Explore the power of the river where it is collapsing the E bank. This place is a rash of chaos, beauty and movement.
**➤ Find** the river that joins the TP (51.710214, -1.417394) by Newbridge and paddle NE.

51.711792, -1.419946

## Windrush Fork, Newbridge

Where the river fork creates a vast island.

51.711477, -1.420192

## Windrush Newbridge Mill and Weir, Newbridge

Access comes and goes; see how far you can get past the A415.

51.714689, -1.419928

 **NEWBRIDGE**

Newbridge spans the River Thames, where it meets the River Windrush, 15 miles from Oxford. The 13th-century bridge is one of the two oldest crossings on the Thames. Newbridge is what remains of the original 51-arch bridge that was built by the monks of Deerhurst Priory in about c1250, on the orders of King John.

51.709850, -1.417433

# 5. NEWBRIDGE TO KING'S LOCK

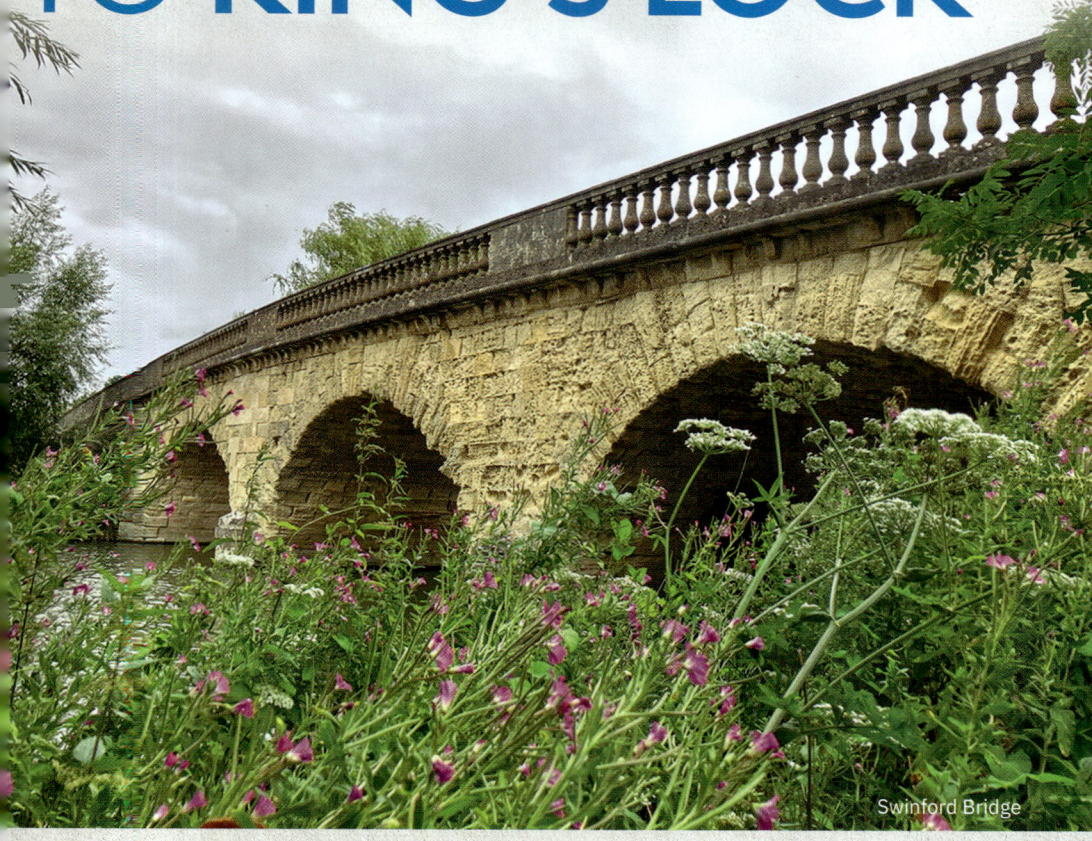

Swinford Bridge

## FERRIES AND FORDS

Almost everything human-made along the Thames is fighting a losing battle for life – even the locks and their keepers. Bablock Hythe is a ferry crossing that has died. Nature flows on regardless, though – moving with the tide, outliving the best ferries, often flooding the shallowest fords. Bring a packraft to paddle across where you can. There's been an inn here for as long as people can remember, if you decide against it.

## 10 STEPPING STONES

Rose Revived Pub
Hart's Weir FB
Northmoor Lock
Bablock Hythe
Skinner's Weir
Pinkhill Lock
Horse Shoe Island
Swinford Toll Bridge
Eynsham Lock
Hagley Pool

Newbridge exit

## New Bridge, Newbridge

Watch swans swim over steely waters around the 12-arch bridge.

51.710049, -1.416944

### → DETOUR – CYCLING ½ – 2 MILES NE

## Moreton Ln, Moreton

Walk or cycle a wonderful boreen. It's dead straight, which suggests it was once important. It leads to Stonehenge Farm – a settlement that is close to a prehistoric site, just to the NE, known as Northmoor Scheduled Monument. There are no standing stones here, but there is a stone circle 2 miles N (see Devil's Quoits, p107). A nice loop into and out of Newbridge, with the river used to return. The 'henge' farm reference is an important precursor of what is to come on this stretch.

➤ **Find** the FP that joins Moreton Ln (51.710833, -1.417189), 90m (295ft) N of Newbridge.

51.710647, -1.411462

## Northmoor Boreen, Northmoor

Cycle the 1-mile boreen from Stonehenge Farm to Northmoor.

51.716385, -1.400509

## ② HART'S WEIR FB, MORETON

Don't resist walking on the concrete arch. Whoever built this thing was an architect of some talent. They say the bridge was built in 1879 on the site of Hart's Weir. However it looks like it was built 100 years later in the 1970s.

51.708528, -1.404642

## → DETOUR – CYCLING ½ – 3 MILES S AND E

### Fyfield, via Hart's Weir FB BW, Fyfield

The bridge provides eight choices: four FPs on the N bank and four paths on the S bank, two of them BWs. Kids, of course, choose none, and in the summer they jump! Inevitably safety is questionable, but that doesn't mean they are not wonderful to watch. Of the BWs, Fyfield is 1½ miles away, via Marsh Ln, which is a lost Ln and BW. There's a church and a sometimes pub. The other BW is two minutes S and then E into the woodland that is Appleton Lower Common (see below).
➤ **Find** the BW that joins the TP (51.706642, -1.393347) and follow S.

51.685721, -1.390288

### Appleton Lower Common BW, Appleton-with-Eaton

A long, wooded BW between the FB and the Appleton Rd. Best in autumn for hazelnuts.

51.704762, -1.383600

### St Laurence's Church, Appleton

An old church full of yew and many original 12th-century fittings. The church is friendly and provides good information on the history of the area.

51.710987, -1.358845

Hart's Weir Footbridge

## Weir BW, Appleton

This riverbank was once a crossing between Appleton and Northmoor. There was public access either side, but that has long gone.

51.714815, -1.378273

 ## Northmoor Weir Island, Appleton

An island is at the head of an old public Rd, where access has been lost.

51.715420, -1.378049

 ## Northmoor Weir, Appleton

Touch one of only two remaining paddle and rymer-operated weirs in the world. They have all been replaced by hydraulic weirs – this one is kept, for now, as a memory.

51.715420, -1.378049

**③** ## NORTHMOOR LOCK, APPLETON

The lock sits on a long, remote island that is shaped like a small boat. It replaced the old flash lock at Hart's Weir, and another downstream at Ark Weir. This one is another living fossil whose days are likely numbered.

51.717110, -1.375368

Northmoor Lock

Ash Copse

### Ash Copse, Appleton

Look for shelter among the N bank's trees.

51.717594, -1.374210

### Eaton Plantation, Eaton

One of the most beautiful, wooded sections along the Thames. Willows of all heights and colours line a ½-mile stretch of the straight river.

51.721455, -1.370777

### Site of Arks Weir (also known as Hart's Weir), Eaton

Touch this large lagoon-like pool. The willow island has almost merged with the mainland. Most of the weir's brickwork was removed in 1910. Look for rubble in the shallows; a stone foundation perhaps or raised turf where the old beams sank into the bank.

51.726227, -1.368495

## THE FERRYMAN INN

A pub beside the river with six bedrooms. The Ferryman Inn is located next to one of the oldest ferry crossings on the river.

Bablock Hythe, OX29 5AT

www.theferrymaninn.co.uk

01865 880028

Eaton Plantation

## Hanging Copse FP, Nr Bablock Hythe

Pink angelica can be found around the hard-edged banks. The river widens here into a lagoon, beside a mile-long stretch of birch, ash and willow trees.

51.724957, -1.369822

## 4 BABLOCK HYTHE

Packraft on to the E bank to walk the riverside FP, rather than following the TP inland. This is a famous Thames crossing that was once used by the Romans. A ferry service operated here for more than 1,000 years.

51.735081, -1.371640

## → DETOUR – CYCLING ½ – 1½ MILES

### Cumnor Well, Cumnor

A beautiful little Anglo Saxon well.
➤ **Find** the riverbank where it meets the TP (51.734368, -1.371097) and paddle the river to the old towpath and the BW E.

51.736399, -1.362462

### Long Leys Farm, Cumnor

A sacred place, linked to springs and wells.

51.737453, -1.354812

### St Michael's Church, Cumnor

A Norman church full of graveyard stories, inscriptions and carved skulls.

51.734162, -1.333051

## Bablock Hythe (E bank), Bablock Hythe

Sit under poplars and weeping willows over the old crossing from the E bank.

51.734276, -1.371053

## → DETOUR – WALKING 1 – 2 MILES N

## Shrike Meadow, Cumnor

Explore a 150m (500ft) lagoon with reeds, gravel islands, mudflats and pools.
➤ **Find** the riverbank on the E side (51.644408, -1.855094) and walk N.

51.75333, -1.366808

## Farmoor Island Waters, Cumnor

Hide in island backwaters when exploring by kayak or packraft.

51.756646, -1.365287

Bablock Hythe

### Farmoor Naze, Cumnor

A grassy river meander over a vast pool of water where fish feed.

51.758297, -1.366060

### Farmoor Reservoir, Cumnor

Tread the reservoir path for ½ mile. This is a detour, and the path rejoins the River Thames at an island of trees (**51.755180, -1.364823**).

51.751420, -1.363781

### Pinkhill Meadows, Cumnor

Several hectares of flood meadow, ponds and reedbeds. Adder's tongue, great burnet and pepper-saxifrage abound; willow, reedbeds and hawthorn, as well as blackthorn and dog rose.

51.757260, -1.364439

Farmoor Reservoir

### Payne's Farm BW, W End

A 4-mile lost Ln and BW between the churches at Eynsham, to the N, and Northmoor, to the S.

51.735355, -1.382144

### → DETOUR – CYCLING ½ MILE W

### Stoneacres Lake, W End

Watch the sun rise over the lake from the Ln. This is a popular spot with early morning anglers.
➤ **Find** the BW that joins the TP (51.735355, -1.382144) and walk W.

51.737705, -1.392550

### Stanton BW Cross, Cumnor

If you carry a packraft, the obvious walk to Farmoor Reservoir is the river towpath on the other side of the River Thames. If you choose to follow the official TP, however, this junction connects to Stanton Cross and the detour that follows.

51.747113, -1.377978

### → DETOUR – CYCLING 1 – 2 MILES W

### St Michael's Church, Stanton Harcourt

Find the famous epitaph by Alexander Pope. It was written when a young couple were struck by lightning and killed while sheltering from a storm. The poem is carved on a stone monument on the outside of the S wall of the nave.
➤ **Find** the BW crossroads that joins the TP (51.746943, -1.378040) and head W.

51.747941, -1.400308

### Stanton Harcourt, Stanton Harcourt

Stanton Harcourt is Old English for 'farmstead by the stones'. The village is famous for a stone circle known as the Devil's Quoits.

51.747941, -1.400308

### Devil's Quoits, Stanton Harcourt

Touch the stone circle SW of the town. The Devil's Quoits were erected more than 5,000 years ago and were in use for over 1,000 years. More than 60 burial mounds, timber circles, pits and grave offerings define this place as one of the most used monuments and sacred sites in English history. Historians restored the original stones at the turn of the last century. They believe rituals here would have involved lighting fires at the entrance, and animal and human bones have been recovered from all over the site. Although fewer than 50 large henge sites exist in the UK, five of them are in the Thames Valley. This henge measures 120m (400ft). It has two entrances, one to the E, the other to the W. You can feel your way around the 28 stones. There used to be more, but the site, inevitably, suffers from neglect, clumsy damage and opportunistic profiteers.

➤ **It** can be hard to find the stones, so look for the Devil's Quoits car park on Google Maps, immediately opposite Dix Pit. Walk in from the church at Stanton Harcourt. Turn R (W) at the TP crossroads to find the medieval chapel and Pope's Tower at Stanton Harcourt. The town is a 1-mile detour of moats, ponds, lost Ln and woodland. Beyond Stanton Harcourt are mile upon mile of more than 50 flooded gravel pits, which line the River Windrush.

51.739891, -1.406022

## Thames Riverbank, Cumnor
Where the TP rejoins the river.

51.753113, -1.368183

## ⑤ SKINNER'S WEIR, CUMNOR
Look for treecreepers along the tree-lined lagoons. The river is deep and wide here.

51.754402, -1.366340

## Farmoor Island, Cumnor
Somewhere to explore, hide and paddle. An 8-acre wooded island of sand pools joined to the TP. Scrub and reedbeds are full of amphibians, birds and dragonflies.
➤ **Navigate** in from the N end.

51.754721, -1.366804

## Pinkhill Weir Crossways, Cumnor
One of the most beautiful locks on the Thames, which can be white and pink with summer flowers. Find the bench opposite the lock house on the other side of the river.

51.759068, -1.362165

## Pinkhill Weir, Enysham
There is deep water beside the pear-shaped lock island. The lock almost completely fills a bulge in the river. Part of the weir stream is known as Luck's or Lot's Hole. The weir has a public FB. The site was once packed with campers, but all is changing as public agencies look to maximise income and restrict public access.

51.760257, -1.364473

Pinkhill Lock

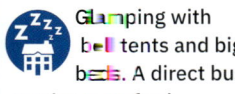

### ⑥ PINKHILL LOCK, ENYSHAM

There are great views of the high ground around Great Wytham Hill and Beacon Hill.

51.761051, -1.362728

### Filchampstead Brook, Enysham

The brook enters the Thames under an oval FB.

51.763475, -1.358894

### Stroud Copse, Enysham

This is not a detour as the TP leaves the riverbank. A FP continues along the riverbank.

51.763444, -1.358617

### Oxford Cruisers, Enysham

Marina and boatyard for repairs and advice.

51.765159, -1.359831

### Swinford Farm Naze, Swinford

Walkers take short cuts around the bends, straight across the meanders. Over time these bends collapse into the water. Little by little we carve away at Beacon Hill, just like the river. Meandering feet, islets, water, erosion.

51.769507, -1.363367

### ⑦ HORSE SHOE ISLAND, SWINFORD

Explore the edges of this small circular island, which has been chiselled by the narrowest of channels. The island is privately owned but beautiful.

51.771910, -1.362706

### ⑧ SWINFORD TOLL BRIDGE, SWINFORD

Watch for the sheer madness of it all... a 5p charge to queue in a car. Swinford Bridge is one of only two remaining Thames toll bridges. The bridge was built over the ford that was once a crossing for pigs. As shallow as the water was back then, the bridge was ordered after the minister John Wesley nearly drowned in 1764. The 'right' to charge a toll was passed by an Act of Parliament. The Act also made it illegal for any other bridge to be built within 3 miles of the toll bridge, either up or downstream. The monopoly of UK trade is more subtle today but no less pervasive than it was in 1764. Cyclists and pedestrians are exempt from the tolls. Almost 300 years of campaigns to abolish the payments have all failed.

51.774299, -1.359121

### Wharf Stream W, Swinford

One of the cleanest streams in England empties into the River Thames at Eynsham Lock. Lots of woodland and wide lagoons.

51.775666, -1.357821

### Eynsham Eyot, Swinford

This is the river's most N point as it turns past the 600-acre Wytham Woods. The island is home to Eynsham Lock.

51.774812, -1.356892

Swinford Bridge

Eynsham Lock

## ⑨ EYNSHAM LOCK, SWINFORD

Walk the permissive path across the lock and weir. The lock was completed in 1928 and was one of the last locks to be built on the Thames. Eynsham was once a trading port on the upper Thames with its own connecting waterway and wharf. The trade lasted for almost 700 years.

51.774812, -1.356892

## Swinford Weir, Swinford

Swinford Weir was used for the loading of stone from Taynton Quarry, which was then taken to London for the rebuilding of the city following the Great Fire of 1666. Coal would then be transported back to Swinford from London. Trade here ended in 1925, and three years later Eynsham Lock was built.

51.775356, -1.356277

## → DETOUR – WALKING ½ – 1 MILE NE AND W

### Swinford Weir Bridge, Swinford

Move across the bridge to explore the Wharf Stream FP.
➤ **Find** the FP on the opposite riverbank (51.775371, -1.356240), and walk NE.

51.776668, -1.354620

### Wharf Stream FB, Swinford

Head over the FB and walk along the Wharf Stream.

51.776654, -1.354622

### Wharf Stream N, Eynsham

Where the stream meets the BW into Eynsham, look for bats and blue tits that feed around the riverside slopes.

51.777310, -1.362697

## Wharf Stream E, Swinford

A beautiful backwater empties into the section of the Thames known as Chil Brook. It loops back to Eynsham Lock to make an island. Wharf Stream tracks back to Eynsham under the ornate bridge.

51.775926, -1.352028

## Chill Brook, Swinford

Lagoon where fish feed in the wide water created by the Wharf Stream.

51.775923, -1.351556

## Further Clay Hill, Swinford

Trees fall down to the water's edge. There are chalk streams around the high ground. April is the best month to visit, when the bluebells are thick. The days and nights are full of moths and butterflies.

51.777241, -1.347189

## → DETOUR – WALKING ½ – 1 MILE SE

### Wytham Woods W, Wytham

You can see Oxford from the high ground, which is called the Singing Way. Pilgrims would sing when they saw the spires of Oxford. There are miles of paths here.

➤ **Find** the FP that joins the TP (51.777391, -1.347081) and follow the woodland S and E.

51.776817, -1.337204

### Wytham Woods E, Wytham

Smell the scent of mushrooms, hazel, oak, pine and birch. There are bluebells in spring. The woods are closed one or two weeks a year for woodland maintenance and deer culling.

51.776817, -1.337204

## Old Canal Beach, Cassington

A sandbank beach to rest and watch the river.

51.780177, -1.343861

## Cassington Cut/Old Canal, Cassington

A willow avenue along the old canal. A good place to hide.

51.780779, -1.342598

## Cassington Cut, Cassington

**Find** the disused canal that joins the River Evenlode. Cassington Lock was once here at the entrance to the cut.

51.781346, -1.343685

### River Evenlode Lagoon, Cassington

Watch fish feeding on a wide stretch of river opposite the
River Evenlode.

51.784981, -1.337753

### → DETOUR – PACKRAFTING 90M (295FT) – ½ MILE W

### River Evenlode, Cassington

Paddle to where the River Evenlode enters the Thames under a
canopy of willow and shallow islets.
➤ **Find** the TP riverbank opposite the River Evenlode and move
across the water.

51.784981, -1.337753

### River Evenlode, Cassington

The source of the River Evenlode is near Moreton-in-Marsh in
Gloucestershire and runs for 45 miles before it reaches the
River Thames. It is the last of the Cotswold waters to enter the
Thames, and the water quality is nitrous like the River Windrush.

51.784900, -1.337800

### Thames Riverbank Bends, Cassington

The waterside edges here are thick with the pink flowers of mint
and blue chicory.

51.785410, -1.332959

### Hagley Pool Weir, Wytham

An old concrete weir at the centre of a wide pool in the Thames.

51.787518, -1.317844

## → DETOUR – PACKRAFTING ½ MILE N

### Yarnton Naze Inlet, Yarnton

A wooded naze with a secret inlet for hiding in.

➤ **Find** the riverbank on the opposite side to the TP (51.787575, -1.316443) and kayak E or W.

51.787576, -1.316443

### W Mead, Yarnton

More than 100 acres of access ground.

51.789659, -1.311013

### Yarnton Meads, Yarnton

Listen for the unmistakable display call of the curlew ('cur-lee'), which can be heard from February through to July.

51.790273, -1.316266

### Oxy Mead, Yarnton

There are masses of cowslips and marsh orchids to be found in this flood meadow next to Yarnton Mead.

51.792091, -1.305578

### Seacourt Stream or Wytham Stream, Wytham

Seacourt Stream or Wytham Stream leaves the Thames on its S bank. Some say this is the old course of the River Thames, which bypasses Oxford. Some of the weir stream can be paddled but it gets very clogged in summer. Seacourt Stream runs parallel to the Thames, bypassing the locks. It's good for fish.

51.787506, -1.317793

### HAGLEY POOL, CASSINGTON

The river becomes a lagoon as it turns the bend. Explore the large willow island on the N bank. The back channel is clogged so it can look like it is part of the mainland.

51.787404, -1.317081

### Hagley Pool, Cassington

Get in the packraft. Seacourt Stream runs 11 miles S, joining the Thames after Oxford. How far you get depends on the rain, the obstacles and the landowners. Hinksey Stream, which is a branch off Seacourt Stream, is less than 3 miles long. You either make it through, or you don't.

51.787269, -1.317129

### Hagley Pool Peninsula, Wytham

A raft of woodland and a beautiful place to shelter from the rain or shine, heat or cold.

51.787783, -1.316746

 ### King's Eyot, Wytham

A secluded island, uninhabited apart from the lock keeper's cottage, immaculate gardens and picnic benches.

51.789317, -1.306348

 ### King's Lock, Wytham

This place is less about boats and more about boots. Spend some time walking the lock and its waters. A public FP crosses both the lock and weir. The connection of the Duke's Cut to the Oxford Canal, via the Wolvercote Mill Stream, is important. This is a single walking and river route that takes you all the way to the N of England, and beyond, via the Coventry and the Trent and Mersey Canal canals.

51.788905, -1.306577

King's Lock

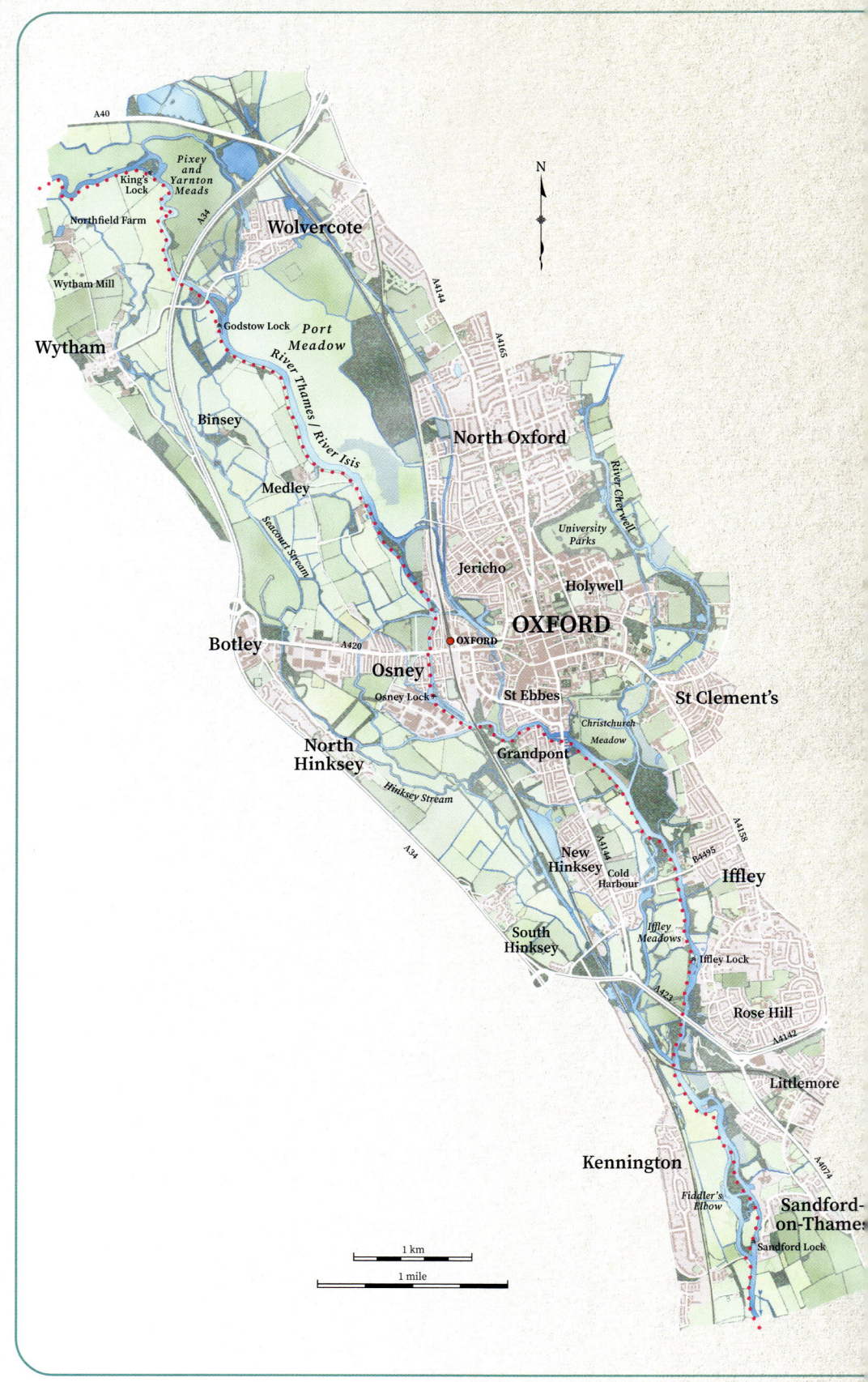

N

A40

King's
Lock

Northfield Farm

Wytham Mill

*Pixey
and
Yarnton
Meads*

A34

**Wolvercote**

A4144

Godstow Lock

*Port
Meadow*

A4165

**Wytham**

*River Thames / River Isis*

*Seacourt Stream*

**Binsey**

**Medley**

**North Oxford**

*River Cherwell*

*University
Parks*

**Jericho**

**Holywell**

**OXFORD**

● OXFORD

**Botley**

A420

**Osney**

Osney Lock

**St Ebbes**

**St Clement's**

*Christchurch
Meadow*

**Grandpont**

**North
Hinksey**

*Hinksey Stream*

A34

**New
Hinksey**

A4144

Cold
Harbour

A4158

B4495

**Iffley**

**South
Hinksey**

*Iffley
Meadows*

● Iffley Lock

A423

**Rose Hill**

A4142

**Littlemore**

**Kennington**

A4074

*Fiddler's
Elbow*

**Sandford-
on-Thames**

● Sandford Lock

1 km

1 mile

# 6. KING'S LOCK TO SANDFORD LOCK

## CITY

Oxford is a grubby place but a friendly one. The second-best city in England (after London) is arguably the most hospitable community of humans and nature living together as one. There are more wild places in and around Oxford than any other riverfront in England. The Hanging Gardens of Babylon, it is not. It's so much better than that.

Bridge to Sandford Pool and island

## 10 STEPPING STONES

- Godstow Abbey
- Port Meadow
- Black Jack's Hole
- Binsey Ford
- Fiddler's Island
- Tunnel to Oxford Canal
- Osney Lock
- Folly Bridge
- Iffley Lock
- Sandford Lock

→ **DETOUR – PACKRAFTING 180M (590FT) – 2 MILES N AND THEN E AND THEN S**

### Wolvercote Mill Stream W, Wytham

Wolvercote Mill Stream branches off the River Thames, N of King's Lock. It's a designated bathing spot, although water quality varies and is at times classified as poor with swimming not advised. Take advice or make checks.
➤ **Find** the riverbank where it meets the TP (51.789280, -1.309100) and paddle NE to the mouth of Wolvercote Mill Stream. The stream loops to rejoin the Thames after 2 miles at Godstow Lock.

51.7906472, -1.3070676

### Ox Hay and Cherry Wood Riverbank, Yarnton

One of several ancient Oxford City 'lot' meadows that date to medieval times. Wildflowers are as high as the swaying grasses, and in early summer, the crimson heads of great burnet tower over low-lying bird's-foot trefoil, fairy flax and yellow rattle.

51.792091, -1.305578

### Wolvercote Mill Stream W, Wolvercote

A clear stream bordered by spring flowers and insects. Look for butterflies – orange-tip, meadow brown and ringlet.

51.791882, -1.302161

### Kingsbridge Brook, Wolvercote

A narrow waterway that moves N and S of Wolvercote Mill Stream. These backwaters are a spaghetti of paths and streams and need to be explored when you have some time. Much like tidal creeks, they are always changing.

51.791147, -1.300011

### Duke's Lake Cut N, Wolvercote

The 450m (1,475ft) Duke's Cut, which branches off the Wolvercote Mill Stream, is named after George Spencer, 4th Duke of Marlborough, who in 1789 oversaw construction of the waterway across his land. The Duke's Cut links the Oxford Canal with the Wolvercote Mill Stream and created a trade route to the River Thames.

51.791277, -1.297138

### Oxford Canal, Wolvercote

If you would like a big detour, you can divert up N up the carless towpath of the Oxford Canal, all the way to Coventry!

51.792580, -1.294096

## King's Weir Lagoon, Wolvercote

Sit in front of the widest stretch of fresh water on the River Thames. At more than 75m (250ft), this lagoon is a place to sit and watch nature and people.

51.789814, -1.305155

## → DETOUR – WALKING ½ – 2 MILES NE AND SE

### Pixey Meads, Wytham

Lay down in the hay meadows. The pleasure of inhaling the scent and flavour of flowers is wonderful. Purple marsh lousewort, yellow buttercups and cowslips can be found here. These meadows have been grazed for more than 1,000 years, which is why more than 100 species of fauna live here. A canvas of green and white, which frames mauve and yellow. This is all Access Land.

➤ **Find** the FP that joins the TP (51.788906, -1.306577) via the lock. Cross the Thames on the King's Weir FB to the other side of the river, and then walk SE to Pixey Meads.

51.786049, -1.304157

### Pixey Lagoon, Wytham

Paddle the shallows and sandbanks around the meadow lagoon. The still water is created by the U-turn in the river. It follows the edge around Pixey Meadow Naze. Find a way down through the reeds to sit by the bank.

51.787295, -1.305164

Thames Bridge

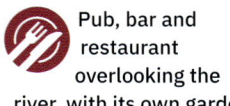

## THE TROUT INN

Pub, bar and restaurant overlooking the river, with its own garden.

195 Godstow Rd, Wolvercote, Oxford, OX2 8PN

www.thetroutoxford.co.uk

01865 510930

## Pixey Meadow Naze, Wytham

Stargaze from a wooded naze. This area is popular with locals who spend the night here in summer under the small willow woodland. I think it's better by day, though.

51.786100, -1.304289

## Thames Bridge, Godstow

Godstow is the perfect entrance to one of the most river-oriented cities in the world. The bridge hangs lows over the water, almost too wide and thin for its weight. The first moorings come into view just past the bridge, the preamble to the city's most prolific symbols of wisdom: communal space, vibrant nature and human endeavour.

51.780706, -1.303260

## Bridge Creek Wood, Godstow

Birch and willow woodland can be found on the N bank of the river. The creek has a wide mouth, although it is sometimes clogged with trees and reeds. The inlet is about 20m (70ft) E of the bridge, but the woodland butts against it. It's a good place to shelter but can suffer at times from the noise of overhead traffic. Narrow boats tend not to moor around the inlet, so it's worth exploring. There is no access from the bridge or Rd.

51.780885, -1.302599

## Wolvercote Bathing Area, Godstow

Another place that is monitored by the Environment Agency for clean water, so that more people can swim safely. Check the water quality before you enter the water and definitely do not swim after heavy rain.

51.780833, -1.295943

## Godstow Bridge, Godstow

Look down over the weir pool opposite The Trout Inn (see left). The pool is full of calm beauty, and the pub alive with the buzz of people. These themes seem to follow the water all around the city. The pub was originally built in 1138 as the hospice for the Godstow Nunnery.

51.779617, -1.299855

## The Trout Weir Pool, Godstow

One of the most beautiful stretches of riverside is across the bank from the old inn. There's a little pebble beach and island beneath the bridge.

➤ **Kayak** access via Wolvercote Mill Stream

51.779756, -1.299351

Godstow Lock

 ## Wolvercote Community Orchard, Godstow

Taste the fruit of benevolent grief. This beautiful orchard is a few metres across the bridge. The land was gifted by Philip Leslie Agnew, the publisher of Punch magazine, and a graduate of New College, Oxford. He dedicated the park in memory of his son, Ewan Siegfried Agnew, who died aged 36 from an illness related to his service with 5th Lancers (Special Reserve) in World War I. There's a memorial stone carved by Eric Gill in the orchard.

51.780141, -1.299530

 ## Godstow Lock, Godstow

The point at which the lower Thames heads into London.

51.775471, -1.297284

 ## GODSTOW ABBEY, GODSTOW

At dusk, look for the bats around the abbey's ruins. Godstow Abbey is also good for wildflowers and featured in Thomas Hardy's Jude the Obscure. The abbey was founded in 1133 by Edith of Winchester, who had a dream telling her to build a place for God near Oxford. Much of it was destroyed by Parliamentary forces during the Civil War in 1645.

51.777985, -1.299095

Godstow Abbey

### → DETOUR – WALKING ½ MILE E

## Wolvercote Common, Wolvercote

Listen to the skylarks behind the gravel beaches where locals and visitors swim. There is a small burial mound called Roundhill here, which was occupied in the Bronze Age. A causeway across the meadow was once a famous trade route.

➤ **Find** the FP that joins the TP (51.779755, -1.299351) at Godstow Bridge and walk E across the bridge to find the FP at the pedestrian crossing (51.783993, -1.290271). Walk E onto the common. Alternatively, packraft across the river anywhere S of here.

51.784000, -1.286000

## PORT MEADOW, WOLVERCOTE

A 340-acre meadow where commoners have grazed their animals, including cattle and horses, for more than 1,000 years. King Alfred the Great, who is said to have founded Oxford in the 10th century, awarded the land to the Freemen of Oxford after

## THE PERCH

A thatched 17th-century country inn with a large garden. This site has been home to a pub for at least 800 years, and it's one of Oxford's oldest.

Binsey Ln, Oxford, OX2 0NG

www.the-perch.co.uk

01865 728891

the city faced numerous attacks from the Danes. According to the Domesday Book of 1086, the Freeman of Oxford could graze their animals on the land without charge, and that rule has never been lifted. The site is said to have never been ploughed, either, and consequently it's home to rare plant species and is a Site of Special Scientific Interest (SSSI). The name Port Meadow is thought to derive from 'portman', an early English word meaning 'freeman of a port', which is also used at towns and cities such as Orford and Ipswich.

51.774668, -1.287528

## Port Meadow S, Jericho

This part of the meadow is most beautiful in the summer mist, post dawn, before the sun has warmed earth and air.

51.764531, -1.279605

## Burgess Field, Oxford

Listen for short-eared owls around the woodland and scrub grass. The meadow is full of white and blue flowers in spring: daisies and chicory.

51.773280, -1.277718

## Hock Meadow and the Trap Grounds, Oxford

Paddle the ditches and walk the flood plain.

51.777768, -1.282452

## Black Jack's Hole N, Binsey

Look for pike around one of the deepest parts of the River Thames. The name Black Jack was intended to scare children from swimming here, as rumour had it a goblin of that name lived in a cave close to the riverbank and would drag them beneath the water.

51.772361, -1.288560

## Godstow Holt, Godstow

Walk the wide dirt tracks between chicory and hemp-agrimony. The riverbank community of nettles and barges is reminiscent of a TV scene of a Wild West series in the 1960s: guitars, fresh coffee and bromance.

51.775429, -1.297275

## BLACK JACK'S HOLE S, BINSEY

Meadow grass, hairy willow herbs and giant eastern cottonwood trees line the riverbank, towering over guelder roses, nettles and barges.

51.770634, -1.289590

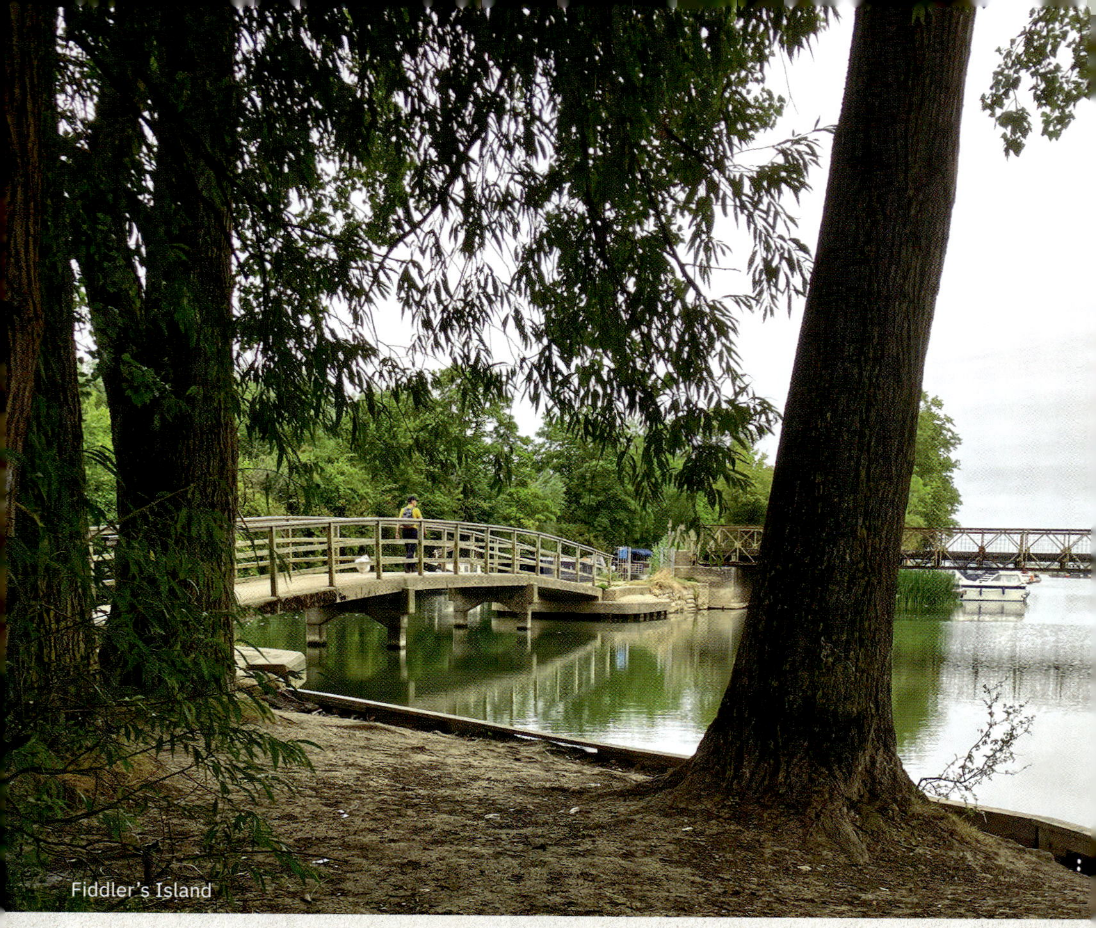
Fiddler's Island

## THE MEDLEY

Wood stove pizzas, salads and garlic bread by the riverside. Open April to September only.

Medley Manor Farm, Oxford, OX2 0NJ

www.themedleyoxford.com

## Binsey Green, Binsey

This green used to have the best view of Oxford, and you can still glimpse it through the gaps in the trees.

51.765716, -1.284680

## St Margaret of Antioch, Binsey

Touch the steps down to Binsey's famous holy well outside St Margaret of Antioch. Henry VIII is said to have brought Catherine of Aragon here hoping the holy water would help produce a son. Medieval texts indicate that the well was blessed by Saint Frideswide, patron saint of Oxford. There's no electricity and services are held by candlelight.

51.768980, -1.297196

## Frideswide's Slab, Binsey

The slab, which is thought to be St Frideswide's gravestone, dates to between 900 and 1099 and was found during the restoration of Christ Church Cathedral in 1869. It's now on display at the Museum of Oxford.

51.768980, -1.297196

###  ④ BINSEY FORD, BINSEY

Paddle into the Thames shallows and what may have been the 'Ox Ford'. The ford stayed in use until the late 19th century so locals could graze their cattle on Port Meadow. Horses were grazed here too, and there is a story that the flood meadow was so enjoyed by the horses that they could never be caught again. They were instead herded back across the Ox Ford onto the more sedate Binsey Green, where they were easily captured.

51.765571, -1.281946

###  Cripley Meadow, Binsey

A large meadow of common land, just to the S of Port Meadow. The adjoining Sheepwash Channel connects the Oxford Canal with the River Thames.

51.762355, -1.274897

###  Medley FB, Binsey

Walk the famous steel bridge. The Rainbow Bridge, as it is also known, was erected in 1865 and restored in 1997 and joins the W bank of the Thames to Fiddler's Island.

51.763888, -1.28030

Castle Mill Stream

## ⑤ FIDDLER'S ISLAND, BINSEY

Fiddler's Island lies at the S end of Port Meadow, lying just to the N of where the Castle Mill Stream branches off the Thames. The rust-red metal-arched bridge known as the Medley FB or Rainbow Bridge (see p125) is uniquely beautiful. Walk avenues of blue chicory flowers. Castle Mill Stream connects back with the Thames further S via the manmade Sheepwash Channel. A path runs the entire length of Fiddler's Island.

51.762437, -1.279116

## Bailey Bridge, Binsey

Bailey Bridge connects the E bank of the Thames with the W bank, via Fiddler's Island.

➤ **Follow** the path E for ⅓ mile to reach the Oxford Canal, over the railway line, or walk N through Port Meadow.

51.762644, -1.278888

## Fiddler's Island Bridge, Binsey

Wild, unmanaged and a wonderful place to rest.

51.762293, -1.279103

## Fiddler's Stream, Binsey

Explore a waterworld and islands on foot or by boat. Try to find Castle Mill Stream.

51.760884, -1.276184

## Fiddler's Path, Nr Botley

Canal-like straight towpath along the Thames.

51.757577, -1.273809

## Sheepwash Channel, Nr Osney

Explore how the Sheepwash Channel connects the River Thames to the W and the Castle Mill Stream next to the Oxford Canal to the E. Spend some time here and get your bearings. It can all get a bit overwhelming if passing too quickly.

51.755544, -1.270961

## ⑥ TUNNEL TO THE OXFORD CANAL, OXFORD

It is possible to travel from Oxford to Cambridge by water... it's only 215 miles with 115 locks to negotiate!

51.755616, -1.271366

## New Osney Bridge, Osney

Walk the iron bridge over the narrow stream. Built in 1888, it replaced the old stone bridge built by the Osney monks.

51.752430, -1.272499

**THE PUNTER**

Vegan and vegetarian dishes by the riverside.

7 South St, Osney Island, Oxford, OX2 0BE

www.thepunteroxford.co.uk

01865 248832

## Bulstake Stream, Osney

A pool of water and willow trees. Take a saw if punting upstream. The current can reverse during high water and floods.

51.746806, -1.2675642

## Onsey Aits, Osney

A group of three islands, mostly grass surrounded by trees. Find the old, disused Osney flour mill.

51.749355, -1.272329

## Osney Lock House Hydro, Osney

Listen to the Archimedes screw as it churns out communal energy. The Osney Lock Hydro was funded by locals and was the first community-owned hydro scheme to be built on the Thames. Electricity generated by the Osney Lock Hydro provides enough energy to supply the equivalent of 50 households.

51.749355, -1.272329

## OSNEY LOCK

At dawn or dusk, look for otters around one of the prettiest locks on the Thames. Explore by packraft if at all possible.

51.749200, -1.271879

Edgar George Wilson Memorial

### Osney Marina, Osney
Clean, well-run marina with slipway, gas, water and boat repairs.

51.748428, -1.269296

### Edgar George Wilson Memorial, Osney
This memorial is to Edgar George Wilson, who in 1889, at the age of 21, lost his life after rescuing two boys from drowning. This obelisk is close to the FB and railway bridge.

51.746898, -1.267554

### St Ebbes Bathing Place (N Bank), Grandpont
A bathing area that was dismantled and closed in 1938. The site is on the E bank of the Thames at Oxpens Meadow.

51.747145, -1.264289

### Grandpont Island, Grandpont
Find the unique stone crossing called Folly Bridge. A timber bridge that dates back to the Saxons stood here originally.

51.745878, -1.264429

### Grandpont Nature Park, Grandpont
Hide in the copses between the marshy grass. A good place for bluebells in spring, this 8-acre green open space on the opposite side of the river to Oxpens Meadow has good cycle links.

51.745878, -1.264429

**THE PAPER BOAT CAFÉ**

Coffee, breakfast and pastries on riverside tables.

Folly Bridge, The Old Toll House, Oxford OX1 4LB

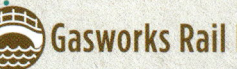

### Gasworks Rail Bridge, Grandpont

A pedestrian bridge that links St Ebbes to the Grandpont Nature Park. It crosses the water on the reach between Osney Lock and Iffley Lock.

51.746030, -1.263634

### Friar's Wharf Bridge, Grandpont

A handy Thames crossing.

51.746981, -1.260704

### Bacon's Tower, Grandpont

The tower that stood here in the 13th century was known as 'Friar Bacon's Study' after the Franciscan monk and astronomer Roger Bacon, who lived here. The original tower on Folly Bridge was demolished in 1779. A new tollhouse, which was named Bacon's Tower in his honour, was built on the bridge in 1844.

51.745873, -1.256599

Folly Bridge

## ⑧ FOLLY BRIDGE, GRANDPONT

This stone bridge, built between 1825–7, apparently stands at the site of a ford over which oxen would have been driven across the Thames.

51.745999, -1.256263

### Trill Mill Stream, Oxford

Walk or packraft one of the least-visited backwaters, which is lined with maple, alder and invasive flowers that have escaped people's gardens.

51.746597, -1.255584

### Jericho, Oxford

Explore a parish that has more churches per square foot than the Holy Land, as more than 20 are dotted either side of the Oxford Canal and County Hall, N of Christ Church Cathedral. The former industrial suburb is located outside of Oxford's city walls, and it was here that medieval travellers to the city would stay while waiting for the city gates to open. In the 1950s it became a red-light district.

51.752725, -1.264393

### Poplar Walk, Christ Church Meadow

This flood meadow is one of Oxford's many watery treasures.

51.745969, -1.254185

### River Cherwell, Nr St Clement's

Packraft the wooded Cherwell River to the point where it joins Shire Lake Ditch. You can also paddle as far as St Clement's Church, although be warned that this stretch is often blocked with trees and angry swans!

51.744955, -1.247336

### Shire Lake Ditch, Nr St Clement's

Paddle the waterway around Christ Church Meadow.

51.738720, -1.244394

### Christ Church Meadow, Oxford

Beautiful, but all a bit over-managed, Christ Church Meadow is owned by the University of Oxford. Sadly, the university chooses to close the meadow at night, which is a rare moment of control in between Oxford's otherwise enlightened embracement of communal 24-hour access. All entrances are via gates that are locked at night.

51.745753, -1.252173

Path out of Oxford

### Christ Church Orchard, Oxford
A wooded orchard on the banks of the River Cherwell, which branches off the Thames. Visit in late summer.

51.742909, -1.247644

### Aston's Eyot, Nr New Hinksey
Look for roe deer between the nettles and wooded plantations. Bats and rabbits come out in large numbers at dusk.

51.741061, -1.247570

### Weirs Ln, Nr New Hinksey
Dog rose and elder bushes flower here in spring. Oxford City Council still cuts the grass around these wide lagoons of willow and nettle.

51.736727, -1.244273

## ISIS FARMHOUSE

Food and drink, and a riverside garden with picnic tables. Free jazz sessions are held here every Sunday from 7pm.

Haystacks Corner, The Towing Path, Iffley Lock, Oxford, OX4 4EL

www.theisisfarmhouse. co.uk

01865 243854

### Shire Lake Ditch, Nr New Hinksey

A beautiful stream that runs through a thin woodland.

51.738777, -1.244404

### The Kidneys, Nr New Hinksey

Possibly the best nature reserve in Oxford. Moorings, deer and badgers under old, creaking willow trees.

51.738521, -1.243993

### Longbridges Nature Park, Nr Iffley

The stream in Longbridges Nature Park was once used as a swimming pool. It's a great place to launch a packraft or kayak to explore the backwaters and weirs.

51.737007, -1.243901

### Iffley Meadows P, Iffley

Listen for the meadow pipits and snipe. They feed in the meadows between the streams. Fritillaries bloom here in spring.

51.734379, -1.242185

### Iffley Meadows, Iffley

Take a 0.2-mile detour from the FP and you will reach Iffley Meadows, more floodplain meadows and a Site of Special Scientific Interest (SSSI).

51.734158, -1.245471

### Meadow Ln, Iffley

Between the boatyard and the stream are some of the thickest stretches of brambles on the Thames. Best when full of berries in September.

51.734071, -1.238089

### Weirs Orchard, Iffley

A maze of streams and dense willow thickets. Places to hide on foot or in packraft.

51.729739, -1.245951

### Haystacks Corner, Iffley

Look for large yellow marsh-marigolds here. *Alice's Adventures in Wonderland* stories were first heard in these meadows, as author Charles Dodgson, otherwise known as Lewis Carroll, is said to have told them here to Alice Liddell and her sisters.

51.730687, -1.240935

### IFFLEY LOCK, IFFLEY

Located near the village of Iffley, Iffley Lock connects a small island with the W bank of the Thames. It was once famous with artists for its 13th-century mill, but this was destroyed by fire in 1908. Built in 1631 by the Oxford–Burcot Commission, Iffley Lock is a pound lock and saw several enlargements and tweaks in the 19th century.

51.729129, -1.240583

### Iffley Mathematical Bridge, Iffley

Built in 1924, this is a smaller version of a bridge built in Cambridge over the River Cam. It was designed by John Griffiths, and although not a direct replica of the James Essex the Younger bridge in Cambridge, which was built in 1749, still incredibly intricate and striking.

51.728980, -1.239934

### Hinksey Stream Wood, Kennington

Run down to Kennington in a kayak or packraft. There are lots of wildflowers on the flood meadow in spring.

51.723053, -1.242468

### Seacourt Stream, Kennington

Seacourt Stream (or Wytham Stream) is the name given to Hinksey Stream where it meets the River Thames. Hinksey Stream then continues NW towards Oxford where it rejoins the River Thames.

51.721000, -1.243000

Bridge to Sandford Pool and island

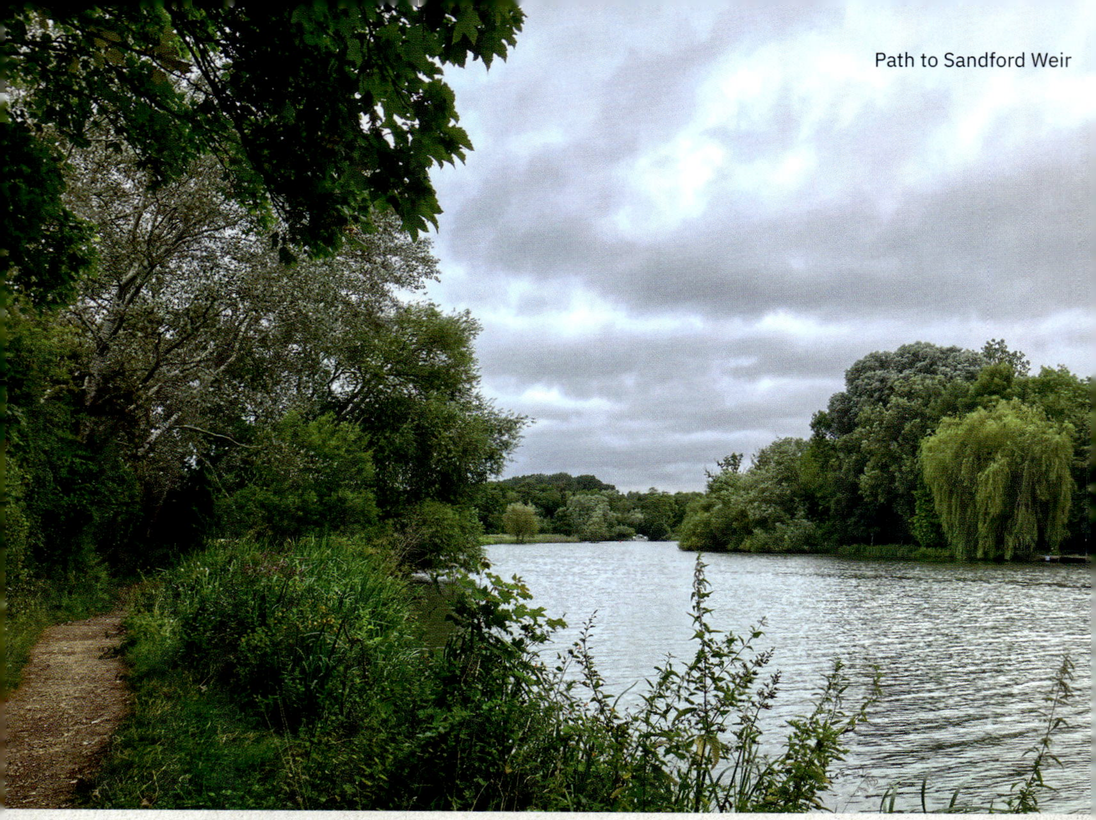

Path to Sandford Weir

## Bagley Wood, Kennington

**Walking out of Oxford is as enjoyable as walking through it, and Bagley Wood should be visited at night. The Victorian poet Lionel Pigot Johnson wrote in 'Bagley Wood':**

The night is full of stars, full of magnificence:
Nightingales hold the wood, and fragrance loads the dark.
Behold, what fires august, what lights eternal! Hark,
What passionate music poured in passionate love's defence!

**The ancient wood is full of bluebells and sunshine in April. Once owned by Abingdon Abbey, it's been open to the public and managed by St John's College, Oxford, since 1557.**

➤ **Find** the TP (51.719369, -1.241308) is ½ mile from the wood.

51.717457, -1.258874

### Rose Isle

Private island of giant Lebanese cedars with an old wooden bridge over the backchannel. In the 1920s it was a hotel – also known as Kennington Island.

51.718346, -1.238343

### Simons Land, Kennington

Half an acre of wooded bog and walkway that weaves its way down to the river, curving around Rose Island. Lovely views over Kennington Meadows.

51.718648, -1.236376

### Kennington Pools, Kennington

A rare wet woodland. Molluscs and dragonflies, are abundant here, surrounded by goat willow and hazel, and bluebells in spring. Snowberry is one of the strange invasive plants that seems to thrive here.

51.717707, -1.242155

### Kennington Meadows, Kennington

People swim here in summer, but there's no indication whether it is safe or not. Meadows are used for grazing and the riverside is good for anglers.

51.720689, -1.242688

### Heyford Meadow, Sandford-on-Thames

A boggy meadow of large trees that soak up the spring water that seeps into the Thames. Grass and boardwalks across the marsh.

51.7143942, -1.234639

### 10 SANDFORD LOCK, SANDFORD-ON-THAMES

Balance along the edge of this island walk. The lock, public house and FB are places to river-watch. The Thames shifts back to rural as fast as it became urban on entering the city. Feel how quickly the path merges back to wild. Sandford Lock and Weir is the greatest fall of water on the Thames.

51.708163, -1.232710

Sandford-
on-Thames

Kennington

Sandford Lock

*River Thames / River Isis*

A4074

Radley

RADLEY

Lower
Radley

Radley College
Boat House

Ferry Cottage

Nuneham
Park

The Old Boat
House

Lock Wood
Island

Lock Wood

Abingdon-
on-Thames

*River Stert*

A4183

*Radley
Lakes*

*Thrupp
Farm*

Abbey
Meadow

A415

*River Ock*

*Nag's Head
Island*

Abingdon
Lock

Rye Farm

*Andersey Island*

*Swift Ditch*

Caldecott

*Culham Brake*

Furze
Brake

New
Covert

Colmoor
Farm

Culham
Campus

Clifton
Hampden

Abingdon Marina
Park

A415

CULHAM

Clifton Hampden
Bridge

Jubilee Junction

Culham Lock

Culham

*Culham Cut*

*Sutton
Pools*

B4016

*River Thames / River Isis*

*Clifton Cut*

Clifton
Lock

Sutton
Courtenay

Long
Wittenham

APPLEFORD

Appleford-
on-Thames

N

1 km

1 mile

# 7. SANDFORD LOCK TO CLIFTON HAMPDEN BRIDGE

Culham Lock

## ACCESS

You won't need a boat today. Sutton Pools and Abingdon have more than six islands between them, all with bridge access. It was here that former Abingdon MP Sir Ralph Glyn founded the Upper Thames Patrol in 1939. The Dad's Army-style Home Guard water-force, cobbled together from watermen and civilians, kept watch over the riverbank and islands of the Thames, from Lechlade to Teddington. Six thousand men and women, helming boats and driving vehicles during the war years, prepared for an invasion that never came.

## 10 STEPPING STONES

The Lasher Pool
Lower Radley Boat House
Lock Wood Island
Abingdon Weir
Culham Old Bridge
Sutton Pools
Culham Lock
Clifton Cut Weir
Clifton Lock
Clifton Hampden Pool

## KINGS ARMS

Al fresco dining on the riverside. Three old open fireplaces for cold nights.

Church Rd, Sandford-on-Thames, OX4 4YB

www.chefandbrewer.com/pubs/oxfordshire/kings-arms

01865 777095

### ① SANDFORD LASHER POOL, SANDFORD-ON-THAMES

The deepest lock on the Thames above Teddington is a dangerous place. Sadly the pool is deceptively calm on hot days, and too many have lost their lives because of undercurrents. A memorial obelisk tells the story of five Christ Church College Oxford students who drowned here between 1843 and 1921.

51.708163, -1.2327105

### Sandford Eyot and Fiddler's Elbow, Sandford-on-Thames

A FB connects to Sandford Lock. The mills were originally built by the Knights Templars in the 13th century. They are now flat conversions. Fiddler's Elbow is the largest of a group of islands that divides the River Thames into two reaches. Sandford Lock stands at the SE corner of the island, while upstream, on the W channel, is Sandford Weir.

51.710504, -1.232733

### Fiddler's Elbow Tip, Sandford-on-Thames

Stand at the tip of the island. It's a bit like flying at the bow of a ship. Mown grass, willow trees and sloping banks, plus lots of benches. An island bridge links to the Sandford Ln cycle way. Sandford takes its name from the sandy ford over the River Thames between Iffley and Radley.

51.706964, -1.233112

### St Andrew's Church, Sandford on Thames

Sit under the shade of the yew tree planted on Good Friday 1800. The church is on a small hill overlooking the river. A lost Ln leads from Sandford Lock to the church. This is more a backwater than the busy Thames.

51.711651, -1.229022

### Church Rd Slipway, Sandford on Thames

River access via a slipway – remnants of what was once an old mill. There used to be a pub opposite the lock on the Sandford side.

51.706979, -1.232436

### → DETOUR – CYCLING 3½ MILES

### Sandford Lock to Folly Bridge Cycle Ln, Sandford on Thames

A 3½-mile track that follows the railway line and River Thames.

51.706985, -1.233727 (Sandford Lock) to
51.745872, -1.256321 (Folly Bridge)

### N Auburn Creek, Sandford on Thames

Find a way into the foliage on the opposite bank, in the mouth of Auburn Creek. This creek once defined the margin of a Celtic common. William the Conqueror granted the manor of 'Newenham' to baron Richard de Courcy in 1086. The parish of Nuneham Courtenay, which borders this stretch of the Thames, retains the combination of Saxon and Norman names.

51.699433, -1.230355

### Riverside Wood, Sandford on Thames

The path is lined with saplings and old dying tree trunks. Look for fungi and Himalayan balsam as the path starts to become more rural. The southern exit out of Oxford is as narrow as the N path out is wide.

51.695492, -1.228316

### LOWER RADLEY BOATHOUSE, LOWER RADLEY

A ferry service ran here until the 1930s. There's not much shelter, so the boathouse is somewhere to duck rain or intense sunshine.

51.685371, -1.222318

### Radley College Boathouse, Radley

Concrete slips, pontoons and racks for rowing sculls line 150m (500ft) of riverbank here. The storage spaces are impressively engineered.

51.685460, -1.222004

## NUNEHAM ESTATE

Holiday lets, weddings and events on an estate that comprises over 1,000 acres of land. The park and garden, which is Grade I listed, was designed by Capability Brown.

Book Repository,
Nuneham Courtenay,
OX44 9PG

www.nuneham.com

Radley Path

 ## S Auburn Boathouse

The boathouse sits at the head of S Auburn Stream. Rest under the willow arches on the N banks.

 ## → DETOUR – PACKRAFTING 180M (590FT) – ½ MILE E

### The Nuneham Estate riverbank

➤ **Find** the riverbank where it meets the TP (51.681062, -1.224955) and paddle E towards the eastern bank and the boathouse.

51.680178, -1.224673

### The Deserted Village, Nuneham Courtenay

The Irish writer, poet and playwright Oliver Goldsmith witnessed the demolition of this village in 1761. He wrote a factual/fictional account of its closure and how people were removed by the landowner entitled 'The Deserted Village'.

51.675266, -1.224397

### All Saints Church, Nuneham Courtenay

The village may be gone, but ghosts remain and so does the church. If you believe in spirits moving over old pastures, this is a Thames highlight. If you don't, you'll enjoy it anyway. The view is stunning.

51.680459, -1.217968

### Lock Wood Island, Nuneham Courtenay

A small heart-shaped island in the middle of the Thames. There used to be a thatched cottage on the island, linked to the mainland by an old oval bridge. Sit here to look up at Nuneham Park's wooded slopes.

51.674436, -1.229295

### Nuneham Woods, Nuneham Courtenay

Trees on a ridge of greensand. They aren't as high or as angular as those at Cliveden but they have as much beauty. You can walk through the park from the Rd. Bikes aren't allowed. The largest trees seem to be oak. There are beech and horse-chestnuts too. The woods were public according to GE Mitton, when he wrote about them in 1906.

➤ **The** nearest bridge from here is 2 miles E at Abingdon. Walk back along the S bank towards Clifton Hampden.

51.672188, -1.230040

### ③ LOCK WOOD ISLAND BANK , NUNEHAM COURTENAY

Lay back among the reeds – and think of all those who have enjoyed sitting here before you.

51.673306, -1.229394

### Lock Wood Stream, Nuneham Courtenay

Come here at sunset. The artist Thomas Gainsborough loved it here.

51.673238, -1.229573

### Lock Wood Ford, Nuneham Courtenay

An ancient ford that once served the now-deserted village that was relocated by force. Find the ford using a packraft.

51.673238, -1.229573

Radley Wood

## Pumney Ditch, Culham

Backwater of poplar and willow. Dense and almost impossible to penetrate. Lots of warblers in spring.

51.669613, -1.239968

## Railway Bridge, Culham

Pastel graffiti meets grass and alder. Human engineering is surrounded by rust and overgrown hawthorn. When this was an old river bridge, it was considered one of the best views of Nuneham's wooded hills.

51.669496, -1.240841

## Orchard Lake Woods, Culham

Smell the pine along more than 2 miles of woodland. There is a large lake (51.669022, -1.249861), which can be spotted through the trees. Orchids grow here in spring and summer.

51.667484, -1.246031

## Thrupp House E, Culham

A dark alder wood by the riverside.

51.666598, -1.250669

## Barton Fields Wood, Abingdon

A riverside wood next to wildflower meadows. A cycle path runs along the northern edge of the Barton Fields from Abbey Stream, Abingdon, to Bullfield Lake. Follow the cycle track to Home Farm Barn, at the end of Thrupp Rd.

51.666598, -1.250669

## Barton Fields, Abingdon

Listen to Roesel's bush-crickets in summer between the geulder roses and hawthorn.

51.666598, -1.250669

## Backwater Woods

Riverside pine and broadleaf woodland. Look for birch leaves and buds in spring – they were used in folklore to make infusions for treating skin problems. They were also thought to ease pain from rheumatism and arthritis.

51.667522, -1.258764

Radley Barton Fields

## → DETOUR – PACKRAFTING 90M (295FT) S

### Swift Ditch, Culham

Swift Ditch is a manmade channel that branches off the River Thames at Thrupp and re-enters the river at Culham Bridge. Running for just over a mile, it provided a short cut for boats travelling to and from Oxford and the first channel dug here originally dates to the 11th century. With the creation of the channel came the formation of the 273-acre Andersey Island (see below).

> **Find** the riverbank where it meets the TP (51.667299, -1.257201) and paddle S.

51.666780, -1.257584

### Andersey Island, Culham

Choose between foot or boat access. Walk along a FP from Abingdon Weir for ⅔ mile. Explore one of the largest islands on the Thames – 273 acres separated from the mainland by the narrow channel of Swift Ditch (see above). The Anglo-Saxon king Offa of Mercia lived here in the 8th century, and the island also has links with William the Conqueror.

51.666392, -1.259441

### Backwater S, Culham

Large trees hang over the waterway. Swift Ditch, or Back Water as it is also known, is sometimes navigable to Culham Bridge, which bypasses Abingdon. There is no FP.

51.667845, -1.259863

### Abingdon Community Woodland, Abingdon

A wet woodland – rare in England. Try to find Barton Ln, a lost Ln, and navigate the greenway around Bullfield Lake. Marsh, nesting birds and frogs.

51.670452, -1.262172

### ABINGDON WEIR (S BANK), CULHAM

Cross the weir (51.670673, -1.269716) to meet the S bank of the Thames and the N shore of Andersey Island. There's a lost Ln/ riverside walk to Abingdon bridge. A good place to explore as there are so many paths, bridges and islands to scramble the senses.

51.670326, -1.269348

### Abingdon Lock Island, Abingdon

Water violets grow around the N tip of Andersey Island from May to July. There are some of the best views of the river along the Abingdon stretch. The weir from Abingdon to the lock island has a pedestrian walkway.

51.671490, -1.271030

Swift Ditch

Abingdon Weir

 ## Abingdon Lock and Weir, Abingdon

Glide across the water or walk along the riverbank. Lots of shades of willow green and yellow. There are free moorings here too. Explore Barton Fields wildflower meadows on the N side. Good cycling to be found.

51.670577, -1.26944

 ## Abingdon Lock Stone, Culham

Look for the stone in the middle of the three weirs that is built into the L-hand side of the lock. There's an inscription carved into the stone that reads:

'This locke was bvilded by Sr George Stonehouse and Richard Adams Ann. 1649'

51.670597, -1.269455

 ## Abbey Stream, Bayworth

The stream follows a course shaped by the monks of Abingdon Abbey in the 10th century.

51 71490, -1.271030

 ## Abingdon Abbey, Abingdon

Built in around 675 AD, Abingdon Abbey stood on land between Abbey Stream and the River Thames. Following the dissolution of the monasteries in 1538, the abbey fell into disrepair. Today all that remains is its outline and some associated domestic buildings, as well as some ruins of the Gothic Trendell's Folly, which was built in the 19th century.

51.671762, -1.274624

**THE NAG'S HEAD**

Pub set on Nag's Head Island, beside the water's edge.

The Bridge, Abingdon, OX14 3HX

www.thenagsheadonthethames.co.uk

01235 639023

## Abingdon Wildflower Maze, Abbey Meadows

Full of flowers and blossom in spring.

51.670341, -1.276028

## Abingdon Bridge, Abingdon

Two bridges that link Abingdon to Andersey Island, via Nag's Head Island. The northern bridge features six arches, while the southern bridge, known as Burford Bridge, and which was built in 1453, has five.

51.668513, -1.279573

## Nag's Head Island, Abingdon

There was once an orchard on this island, which is named after the pub here (see left). The river has strong currents in this area.

51.668413, -1.279748

## St Helen's Church, Abingdon

Look for the Tree of Jesse dating from around 1390 on the painted ceiling panels of the N aisle. J.M.W. Turner featured the spire of St Helen's Church in his c.1806 painting Abingdon, which also pictured the area around Dorchester on Thames.

51.667606, -1.282844

## THE CROWN & THISTLE

Historic pub and hotel.

18 Bridge St, Abingdon, OX14 3HS

www.crownandthistle abingdon.co.uk

01235 522556

## ST ETHELWOLD'S HOUSE

A retreat and meditation centre by the river. Rooms can be hired at affordable rates.

30 East St Helen St, Abingdon, OX14 5EB

www.ethelwoldhouse.com

01235 550139

## Long Alley Almshouses, Abingdon

Three sets of unique almshouses around the church.

51.667606, -1.282844

## Abingdon Bridge Woods, Abingdon

Lovely wooded walk along the rural riverbank of Andersey Island that looks back across the water into town.

51.667400, -1.281539

## River Ock, Abingdon

The River Ock flows into the Thames on the reach above Culham Lock.

51.666500, -1.283800

## Abingdon Village Green, Abingdon

Sit on of the best village greens in England – the village focal point for 1,000 years. Geese and swallows fly overhead.

51.665974, -1.283364

## Abingdon Marina Slipway, Abingdon

A small slipway, good for launching smaller boats.

51.656983, -1.281365

## CULHAM OLD BRIDGE, CULHAM

Culham Hythe ford was the main crossing over Swift Ditch until the 15th century when Culham Old Bridge was built in 1416 by the Guild of the Brotherhood of Christ. The stone bridge was later the scene of the Battle of Culham Bridge during the English Civil War when Royalists and Parliamentarians tried to seize it. It was used by Rd traffic in and out of Abingdon until 1920 when the new Culham Bridge was built to the N. Culham Old Bridge is now pedestrian only.

51.658442, -1.277342

## Wilts & Berks Canal, Sutton Courtenay

To the S of Abingdon is the entrance to the Wilts & Berks Canal. This canal, which ran for 52 miles between Abingdon and Semington in Wiltshire, and had 45 locks, connected the River Thames to the Kennet and Avon Canal. It was opened in 1810 to move coal and corn from Somerset. It closed in 1914, and since then much has become unnavigable. The Wilts & Berks Canal Trust has since been formed with the aim of reopening the canal. A new entrance to the Thames, the Jubilee Junction, was opened in 2006 and there are plans for a new route to connect existing, but inaccessible parts with the Thames.

51.651000, -1.282700

## ENDURANCE BOAT CAFÉ

A pop-up café on board a canal boat called *Endurance*. Open on Sundays only.

Sutton Courtenay Pools, Abingdon, OX14 4NJ

www.annashackleton. co.uk/endurance-boat-caf

07740 137151

### → DETOUR – PACKRAFTING 90M (295FT) – 1 MILE SE

## Old River Thames Loop, Sutton Courtenay

Virgin riverbank around an old river loop.

➤ **Find** the riverbank where it meets the TP (51.650394, -1.282025) and paddle S and then E along the Thames.

51.648413, -1.282980

## 6 SUTTON POOLS, SUTTON COURTENAY

A Thames backwater that takes you away from the main navigation channel that runs along the 19th-century Culham Cut to Culham Lock. Here you will find a waterway of islands that have been hijacked, not unlovingly, with a series of FBs and weirs. A Saxon causeway separates the lower pools from the river.

51.645558, -1.275619

## Sutton Bridge, Culham

Built in 1807, the stone, three-arched Sutton Bridge lies to the E of Culham Lock. Rd users were charged tolls to cross it until 1939.

51.650613, -1.266178

## Sutton Lasher Pool, Sutton Courtenay

The reach below the Lasher Pool is extremely pretty and winding and fringed by willow trees on the L. It's thick with alder, aspen and willow on the R.

51.646715, -1.269749

## Culham Island, Culham

Look for cormorants, herons and kingfishers. There is a FP across the island to Sutton Pools from the FB.

51.649354, -1.273394

## St Paul's Church, Culham

Standing at the SW end of Culham village green, St Paul's Church was originally built in the 12th century, but the current church dates to the Victorian era. The tower was built in 1710.

51.651363, -1.276061

## THE SWAN FOODHOUSE & BAR

A country pub serving decent seasonal and local produce. Lots cf outdoor seating.

The Green, Sutton Courtenay, OX14 4AE

www.theswanfoodhouse.com

01235 847446

## → DETOUR – WALKING ⅔ MILE S

### Sutton Weir, Sutton Courtenay

If you don't explore Sutton Pools by boat, you can reach Sutton Weir via a FP across Culham Island.

➤ **Find** the FP that joins the TP (51.649353, -1.273394) and walk S.

51.645538, -1.275656

### Church of All Saints, Sutton Courtenay

Look for the grave of the novelist Eric Arthur Blair, otherwise known as George Orwell, who is buried at the Church of All Saints in Sutton Courtenay. Former British Prime Minister Herbert Asquith and his second wife, Margot, are also buried in the churchyard. The Norman arch over the tower's W door features carved crosses, which are said to have been made by soldiers at the time of the Crusades.

51.644207, -1.271703

### Sutton Courtenay

Tall chestnuts, limes and elms fill the village green.

51.641222, -1.277803

## ⑦ CULHAM LOCK, CULHAM

Located at the E end of Culham Cut, this lock opened in 1809 so barges could avoid the tricky navigation around Sutton Pools.

51.650451, -1.267542

### Culham Weir, Culham

Listen to the water around the great pool, with its miniature bays and tumbling water.

51.650467, -1.266974

### Culham Straight Pylons, Culham

Look for the dead ash wood, and the King Alfred's Cakes fungi it hosts. Look for new ash keys in spring, too.

➤ **Find** the ash trees just E of the pylons.

51.647701, -1.252084

### Appleford Ford, Appleford

In dry summers, look for the ford, which was used for the transportation of apples from Harwell Orchards. The graves of early Roman and Saxon settlers have been found here where the riverbank is highest.

51.643079, -1.237930

Culham Lock

### Appleford Wood, Appleford
Somewhere to shelter among the willow and ash trees.

51.644516, -1.242153

### Culham Wood, Culham
Forage for green and kindling wood and willow.

51.643122, -1.237659

### St Peter's & St Paul's Church, Appleford
One of the Thames' most sacred churches. The church shares the chalk river and springs with the neighbouring farm.

51.639537, -1.234920

### Appleford Well, Appleford
The largest of five springs that defined this place as sacred to Celtic settlers. The springs bubble to the surface less than 35m (115ft) from the River Thames. A good place to shelter if in a small boat or to investigate plant life. It's quite overgrown where the springs empty into the Thames.

51.641288, -1.233611

### → DETOUR – PACKRAFTING 3 MILES S AND E

### Clifton Cut FB, Clifton Hampden
A bridge to an island created by a cut. The River Thames proper is on the other side and runs around Long Wittenham.
➤ **Find** the riverbank on the opposite side to the TP (51.642931, -1.220608), and kayak S into the old Thames. There is no foot access across the weir.

51.645811, -1.213942

### Clifton Pool, Nr Long Wittenham
A 7m (22ft)-wide pool, lined with small trees along the W bank. Much care needed around the weir if this section of river is accessible. There is a tiny island to the E, set into the shallows.

51.642357, -1.219468

### Moor Ditch, Nr Long Wittenham

Shallow stream of clear water in which to look for silver fish fry. About 75m (250ft) of wide water. If possible, follow the water to the Moor Ditch BW (51.637516, -1.224907).

51.639982, -1.221363

### Moor Ditch BW, Nr Long Wittenham

A 1-mile lost Ln between St Peter's & St Paul's Church, Appleford-on-Thames, and Long Wittenham.

51.637516, -1.224907

### Long Wittenham Ditch, Long Wittenham

Backwater and tree-lined avenue to hide and shelter in by a FP.

51.639529, -1.220919

### Long Wittenham Creek, Long Wittenham

A snake-like backwater that provides a beautiful tree-lined place to paddle.

51.640153, -1.216677

Appleford

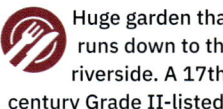
## St Mary the Virgin Church, Long Wittenham

A 13th-century church. The rare S porch was donated by Lincoln Cathedral.

51.642560, -1.208844

## Long Wittenham Island, Long Wittenham

Between 1891 and 1914, the Long Wittenham History Society held summer camps for schoolboys here. The vast meadow island, which was created by the Clifton Cut, was used by the boys between July and September for a range of activities, including cricket. They also went boating and fishing on the Thames.

51.641031, -1.214939

## Long Wittenham Thames, Long Wittenham

A 19th-century writer once said the river between Culham and Clifton was boring. That's because the best bit has been cut out. So, ignore the Clifton Cut, and go and walk or paddle a part of the Thames that is one of the best backwaters on the river.

51.639618, -1.219213

## Clifton Lock Island and Long Wittenham Island, Nr Long Wittenham

Find the small sandy beaches along the Wittenham bank. The uninhabited island is grazing land.

51.648424, -1.210094

## 8 CLIFTON CUT WEIR, NR LONG WITTENHAM

Find where the FP joins the TP. The FP diverts to Culham Station, 2 miles away, zigzagging past Lower Town Farm.

51.641508, -1.222814

## 9 CLIFTON LOCK, CLIFTON HAMPDEN

The lock marks the start/end of the Clifton Cut. The lock and cut were designed to help navigate what was an otherwise difficult section of the Thames. The river past Long Wittenham was considered unruly as it is prone to strong currents, so the lock was opened in 1822.

51.648937, -1.210634

## Clifton Lock Garden, Long Wittenham

Smell the camellias, dahlias, and the sharp tang of red-hot peppers. Large pot plants are scattered about, framing impressive plants. It's as much a feast for the eyes as for the bees.

51.648598, -1.210576

**BARLEY MOW**

 A thatched country tavern that is more than 650 years old. Serves traditional British dishes.

Clifton Hampden Rd, Clifton Hampden, OX14 3EH

www.chefandbrewer.com/pubs/oxfordshire/barley-mow

01865 407847

 ### St Michael's & All Angels Church graveyard, Clifton Hampden

A sacred site that predates the Saxons, and the churchyard dates from 1819. Many casualties of war are buried here, including Sergeant William Dyke, whose accidental discharge of a gun in 1815 is said to have started the Battle of Waterloo.

51.655831, -1.210332

 ### CLIFTON HAMPDEN POOL, CLIFTON HAMPDEN

A river lagoon, more than 60m (200ft) wide. Watch fish and boaters from either the bridge or the riverbank.

51.654654, -1.210893

 ### Clifton Hampden Bridge, Clifton Hampden

This crossing was designed by the brilliant architect Sir George Gilbert Scott, a Gothic Revivalist who was influenced by Augustus Pugin. Scott's main work was renovating churches and cathedrals, and he is arguably best known for his work on Westminster Abbey between 1849–53, where he is buried. He also designed the Martyrs' Memorial on St Giles' boulevard in Oxford, which remembers three Protestant martyrs from the 16th century. Clifton Hampden Bridge opened in 1867 and has the look of a wall that the poet John Clare might have climbed over as a boy to trespass. Originally a toll bridge, fees to cross were removed in 1946 when the bridge was sold to the local councils.

51.654596, -1.210488

### Clifton Hampden Ford, Clifton Hampden

Cattle and people on horseback used the shallow ford before the bridge was built.

➤ **Taste** apples from the tree on the ford's W bank. This may once have been an orchard.

51.654596, -1.210488

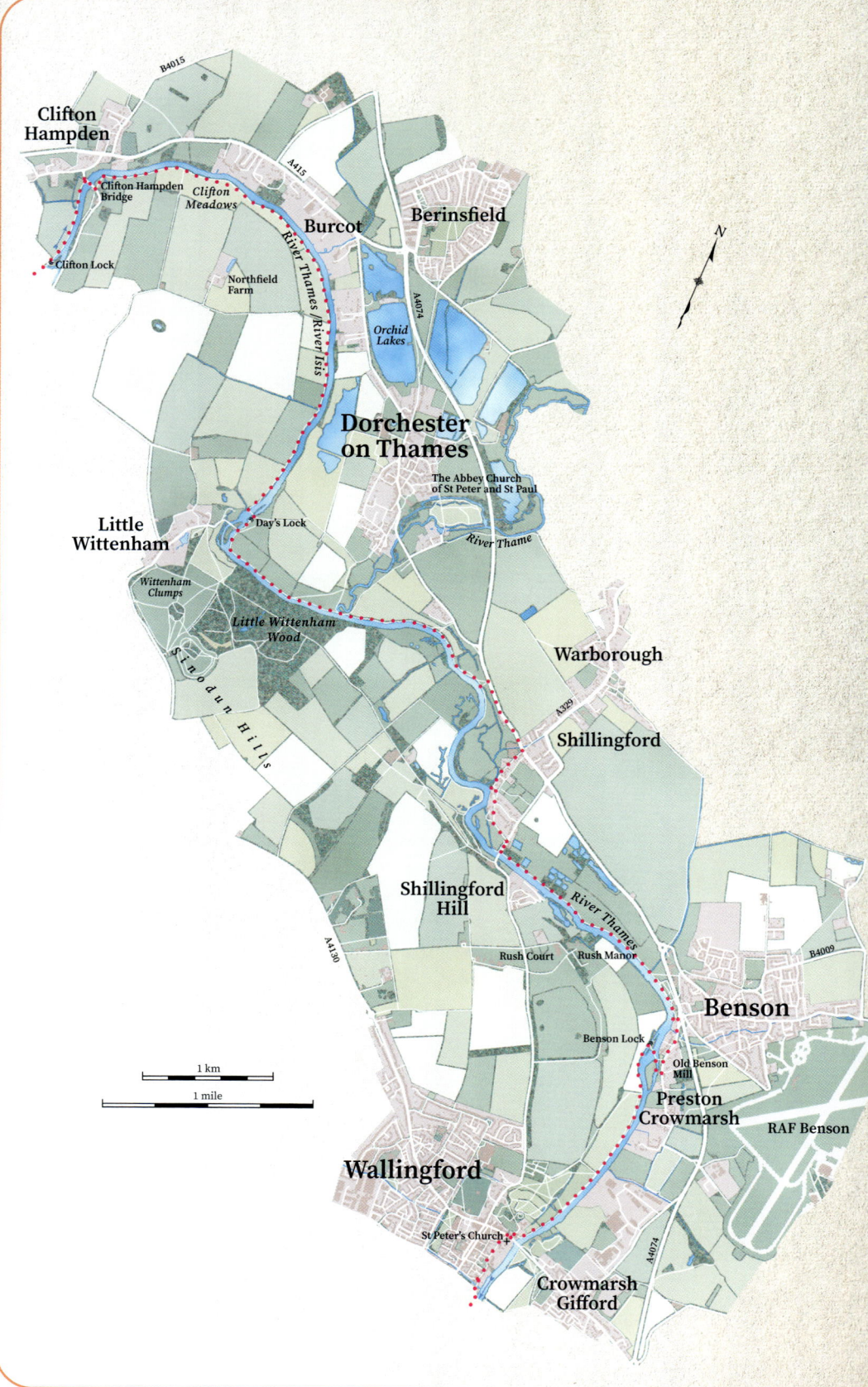

# 8. CLIFTON HAMPDEN TO WALLINGFORD

## HILLS

The two wooded chalk hills of the Wittenham Clumps tower over this section of the Thames. People lived among the beech and yew woodland for more than 7,000 years. A plaque commemorates the Poem Tree, a 500-year-old beech tree that stood here until the 1990s, on which Joseph Tubb, in the 1840s, carved a 20-line poem celebrating the local area. During this time many areas of common land were being enclosed by English landowners, and commoners were being evicted, something that Tubb objected to. His protests against the enclosures, which included pulling down fences, led to him being sent to jail in Oxford.

### 10 STEPPING STONES

St Michael's & All Angels Church
Burcot Wharf
Days Lock
Wittenham Clumps
The River Thame
Shillingford Towpath Exit
Shillingford Wharf
St Helen's Church, Benson
Benson Lock
Wallingford Castle

**THE PLOUGH B&B**

A 16th-century inn, a short walk from the river and path.

Abingdon Rd, Clifton Hampden, Abingdon, OX14 3EG

www.ploughbnb.com

01865 409976

Clifton Meadow

### ① ST MICHAEL'S & ALL ANGELS CHURCH, CLIFTON HAMPDEN

Beautiful church that stands on a small rocky cliff overlooking the Thames. Look for the stained glass of St Michael slaying a blue dragon.

51.655831, -1.210332

### Clifton Hampden Riverbank, Clifton Hampden

Stone cliffs are unique along the Thames, so this is worth exploring: a sandstone riverbed and bank surrounded by trees. The steep river sides lead up to St Michael's & All Angels Church at Clifton Hampden – a rare example of a Thames church that hasn't sold its river frontage.

51.655640, -1.210047

### Clifton Shallows, Clifton Hampden

A solid sandstone riverbed, so not something that can be dredged. Try to paddle the edges in summer where there are shallows. The water is clear, although there is some green weed.

51.655465, -1.209431

### New Barn FP, Clifton Hampden

Pools, clear water, and the first view of Wittenham Clumps to the S.

51.658054, -1.201651

## Burcot House, Burcot

For hundreds of years, this was the furthest upstream that barges could travel because of the sandstone rock at Clifton. The writer John Masefield lived at Burcot House, overlooking the river, until his death in 1967.

51.657833, -1.193253

## ② SITE OF BURCOT WHARF, BURCOT

This stretch of the river is where it's thought Burcot Wharf stood, and where barges would have been unloaded. No evidence now remains, however.

51.657931, -1.1921082

Clifton Meadow

### Burcot House Ditch, Burcot

Look across the water at Burcot Boathouse, a few metres short of the wooded ditch. Then turn around and look behind you and you get a good look and feel for Wittenham Clumps. Those hills define the walk on this stretch.

51.657894, -1.192552

### Dorchester on Thames Back Gardens, Dorchester

There are no brick walls or hawthorn hedges here, just water and the occasional jumping bream. Gardens of mown lawns and magnolias run down to a riverbank of common knapweed, meadow vetchling and meadowsweet. It's all very beautiful, whichever side you're on.

51.652833, -1.180387

**THE GEORGE HOTEL**

 A 15th-century coaching inn with rooms, open fires and seasonal menus.

High St, Dorchester, OX10 7HH

www.george-dorchester.co.uk

01865 340404

## Dorchester FB, Dorchester

Roman coins have been found around the shallows of the old Roman town.

51.646912, -1.177568

## Riverbank Walk, Dorchester

Slip into the water from the riverbank. There are lots of hiding places along the damp edge of maple and willow trees, particularly in the midsummer. You can spend all day here, bathing in dappled sunshine alongside lazy fish.

51.644070, -1.177706

## Hurst Water Meadow, Overy

Look for kingfishers and herons around the island's edge. Giant black poplars are of interest. Hurst Water Meadow is to the E of Dorchester, between the River Thames and the Overy mill stream.

51.641371, -1.163660

## Little Wittenham Weir Pool, Little Wittenham

Explore the inlets and springs that bubble around the edges of this deep water. Access is restricted, with lots of spiked gates and railings, but look for the wet and wooded areas where there is some access or get on the water.

51.638425, -1.180357

Dorchester

### ③ DAYS LOCK, LITTLE WITTENHAM

Find the shade of giant horse chestnut trees. The lock is across the river from Little Wittenham and is overlooked by the Wittenham Clumps. The lock weir runs across the river from the opposite side of the island. The TP crosses the river here and for many years was the location of the World Poohsticks Championships, which raises money for the RNLI. The 42-year-old event is now held further upstream at Sandford Lock.

51.637318, -1.181040

## St Peter's Church, Little Wittenham

A 19th-century church with loads of things to see: the 14th-century W tower; two watercolours of the old church in the vestry; a 15th-century octagonal font, and lots of brasses and monuments.

51.637012, -1.182995

## → DETOUR – CYCLING ¾ – 1½ MILES W

### Little Wittenham Rd, Little Wittenham

Cycle the lost Ln across the neck of the peninsula that is created by the vast Thames U-bend that you've just walked.
➤ **Find** the lost Ln that joins the TP (51.637162, -1.179995) on the E side of the lock. Cross the lock and follow the Ln S of the church and then turn NW at the first junction.

51.640200, -1.193923

### Neptune Wood, Little Wittenham

An orchard walk that provides shade with wildflowers in spring, just E of Long Wittenham.

51.641341, -1.200896

### Little Wittenham Wood, Little Wittenham

Mixture of pine and broadleaf woodland. Lots of dead birch, so look for fungi around the tree roots or on the bark. Birch trees seem to attract more than most. The Druids associated birch trees with purification. However, as cleansing and purification is often associated with altered states of consciousness, it's possible this link had more to do with the fungi that live on the birch than the trees themselves.

51.633329, -1.178110

Wittenham Clumps

### → DETOUR – WALKING ½ MILE S

## Wittenham Clumps E, Little Wittenham

Tread barefoot around these hills if you dare. The grass can be soft, but the ground uneven over a mix of gritty chalk, springs and soft soil. Beware occasional jagged rocks, thorns and others.
**➤ Find** the lost Ln that joins the TP (51.637162, -1.179995) on the E side of the lock. Cross the lock and follow the FP for ½ mile S.

51.630675, -1.183083

## 4 WITTENHAM CLUMPS W, LITTLE WITTENHAM

People lived here from 6000 BC until the medieval period – and then the Normans arrived with new ideas of rewilding and enclosure. Both are coming back now under the same banner of 'conservation'. Look for a scatter of flints left by Mesolithic hunter-gatherers. 'Beech' is the origin of the word 'book'. These beech hills are the UK's oldest library.

51.633583, -1.183756

### Little Wittenham Ponds, Little Wittenham

Look for frogs and toads around the ponds from late February and early March. The pools are set inside one of the thickest parts of the woodland.

51.632944, -1.173806

### Little Wittenham Pools, Little Wittenham

Touch the water in the vast area of pools that once hydrated the people who lived here.

51.631290, -1.174843

### Brightwell Barrow, Brightwell-cum-Sotwell

A third hill, but not normally considered one of the Clumps, is Brightwell Barrow, further to the SE.

51.622961, -1.169473

Day's Lock

### The Poem Tree, Little Wittenham

Joseph Tubb carved a poem into a beech tree here (the Poem Tree) between 1844 and 1845. The beech tree is no longer standing, but a rubbing of the poem was taken and can now be seen on a commemorative plaque that stands nearby. The plaque was installed in 1994 to mark the 150th anniversary of the poem's creation.

51.628237, -1.178578

### Castle Hill, Little Wittenham

Sadly, you can't walk around the beech trees any more as the area is so often closed because of the 'danger of falling trees'. Planted 300 years ago, the clumps on Castle Hill and Round Hill are considered the oldest beech hangers in England. Wittenham Clumps is formed of two chalk hills, the smaller of which, Castle Hill, is home to an Iron Age fort. Views via Little Wittenham church and Wittenham Clumps are best at sunset or sunrise. It's a steep 2-mile detour, but worth it.

51.627791, -1.178710

### Round Hill, Little Wittenham

The higher of the Wittenham Clumps, Round Hill, has views over the Thames towards Buscot and the meadows. Lots of downland wildflowers in summer. Good path access all year round.

51.630446, -1.182987

### Dyke Hills, Dorchester

Explore the prehistoric groundworks and the plants and grasses that surround them.

51.638313, -1.167052

## → DETOUR – CYCLING 1 MILE NE

### Dorchester on Thames, Dorchester

Where the River Thames joins the River Thames. In his book *Three Men in a Boat*, Jerome K. Jerome said that 'Dorchester, like Wallingford, was a city in ancient British times; it was then called Caer Doren, "the city on the water".' The Romans camped here, and it was the Anglo-Saxon capital of Wessex until Winchester replaced it in 871 AD. Very old, very holy, and very much worth a visit.

➤ **Find** the lost Ln that joins the TP (51.637162, -1.179995) on the E side of the lock. Walk or cycle NE across Dyke Hills into the village.

51.644326, -1.168567

### St Peter and St Paul's Abbey Church, Dorchester Abbey

Note the Jesse Tree window on the chancel's N wall. The church was built by the Augustinian Canons, although there are traces of Saxon masonry linked to an ancient temple or cathedral. In more recent times, the abbey has been used by musicians for its acoustic qualities, including the band Radiohead, who originally hailed from nearby Abingdon. The band recorded orchestral parts for two of their albums, 'Kid A' and 'Amnesiac', in the abbey. The abbey is open every day from 8am until dusk.

51.643700, -1.164400

### River Thame Bridge, Wallingford

Cross and explore, under and over, this beautiful reed-laden mouth of the River Thame.

51.634819, -1.166404

### → DETOUR – WALKING ⅔ MILE N

### ⑤ THE RIVER THAME, WALLINGFORD

If exploring the river by boat, be wary of swans in nesting season. The village of Dorchester can be reached by paddling ½ mile up the Thame. The River Thame runs for 40 miles from where it enters the Thames to Aylesbury in Buckinghamshire. Interestingly, the River Thames has in the past been referred to as Isis from the point where the two rivers meet to the Thames' source near Cirencester. It's only here, at the mouth of the River Thame, that references to the River Thames were originally made.
➤ **Find** the FP that joins the TP (51.634829, -1.166707), just before the river mouth, and walk N.

51.634819, -1.166404

### Dyke Hills, Dorchester

The groundworks dug by ancient Britons included a dyke with high embankments on either side. Similar in structure to the earthworks known as Grim's Dyke or Grim's Ditch, near Wallingford, the banks are 6m (20ft) in length. Lots of Roman pottery, glass bottles and other things have been found here, including, in the 19th century, some by the Reverend W.C. MacFarlane, vicar of Dorchester.

51.636607, -1.166789

### Spring Wood, Brightwell-cum-Sotwell

Listen to the blackbirds in the wet woodland – they sing here all day. The woodland is fed by streams and springs. It's a good place to shelter but it can be difficult to make progress across the water.

51.635704, -1.154988

### A4074 FP, Nr Shillingford

You must now decide what to do: either navigate into Shillingford by Rd or by river; whether to follow the dead-end river path and packraft to the other side, or take to the unfriendly A4074 Rd.

51.634254, -1.148896

### 6 SHILLINGFORD TOWPATH, BRIGHTWELL-CUM-SOTWELL

Walk along the FP on the W bank, an old towpath, for 1 mile to Shillingford Bridge.

51.630558, -1.149204

## SHILLINGFORD BRIDGE HOTEL

A 16th-century Georgian coaching inn surrounded by woodlands. Forty bedrooms close to the river.

Shillingford Hill, Wallingford, OX10 8LZ

www.shillingfordbridge hotel.co.uk

01865 858567

## → DETOUR – PACKRAFTING 90M (295FT) – 1 MILE SW

### Shillingford Drain, Brightwell-cum-Sotwell

A 150m (500ft) canal-like backwater. Limited overhead cover other than a few low willows. Shillingford Drain provides minimal shelter but is an interesting place on the W bank to explore by boat.

➤ **Find** the riverbank where the TP turns away from the riverbank (51.634254, -1.148896), launch your packraft and explore the backwater. Alternatively, head S down the river to Shillingford Bridge.

51.633259, -1.149433

### Shillingford Creek, Brightwell-cum-Sotwell

A snake-like backwater that curls ¼ mile inland, along mostly open meadow.

51.633259, -1.149433

### Shillingford Farm Crossing, Warborough

The problem here is not the lack of bridge or ferry, it's the being forced onto the alternate bank when the E side is perfectly adequate as a riverbank on which to walk to Shillingford Bridge.

51.630627, -1.148313

## ⑦ SHILLINGFORD WHARF, SHILLINGFORD

One of the best views from the Thames riverbank, and all the better if you can arrive by packraft. Stay a while if you can. It's not a place to rush, albeit it's very small. Might be one of the most welcoming neighbourhoods on the Thames. Locals are friendly and have much knowledge to share about the history of this piece of river.

51.628069, -1.143273

### Shillingford Pool, Warborough

Fish feed in warm summer shallows. The Thames flows across a 90m (295ft) marsh to create a shallow lake. The surrounding area was once a reed island dissected from the mainland by a narrow backwater. The island's banks have since been raised and developed, with an access Rd adjoining the TP. Best seen from the river in winter when the pool is at its highest. It dries out in summer.

➤ **Find** the riverbank at the end of Wharf Rd (51.628159, -1.143214), and kayak S and E.

51.625170, -1.143004

### Shillingford Bridge, Shillingford

This stone bridge seems happy to hold the weight of time. It was built in 1827, its arches framing an era that has long gone.

51.624447, -1.139553

### Brightwell Vineyard, Wallingford

Sixteen acres of vineyard can be found just a mile N of Wallingford, producing red, white, rosé and sparkling wines. www.brightwellvineyard.co.uk

51.619062, -1.132211

### Rush Court Landing, Wallingford

Palace-like stone steps and walls on the riverbank where the water widens. The old Rush Manor was apparently moated. Three ceremonial stones are a mystery. Get into the reeds around the steps if you can by packraft.

51.621857, -1.126281

Benson

## Littleworth FP, Nr Benson

Cormorants often perch like undertakers on dead trees. The river bends towards Benson here, where birds and leafless trees form silhouettes on blue and grey skies. Look for wild angelica, with its purple-white umbels, ragged robin and marsh marigold, too. These three plants seem to find the fertile gaps along the ditches and riverside clearings.

51.621147, -1.119029

## Ewelme Brook Mouth, Benson

Where the chalk stream empties into the Thames.

➤ **Paddle** across or cross the weir FP and find where the brook empties into the Thames.

51.618221, -1.114709

## ST HELEN'S CHURCH, BENSON

The church in Benson was founded by the Celts on the confluence of the river and Ewelme Brook. This 12th-century Norman church replaced the Saxon one before it.

51.620129, -1.113075

## Benson, Wallingford

Lots of places to buy cake and sit by the river.

51.620557, -1.106860

## ➔ DETOUR – WALKING 2 – 2½ MILES

## Brook Street, Benson

Find Brook Street and walk along the waterway that Benson was founded on. Care is needed as there is no pavement from which to escape the traffic.

➤ **To find** Brook St, walk E along Church Ln into High St. Keep following High St E into Brook St. After 1¼ miles Brook St leads to the watercress fields.

51.624328, -1.094924

## Ewelme Watercress Beds & Local Nature Reserve, Ewelme

The watercress beds are free to explore.

➤ **Find** Church Rd (51.619417, -1.114015) and walk E to the nature reserve.

51.622515, -1.079926

**BOAT HOUSE**

A large garden and riverside terrace for lunch and dinners.

103 High St, Wallingford, OX10 0BL

www.greeneking.co.uk pubs/oxfordshire/boathouse

01491 834100

### St Mary the Virgin Church, Ewelme

Find the alabaster tomb. It is an elaborate chest tomb that dates to 1475, which was created for Alice de la Pole, wife of William de la Pole, Duke of Suffolk, and daughter of the poet Geoffrey Chaucer. What makes it unusual is that on top of the tomb is an alabaster sculpture of Alice, reclining with her hands closed as if resting in quiet prayer, while below, lying on the floor, but hidden behind arched panels, is a sculpture of her decaying corpse. Granted Order of the Garter in 1432, the upper effigy of Alice wears the honour on her left arm, and it is said that officials of Queen Victoria viewed the sculpture to determine how it should be worn by a woman in order to maintain dignity.

51.617887, -1.067271

### Ewelme Pool, Ewelme

Henry VIII is said to have bathed his ulcerous legs in the spring water here. There are watercress beds just to the NW, less than ½ mile.

51.618874, -1.070786

### Ewelme Almshouses, Ewelme

Fabulous almshouses. These were funded by William de la Pole and his wife, Alice, in 1437 after Henry VI granted them a licence to set up a chantry foundation. The money they donated paid for a number of endowed buildings to be built, including the almshouse that provided accommodation for 13 impoverished local men and a school, as well as the running costs. They also paid for the church to be rebuilt.

51.617468, -1.068044

### BENSON LOCK, BENSON

Cross the lock FB to get a view upriver. Things are quieter here since the old mill stopped running. Six and a half miles lie between Benson Lock and the next downstream lock, Cleeve Lock, which is the longest stretch without locks on the river.

51.616486, -1.115988

### Wallingford Boathouse, Wallingford

River access, albeit it's a bit high, from the old coal wharf. The boathouse is no longer, but it has become a pub in recent years (see left). Sitting against the old wharf's red brick wall in the sunshine is quite nice.

51.601191, -1.120453

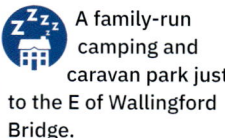
Wallingford Castle site

## Wallingford Bridge, Wallingford

Like most Thames bridges, this one sits across the site of an old Celtic ford that is surrounded by weeping willows. It is still shallow in summer.

51.600746, -1.121006

## WALLINGFORD CASTLE, WALLINGFORD

Built by the Normans in 1067, Wallingford Castle is a motte-and-bailey design. It was used by Henry VIII in the 16th century until it fell out of favour. Stone from the abandoned castle was reclaimed for the construction of Windsor Castle. The Royalists used it as a stronghold during the English Civil War of 1642–51, but it was eventually demolished by Cromwell in 1652. The meadows contain two sections of wall, but that's all that's left. Look for the ditches and castle wall ruins. The grasses and flowers are probably much as they were 500 years before Cromwell's army turned up to destroy it.

51.602234, -1.121700

### St Peter's Church, Wallingford

Look out for the spire as a marker. This church is worth getting up close to, although access is limited. The flint tower isn't liked by most people, but the spire and church were designed by English architect and sculptor Robert Taylor. He served as a Sheriff of London in 1783. Look for the stained glass in the E window. It was produced by Morris & Co in 1918.

51.597051, -1.122595

 ### Wallingford, Wallingford

Lots of famous places to buy cake and food and then sit by the river. Camping and B&Bs are both available, depending on the time of year and season.

51.600745, -1.128224

St Peter's Church, Wallingford

**Wallingford**
Crowmarsh Gifford
St Peter's Church
WALLINGFORD
Winterbrook
A4130
A4074
Mongewell Park
River Thames
North Stoke
A329
**Cholsey**
Cholsey Meadow
CHOLSEY
Little Stoke
**Moulsford**
South Stoke
B4009
A417
Cleeve Lock
B4526
**Goring-on-Thames**
Great Chalk Wood
Goring Lock
GORING AND STREATLEY
**Streatley**
*Chiltern Hills*
Lower Basildon
A329
Hartslock Wood
Coombe Park Farm
B471
**Whitchurch-on-Thames**
A329
River Thames
Beale Park
Basildon House
*Basildon Park*
Pangbourne Meadow
Whitchurch Lock
Whitchurch Bridge
PANGBOURNE
**Pangbourne**
A340

N

1 km

1 mile

# 9. WALLINGFORD TO WHITCHURCH

Whitchurch Bridge

## DETOURS

More than a third of this path section trails away from the river – and it's all the better for that. Short Thames detours can be disappointing; this is a permanent wonder.

Goring is an old ford – a water crossroads that accommodates the TP and The Ridgeway, an 87-mile NT along a chalk ridge. The Thames crashes through the Chiltern Hills like a bulldozer. Chalk hills and their FPs, held together by yew roots, are the grounds that carry you into and out of Whitchurch-on-Thames.

## 10 STEPPING STONES

Wallingford
Old Papist Way Slipway
The Beetle and Wedge
Cleeve Lock
Goring and Streatley Bridge
Gatehampton Railway Bridge
Hartslock Wood
Hartlock Meadow
St Mary's Church, Whitchurch
Whitchurch Bridge

###  WALLINGFORD

Wallingford was an important port long before the Norman Conquest, and it had its own mint. The town was one of the most secure garrisons in England. It was double walled and double ditched. All walls and ditches have since been removed or replaced by time.

51.600745, -1.128224

###  St Leonard's Church, Wallingford

St Leonard's Church in Wallingford is the town's oldest church, with parts of the tower dating to the 11th century. A herringbone pattern in the stonework is identifiable as Saxon, although much of the church was rebuilt in the 17th century. It was rebuilt again in 1849 in the Gothic Revival style. Look for four murals of angels, which were created by the artist George Leslie in 1889.

51.597220, -1.122894

###  Oxford University Boat Club, Wallingford

A nice place to sit and watch the river at the weekend or during late summer evenings.

51.594893, -1.122522

###  Watermead Nature Reserve, Wallingford

Riverbank meadows and a nature reserve that floods in winter.

51.590227, -1.122439

### White Cross Farm, Wallingford

Look for Bronze Age flint flakes around the riverbank just N of Winterbrook Bridge.

51.588750, -1.124539

### Winterbrook Bridge, Wallingford

Steel plate girders lie beautifully low over the river, peppered in graffiti. The bridge, which is also known as the Wallingford Bypass Bridge and the Nosworthy Mamum Bridge, carries the A4130 around Wallingford. There may once have been an island here that was a Bronze Age settlement, and late Bronze Age artefacts have been found along the W bank.

51.588323, -1.123977

### → DETOUR– PACKRAFTING, WALKING & CYCLING 45M (150FT) – ½ MILE E AND THEN S

### Grim's Ditch, Crowmarsh

Find the FP on the E riverbank that connects to the Grim's Ditch earthworks and The Ridgeway path. The long series of ditches and banks that run for 11 miles between Bradenham and Berkhampstead, through the Chiltern Hills, are thought to be Bronze Age or Iron Age in origin. Their construction would have involved the removal of thousands of tonnes of earth and chalk, but the reason for the earthworks is unknown. Part of the earthworks is now listed as a Scheduled Monument.
➤ **Find** the riverbank where it meets the TP (51.589738, -1.124080) and paddle E for 45m (150ft) to meet the dead-end FP on the other side.

51.589659, -1.123351

### St John the Baptist, Mongewell

Touch the ruins of the church, parts of which are thought to date to the 12th century. The Norman-style chancel is home to the 18th-century tomb of John Saunders, who is represented by a life-sized effigy, dressed in oriental robes and a turban, reclining on the tomb.
➤ **Find** the riverbank where it meets the TP (51.585621, -1.125174) and paddle E for 45m (150ft) to the opposite riverbank. It was restored in 1849 but looks unloved. Don't neglect to visit.

51.586269, -1.123307

### Church Stream, Mongewell

Stream access can be tricky but visit if you can as it is Thames water. The Boathouse is pretty.

51.585778, -1.124093

St John the Baptist Church, Mongewell

### Mongewell, Wallingford

A spa village. The springs are prolific, but they are lost into lakes that form because of the sheer volume of water that floods this area in winter. Access is poor, unless you have a punt or packraft.

51.585778, -1.124C93

### The Lake, Mongewell

Cycle 3 miles of lost Ln from Wallingford Bridge to Littlestoke Manor (51.560550, -1.133846). The lake is a water bowl fed from the springs at Mongewell.

51.586191, -1.120C11

 ### Bow Bridge, Cholsey

Look for lamprey and bullhead swimming in the shallows near Wallingford. This wooded riverside path is an important moment in the NT canon: where the TP meets the Ridgeway on the opposite bank.

51.576805, -1.126552

 ### Bow Bridge Wood, Cholsey

In late March and early April, this area is awash in white tree blossom. The blackthorn dominates and it's surprising just how much is in flower. Looks like snow – feels like it, too, when you find the shade.

51.576796, -1.126289

### → DETOUR – PACKRAFTING, WALKING & CYCLING  ½ MILE E AND THEN S BY PACKRAFT OR 1½ S OF NOSWORTHY WAY BRIDGE ON THE E BANK.

## Church of St Mary, N Stoke

The meeting of the two NTs across the river. N Stoke church is on the other side of the river (The Ridgeway runs through the churchyard). The two trails meet fully at Goring. Look for the tithe remains of a Saxon piscina, a 13th-century crusader chest, and 14th-century wall paintings.

➤ **Find** the riverbank and dead-end FP (51.574773, -1.125218) on the opposite side to the TP (51.574715, -1.126072) and walk and then cycle to the church. Lost Ln S of the church follows the Ln to Littlestoke Manor.

51.571731, -1.122656, 1 mile E and S

## N Stoke (E bank), N Stoke

The Thames curls past N Stoke. Private homes and a private boathouse line its banks; there's no public slipway here.

➤ **Find** the riverbank on the opposite side to the TP (51.572189, -1.126284), and kayak E for 45m (150ft).

51.572189, -1.126284

## Muire Sruth (stream), S Stoke

An island of woodland and pools. This northern stream connects with The Ridgeway trail. Access comes and goes between the water levels and fallen branches.

51.567401, -1.128660

North Stoke

### Mór Ait, S Stoke

Small island, large backwater. Wonderful to explore the trees and shallows by punt.

51.569771, -1.125995

### Maria Eyot, S Stoke

A wooded hideaway along what is otherwise a relatively open stretch of river. The island is mostly closed with foliage at the N end, but there is access at times from the southern waterway.

51.567401, -1.128660

## ② OLD PAPIST WAY SLIPWAY, FERRY LN, CHOLSEY

A rare treasure – a slipway and parking. Use the Cholsey slipway to launch from and paddle upstream to Mongewell. Or just paddle to the other side to meet The Ridgeway path at Littlestoke Manor Farm. The ferry Ln here became known as the Papist Way because it was used by a family of Roman Catholics who lived at Littlestoke Manor, on the opposite bank of the river. Hostilities towards Roman Catholics in the 16th century led to them being referred to as 'Papists', a derogatory term.

51.565044, -1.134296

Moulsford Railway Bridge

### Cholsey Marsh, Cholsey

Best in early to late April when the blackthorn thickets are full of fat white blossom. Loddon lilies and warblers in spring and summer, too.

51.564180, -1.137154

### Moulsford Eyots, Cholsey

Three uninhabited islands – haunted, they say – are accessible by boat. Densely wooded with old crack willow. A bridge hangs over the islands. This is the site of the old Moulsford Flash Lock and there was a mill and weir here too.

51.559753, -1.142226

### Moulsford Railway Bridge, Cholsey

The TP detours from here. This is the point that the Great Western Main Line, which runs from Paddington to Bristol, crosses the River Thames, via the Moulsford Railway Bridge, or Four Arches Bridge as it is also known.

51.559296, -1.143544

### St John the Baptist Church, Moulsford

The river is enclosed behind a fence a few metres from the riverbank. It's a crying shame, but no doubt ministers and vicars many generations ago felt the need to cash in the riverbank asset to grateful neighbours. Interesting features to note include 17th-century wall monuments and a carved octagonal font from the 19th century.

51.552896, -1.148262

### → DETOUR E 80M (260FT)

### S Stoke Slipway, Ferry Ln

A communal slipway at S Stoke village. Ferries stopped running across the river here in 1962, but there is access to the TP and riverbank at the Beetle and Wedge pub on the opposite bank to the S Stoke slipway. It's very rare to have a pub built over and around a NT, and the food here is wonderful; as is the view.
➤ **Find** the riverbank where it meets the TP (51.548286, -1.145687) and paddle NE to the slipway.

51.549296, -1.145270

### St Andrew's Church, S Stoke

Cycle or walk the 2-mile BW/lost Ln from S Stoke to Goring via St Andrew's Church.

51.543076, -1.134363

## THE BEETLE & WEDGE

**3** A wonderful place to sit at dusk to watch geese and ducks flying downriver to roost. Good food, either before or after a paddle, and extremely friendly staff.

Ferry Ln, Moulsford, Wallingford, OX10 9JF

www.beetleandwedge.co.uk

01491 651381

## River access

The water is often shallow here, so it's perfectly OK to launch a packraft into the river from the FP. The Beetle and Wedge pub upstream owns some mooring rights, but not river access. Alternatively, there are steps on the riverbank downstream (51.547565, -1.144872), albeit some boat owners can forget to leave room for those who want to get onto the water. There's also easy access in the trees (51.547039, -1.144515).

51.548002, -1.145427

## Moulsford Riverbank, Moulsford

Sit here, and listen. The wings of geese and swans cut the air along the best reach of this stretch of river. The river spreads out like a lake, with little or no current.

51.548553, -1.145935

## Sphinx Hill, Moulsford

Built for Egyptology-enthusiasts Christopher and Henrietta McCall, Sphinx Hill was designed by postmodernist architect John Outram. The symmetrical house is not only heavily influenced by the Egyptian style, but also by the Thames. Limestone tiles downstairs represent the Thames chalk bedrock, while wooden floors upstairs match the yew and beech trees that grow up from the chalk. The garden is designed around a Babylonian-Egyptian-style channel of water that leads from the central back wall of the house to the River Thames, via a series of waterfalls. Built in the late 1990s, Sphinx Hill is the youngest Grade II*-listed building in the UK. In the spring, the water pools in a grass dell just next to the TP at the bottom of the garden. Huge marsh marigold flowers are surrounded by giant leaves of cow parsley.

51.546265, -1.144275

## Runsford Hole, S Stoke

The best place on the river to see kingfishers. A fat river inlet of still water and dead wood. Packraft across to the wide entrance into the stream towards S Stoke.

51.540788, -1.136542

## Withymead Nature Reserve, S Stoke

See fields of Loddon lilies over the 13-acre nature reserve of fen and wet woodland, which is managed by the Anne Carpmael Charitable Trust. Visitors can access the site from the riverbank or the Ridgeway BW.

51.541109, -1.136149

## Cleve Eyots, Goring

These three islands just before Goring Lock are best in summer when the water is low and little sandy beaches appear. Views over the Berkshire Downs.

51.529461, -1.136759

## CLEEVE LOCK, CLEEVE

The lock, built in 1787, is named after the hamlet of Cleeve, which no longer exists, since it merged with Goring. The 6½-mile stretch between Cleeve Lock and Benson Lock to the N is the longest lock-free reach on the non-tidal part of the River Thames. The shortest one runs from Cleeve Lock, too, and it is just ¾-mile downstream to Goring Lock.

51.531906, -1.135866

## GORING AND STREATLEY BRIDGE, GORING GAP

Built in 1923, Goring and Streatley Bridge is formed of two parts. The W bridge runs from the village of Streatley to the island that divides the river, while the E bridge runs to Goring on the opposite bank of the Thames.

51.523156, -1.141952

## Goring Lock, Streatley

Located on the E bank of the Thames, Goring Lock was originally just a weir, with a ferry boat operating across the river. In 1674, however, tragedy struck when 60 men, women and children drowned after the ferry they were travelling on overturned near the lock. The lock doesn't change the river too much. Always moving.

51.523298, -1.141266

## Swan Eyot, Goring Gap

A small, wooded island that was named after the Swan family who operated a ferry here in the 1780s. The island divides the River Thames at Goring.

51.523225, -1.142367

## Goring Weir, Goring Gap

A shallow waterfall surrounded by weeping willows and posh dining.

51.522877, -1.141591

## Heart Eyot, Goring

An island in the shape of a human heart. Access by FB from the Streatley bank.

51.522067, -1.142890

## THE MILLER OF MANSFIELD

An 18th-century Grade II-listed coaching inn. This used to be singer-songwriter George Michael's favourite pub when he lived in Goring. Apparently, he only ate starters!

High St, Goring, RG8 9AW

www.themillerofmansfield.com

01491 913990

## YHA STREATLEY-ON-THAMES

Superb-value accommodation within a short walk of the river.

Reading Rd, Streatley, RG8 9JJ

www.yha.org.uk/hostel/yha-streatley-on-thames

03453 719044

## Icknield Way Ford, Goring

The Icknield Way crosses the Thames at a now-redundant ford at the foot of Ferry Ln (51.520583, -1.143962). The Goring side of the ford has been defined as public open space and is a good place to paddle after a long hot summer's day.

51.520618, -1.143103

## Streatley Meadows, Streatley

Grassland at the centre of the village, with views of the church and river.

51.522991, -1.145890

## St Mary's Church, Streatley

Ancient church where Lewis Carroll, author of *Alice's Adventures in Wonderland*, once preached. He gave sermons here in the late 19th century in between writing and tours of the River Thames. Carroll's real name was Charles Dodgson. The church lies just behind the Swan at Streatley.

51.523576, -1.144724

St Mary's Church, Goring

St Thomas of Canterbury Church

### Goring, Reading

The Ridgeway trail crosses the Thames at Goring. There is high ground to the NE and high ground to the SW, and between the two the river forces its way through the Goring Gap. Two villages, two counties, two NTs, a river, Rds, houses and a station squeezed between the narrowest part of the Thames Valley – the Chiltern Hills to the E and the Berkshire Downs to the W.

51.522974, -1.137397

### St Thomas of Canterbury Church, Goring

Church surrounded by yew trees and character, built about 1100. Fourteenth-century features include the N porch and doorway.

51.522166, -1.140176

The Grotto walk

## St Thomas of Canterbury Church Lake, Goring
Paddle or walk here to look up at the church. Beautiful.

51.522708, -1.141279

## Grim's Ditch Eyots, Basildon
Three small islands on S southern bank, close to Grim's Ditch.

51.513024, -1.137807

## Towpath Walk, Nr Goring
Best in May when the mayflower is out. Look across the river to the high ground above the Grotto that runs into Streatley Hill.

51.512611, -1.136214

## Little Meadow, Goring
A hay meadow that the TP passes through. Lots of wildflowers in summer.

51.511228, -1.133378

### Gatehampton Eyot, Basildon

Large, wooded islands on the S bank formed by the breakaway of a naze. Possibly the most beautiful woodland before you reach Cliveden. The channel has been taken over by riverboats, and the E side of the island is a jungle of fallen trees, fences and fun. Take a saw. This small uninhabited woodland rests in the bend just before the Brunel-designed Gatehampton Railway Bridge.

51.510882, -1.131975

### GATEHAMPTON RAILWAY BRIDGE, GORING

This place, for all its brick and offensive size, is one of the calmest places to sit and enjoy the Thames. Even the river water seems unusually still. The Gatehampton Bridge, or Gatehampton Viaduct as it is also known, was designed and built between 1838 and 1840 by civil engineer Isambard Kingdom Brunel, which is probably why it is such a relaxing place. Brunel used nature as inspiration, canvas and frame for everything he designed.

51.511858, -1.128070

### Gatehampton Ferry, Goring

Site of the old Lower Basildon to Gatehampton ferry service. The TP is forced to leave the river at the point the old ferry service ran from. The crossing point leads to a public landing point and FP (51.511266, -1.121033), which also provides access to St Bartholomew's Church.

51.512033, -1.1227193

Gatehampton Failway Bridge

## Gatehampton BW, Goring

Cycle almost 3 miles of BW and lost wooded Ln from S Goring to Whitchurch-on-Thames. There will be much pushing uphill, as the climbs are steep and the narrow paths are perhaps not ideal, with steep cliffs down to the river. The yew and beech scenery down to the river is breathtaking.

51.512875, -1.122065

## Hattonhill Shaw Wood N

Climb through the trees to a find a spot overlooking the river and Goring Gap. Lovely to sit here in the moment.

51.510650, -1.114954

### → DETOUR – PACKRAFTING 275M (900FT) – 1½ MILES S

### St Bartholomew's Church, Lower Basildon

This 700-year-old church near Lower Basildon is now looked after by the Churches Conservation Trust. Built of flint and brick, it also features several significant memorials, including one to Jethro Tull, who is said to have been buried here. Jethro Tull is known as the father of modern agriculture, who designed the horse-drawn seed drill. There is also a memorial to politician Sir Francis Sykes by John Flaxman, a designer at the Wedgwood pottery factory.

➤ **Find** the riverbank where it leaves the TP (51.511928, -1.122030) and paddle SE to the church FP (51.511340, -1.121078) on the S riverbank.

51.508950, -1.120008

### Berkshire Towpath, Basildon

We could argue that leaving the river to follow the TP for an inland detour is an unpleasant chore. It's not. It's a joy. But life is about options. You're given three here: walk the W bank, kayak the river, or walk the chalk hills. The fourth option of walking the E bank isn't possible, unfortunately. Beech trees line the chalk cliff and meadow all the way to Pangbourne Station. The walk either side of the Thames makes a perfect circle if you can carry a packraft to navigate the old ferry crossing. Walk the 2½-mile towpath on the W bank. Accessible from the old ferry crossing, but well worth it as you can explore the wooded side of the path that has no river access. A triad of good choices.

51.510772, -1.117669

### Basildon Creek and Lake, Lower Basildon

A creek on the Berkshire towpath that opens into Basildon Lake.
Get in and packraft around.

51.500778, -1.108029

### Hartslock Aits, Basildon

Uninhabited islands with boat access. The islands take their
name from the ancient wood on the E slopes, Hartslock Woods.
There was once a lock and weir among these aits. A few old
wooden stumps of piles remain to mark the spot.

51.504586, -1.109716

### Basildon Park, Basildon

The 400-acre park was improved by Capability Brown in 1778.
It is now owned by the National Trust. Ancient trees, a second
hand bookshop and den building for kids.

51.500778, -1.108029

Hartslock Wood

### Lower Hartslock Wood, Lower Basildon

A yew woodland that is best seen before the beech trees start to unfurl their leaves in late April. Beech and yew share these chalk hills. The vast tangle of yew roots embedded in the cliffs is impressive.

51.508581, -1.111859

### ⑦ HARTSLOCK WOOD, LOWER BASILDON

Look for old messages and initials carved into the ancient beech trees here, sometimes halfway up the tree trunks. These giants tower over everything.

51.502723, -1.106871

### Wheatley's Pine BW, Nr Whitchurch

Follow the wooded lost Ln. Maple, beech and birch.

51.499935, -1.101179

### Hartswood Reach, Nr Whitchurch

Walk or paddle the miles of woodland. Look for the Thames through gaps in the trees.

51.505374, -1.109742

St Mary's Church, Whitchurch

Whitchurch Bridge

## THE GREYHOUND INN

Located in Whitchurch-on-Thames, this pub offers a large, sunny garden and a number of different street food vendors. A good place to rest on your way to the church.

High St, Whitchurch-on-Thames, RG8 7EL

www.thegreyhoundwhitchurchonthames.co.uk

01189 841485

## Hartswood, Nr Whitchurch

The path reaches the summit of Hartswood with good views. Best in autumn, when the beech woods are in gold and red leaf.

51.508009 -1.111094

## HARTSLOCK MEADOW, NR WHITCHURCH

The hill is full of summer scent when mauve marjoram flowers are in bloom. Hillside orchids in spring. Thames views all year.

51.509458 -1.106382

## ST MARY'S CHURCH, WHITCHURCH-ON-THAMES

Find the 11th-century flint and stone wall on the S side of the church. Look for plaques commemorating famous figures such as Sir John Forbes, Queen Victoria's physician, and the missionary Captain Allen Gardiner. Relatives of the American artist James McNeill Whistler are commemorated with family shields that are laid in the nave. The giant yew tree is impressive and flowers in February.

51.488194 -1.086924

## WHITCHURCH BRIDGE, WHITCHURCH-ON-THAMES

The toll bridge connects the villages of Pangbourne, in Berkshire, and Whitchurch-on-Thames, in Oxfordshire. It replaced the ferry in 1792 and is one of only two remaining private toll bridges on the Thames, the other being the Swinford Toll Bridge (see p110).

51.486509 -1.085116

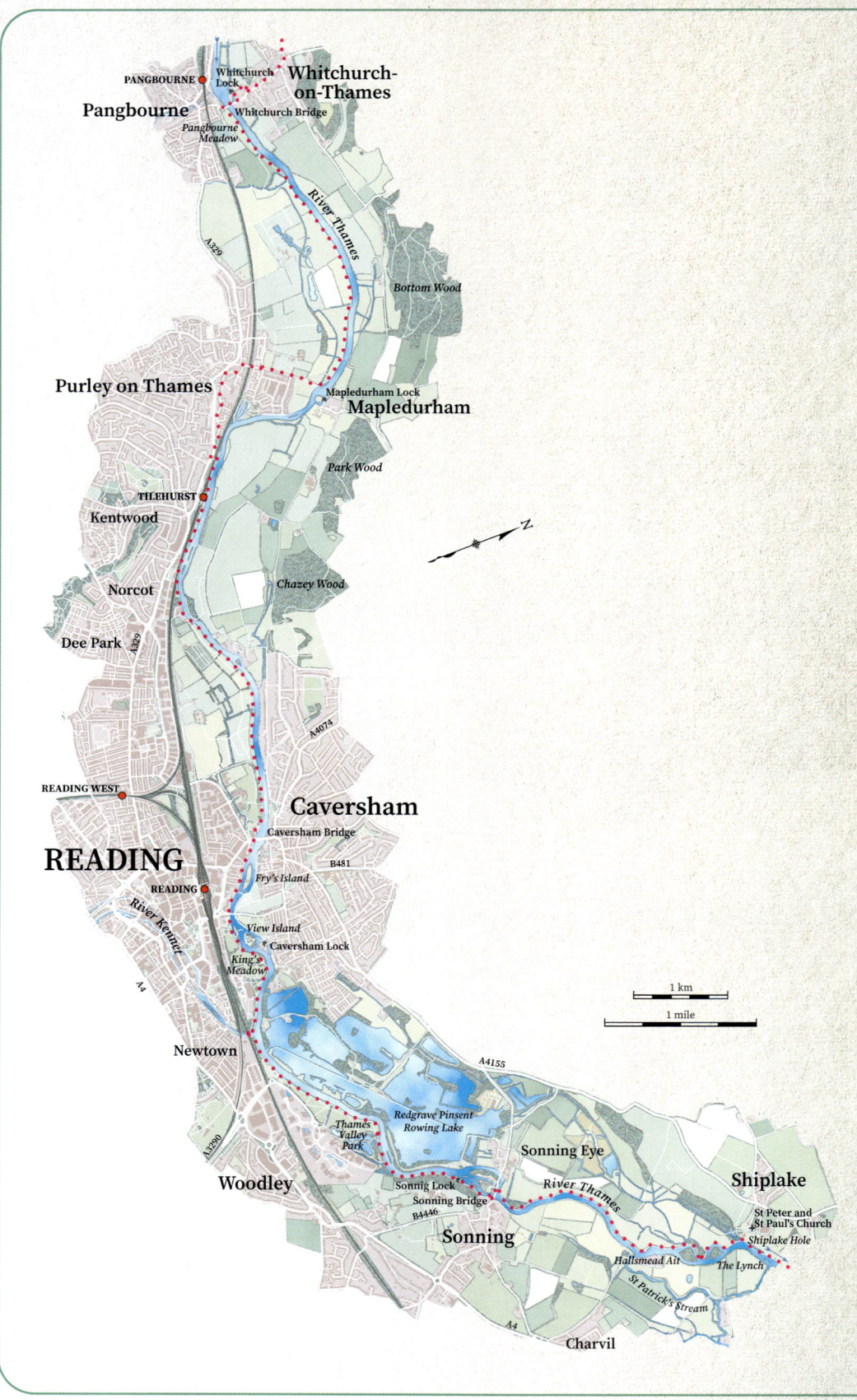

PANGBOURNE

Pangbourne

Whitchurch Lock

Whitchurch-on-Thames

Whitchurch Bridge

Pangbourne Meadow

River Thames

Bottom Wood

Purley on Thames

Mapledurham Lock

Mapledurham

Park Wood

TILEHURST

Kentwood

Chazey Wood

Norcot

Dee Park

A329

A4074

READING WEST

Caversham

Caversham Bridge

READING

B481

Fry's Island

River Kennet

View Island

A4

Caversham Lock

King's Meadow

Newtown

A3290

A4155

Thames Valley Park

Redgrave Pinsent Rowing Lake

Sonning Eye

Shiplake

Woodley

Sonning Lock

Sonning Bridge

River Thames

St Peter and St Paul's Church

B4446

Shiplake Hole

Sonning

Hallsmead Ait

The Lynch

St Patrick's Stream

A4

Charvil

1 km

1 mile

# 10. WHITCHURCH TO SHIPLAKE

## PUNTS

There will be moments in your life when you realise that not all paths can be completed on foot alone. This is one of them. More than 11 miles of the best navigable river and pathless chalk backwater.

There are three fonts of water: Thames, Kennet and St Patrick's Stream, a triad of gateways to the illusive Loddon lilies.

Yachts race over the flooded Thames gravel pits of Caversham. For all their skilful speed, it's the slow-paced resident barges of Reading that define this place.

## 10 STEPPING STONES

Whitchurch Lock
Mapledurham Mill
Roebuck Railway Steps
Poplar Island
Scours Ln Slipway
St Mary's Island
Christchurch Bridge
Brunel Bridge (Horseshoe Bridge)
Sonning Mill
The Lynch

## THE ELEPHANT HOTEL

 Twenty unique boutique rooms are adorned with quirky designs, beautifully handcrafted Indian furniture, oriental rugs and delicate fabrics. The owner enjoys sourcing unique items for the hotel at auction. Good food.

Church Rd, Pangbourne, Reading, RG8 7AR

www.elephanthotel.co.uk

01189 842244

## THE GEORGE HOTEL

 An old coaching inn established in the 1600s. The interior is inspired by Kenneth Grahame's *The Wind in the Willows*.

The Square, Pangbourne, Reading, RG8 7AJ

www.georgehotel
pangbourne.com

01189 842237

Whitchurch Lock

 ## WHITCHURCH LOCK, WHITCHURCH-ON-THAMES

No foot access but can be reached by boat.
The only lock on the Thames without a PRoW. The lock island is a lock keeper's cottage surrounded by garden and woodland.

51.486735, -1.088376

 ## Pangbourne Weir, Pangbourne

Large pike fish here because of the great depth of the pools. They hide under the banks. The lock is in the middle of the river; the weir is on the Pangbourne side, with its deep pool.

51.485758, -1.088066

 ## River Pang, Berkshire

Find where the chalk stream enters the Thames. The river runs for about 14 miles from its source near the village of Compton to Pangbourne.

51.485800, -1.088000

 ## Pangbourne, Ferry Ln, Slipway

There's a FP and PRoW down to the riverbank. A handy place to launch.

51.486111, -1.086332

### Pangbourne Steps, Pangbourne

Find the old concrete steps that fall to the river where the weir and Swan pub sit. The hills are high and healthy.

51.486153, -1.089882

### Pangbourne Meadow, Pangbourne

Riverside alder trees, with reeds and scrub providing cover to hide in.

51.487302, -1.078598

### Mill Pool, Whitchurch-on-Thames

Walk through the mill. It's private so no fishing or mooring. But there's a wonderful public ramp into the river.

51.487620, -1.085564

### Ford Ln, Whitchurch-on-Thames

The clue is in the name. An ancient ford that has been closed on the N bank. We can explore by boat or boot. The path on the S bank has also been removed.

51.491830, -1.062971

Pangbourne

→ **DETOUR - CYCLING**

## Bottom Wood, Collins End

The chalk hill hangers here are home to many BWs and hiding spots. A strange detour in that however far you cycle, there's almost no public access to the TP or the opposite bank for over 6 miles. A nod to protecting the toll at Whitchurch, perhaps? The only access is a narrow FP down to the riverbank (51.495829, -1.063606), 1 mile E of Whitchurch (see Ford Ln, p193).

➤ **Find** Hardwick Rd where it meets the TP (51.492595, -1.088057), and cycle 3 miles to Mapledurham via Bottom Wood.

51.498439, -1.048792

## Hardwick House, Sadhama Rewild Retreats

A yoga retreat set beside a chalk stream. Once a monastery, now long gone. The name 'Hardwick' means a 'hard spring'. Similar spellings like wick, wyke, wich and wych appear in many place names of Old English or Celtic origin, all referring to springs or places near water – fitting, as natural springs here run down to the river.

51.493296, -1.053462

## Hardwick BW, Hardwick

Superb views of the Thames from the chalk hills.

51.495449, -1.053509

## Straw Hill, Mapledurham

Fabulous views of the Thames. Good for star watching.

51.494572, -1.042606

## Mapledurham Mill, Mapledurham

Once a favourite with artists who favoured working in watercolours – both pre- and post-Turner.

51.485855, -1.037545

## Hardwick Pool, Hardwick

A wide section of river to sit and watch fish and birds. There's a small place to launch a packraft on the opposite banks. The area is occasionally used by paying campers who rent moorings along the bank.

51.492601, -1.053988

## Otter Island, Nr Mapledurham

Named after the otter that was shot in the early 19th century. Otters are making a comeback.

51.491068, -1.048398

## → DETOUR – PACKRAFTING 365M (1,200FT) E

### Mapledurham Mill, Mapledurham

A view of the mill from the river is as impressive as it is from on shore.
➤ **Find** where the TP leaves the riverbank (51.485873, -1.039978), and kayak E towards the mill riverbank.

51.485857, -1.037545

### Mapledurham Lock Pool, Mapledurham

A perfect pool for fish watching. The mouth of this water down to the tail of the eyot opposite the Roebuck Inn (51.482024, -1.037017) was once considered the best trout water in England. Chub and perch still feed here.

51.486526, -1.040097

St Margaret's Church, Mapledurham

### THE MAD DUCK CAFE

Somewhere to escape the path detour away from the river. An excellent café and tearoom – an ideal stopover for walkers.

84 Wintringham Way, Reading, RG8 8BG

www.themadduckcafe.co.uk

07377 879679

## ② MAPLEDURHAM MILL, MAPLEDURHAM

The last commercial watermill left on the Thames. Dating back to the English Civil War, it still produces flour today. It sits next to St Margaret's Church (see below). Check opening times and tours. The two islands are linked by a large weir that dates from the 13th century. The mill is featured in Black Sabbath's 1970 debut album. It's all a bit Walt Disney, if I'm honest.

51.485857, -1.037545

### St Margaret's Church, Mapledurham

The only way to truly enjoy the majesty of this place is from the river on a boat under your own steam.
When Eton College was founded in 1440, Mapledurham was one of the parishes Henry VI used for its endowment. A direct connection between the college and the parish endures to this day. The church featured in the Michael Caine movie *The Eagle Has Landed*.

51.485857, -1.037545

### Mill Pool, Whitchurch-on-Thames

This mill pool is pretty. Like a beauty pageant for billionaires with too much money and too few great-grandchildren.

51.485438, -1.037232

### Mapledurham House, Mapledurham

You can view this stately home from the Berkshire riverbank (51.484027, -1.03786). Paddle over for a closer look. Otherwise pay to get a mooring.

51.484706, -1.035749

###  Hardwick Ait, Mapledurham

A mid-river islet, with a small sandy beach on the Berkshire bank.

51.485438, -1.037232

###  Mapledurham Lock, Mapledurham

The lock dates back to 1908. Illustrations for *The Wind in the Willows* were supposedly inspired by this setting before it became heavily 'conserved'. National Trust now maintains a presence here. The weir stretches across Berkshire and Oxfordshire. No public access exists. You'll need to make a detour via Reading or Pangbourne to travel between the two villages.
The weir still drives Mapledurham Watermill. It's the furthest upstream mill on the Thames with a salmon ladder.
*The Wind in the Willows* illustrator, E.H. Shepard, is said to have based Toad Hall on either Mapledurham or Hardwick House.

51.485438, -1.037232

## → DETOUR - WALKING 100M (330FT) – 1 MILE S AND E

### Towpath, Mapledurham

Follow the towpath or paddle instead of continuing on the TP diversion away from the river. You'll need a packraft at some point to cross the river to the towpath on the opposite bank. Otherwise walk back.

**> Find** the FP that follows the riverbank and leaves the TP (51.485731, -1.039961) and follow SE until the FP ends and crosses the river.

51.484638, -1.038480

### Ferry Eyot, Mapledurham

A tiny uninhabited, wooded island – named after the ferry that once crossed here to Mapledurham House.

51.482466, -1.036867

### Towpath River Crossing, Purley on Thames

Find the end of the W bank FP, where ferries once carried barge horses across the other side. There's no bridge for the walker, but if you carry a packraft, the landing point is here (51.475732, -1.036521).

51.479866, -1.038862

### Towpath W Bank, Purley on Thames

Kayak to the towpath on the opposite bank. The E bank is steep, so it can be difficult to get out. The W riverbank once led onto land belonging to St Mary's Church (see p198), but it has been sold long ago, and there is no foot access anymore.

51.479788, -1.038776

### Kentwood Dell, Mapledurham

Find woodland and springs where the towpath FP ends on the E bank. Long-term moorings occupy some parts of the FP, but this small community of boaters are friendly and knowledgeable. There's a small well and spring along the NE edge of the copse. There's also a small island about 180m (590ft) after the FP ends. The towpath continues on the opposite bank, directly across the riverside of the railway line. A packraft is required, but you wouldn't be here if you didn't have a boat in your bag.

51.475716, -1.036530

### Thames Bend, Purley on Thames

There's a postbox here on the W bank, just short of where the towpath starts and then joins the TP again. The towpath rejoins the TP at the Elsley Rd/Oxford Rd railway bridge (see p198).

51.475603, -1.037739

### St Mary's Church, Purley on Thames

This small church is on the riverbank, but there's no direct river access.

➤ **Find** the finely carved Norman font, dating to 1150.

51.479497, -1.040212

### Elsley Rd/Oxford Rd railway bridge, Tilehurst

Smell the hawthorn hurrah of white blossom, nettles and dandelion flowers in spring. Where the TP rejoins the river.

51.474134, -1.034719

### ROEBUCK RAILWAY STEPS, TILEHURST

Stand on the steps waterside. A small boat launch marks the point where path rejoins river, albeit there are sometimes moored boats blocking river access.

51.474239, -1.034503

### Roebuck Ait, Mapledurham

Explore the wooded back channel and riverbank of this tiny island. The scrubland is separated from the N bank of the river by a narrow channel.

51.474512, -1.033978

Roebuck Railway Steps

Appletree Eyot Riverbank

### ④ POPLAR ISLAND RIVERBANK, BERKSHIRE

A popular mooring place. The bank is littered in large fallen branches for mooring and hiding places.

51.468632, -1.022041

### Appletree Eyot Riverbank, Berkshire

An uninhabited, wooded islet.

51.467587, -1.020164

### Thames Canoe Hire, Reading Marine Chandlery

Boats can be hired for half a day, a full day, a weekend or for a week. Drop offs or pick-ups are also available.
www.thamescanoehire.com

51.466187, -1.014243

### ⑤ SCOURS LN SLIPWAY, NR NORCOT

A public slipway into the Thames.

51.466247, -1.014136

## ⑥ ST MARY'S ISLAND, READING

A pretty, wooded island thick with osiers, reeds and wildlife. There are two other islands on the W end, but the overhanging trees make them all look like one island.

51.469189, -1.003544

## Fishery Backwater, Reading

A launch for small boats. Old signs used to warn boaters against loitering, as this was a popular beauty spot. Get behind the backwater.

51.469189, -1.003544

## → DETOUR - CYCLING 275M (900FT) – 2 MILES

### St Peter's Church, Caversham

Stand in the hillside setting above Caversham Gardens, with fabulous views of the Thames. Royalists stationed troops in the 12th-century church during the Siege of Reading in 1643 and placed a cannon atop its tower.

➤ **Find** Caversham Bridge N bank (51.466320, -0.976850) and follow the Rd W to church. From the church find the river path E that leads to the Warren.

51.468508, -0.980913

### Reading Canoe Club, Caversham

A friendly club over the river. Courses and beginner sessions are available.

51.46786083691888, -0.9821717641705295

### The Warren, Caversham

A 1-mile lost Ln from Faversham Church (51.468511, -0.981111) to Gravel Hill (51.472825, -1.004868).

51.469787, -0.991409

### Chazey Wood, Mapledurham

A 1 ½ mile BW from The Warren to Mapledurham Church.

51.475457, -1.012641

## Rivermead Park W, Reading

Listen to honking geese. Sit on benches beside big daisies along Reading's rural N fringe.

51.467582, -0.987812

## Rivermead Park E, Reading

Smell wildflower meadows where they fall down to riverbank.

51.466831, -0.981602

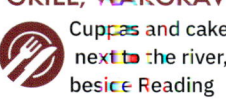

## LEO'S CAFE AND GRILL, WARGRAVE

Cuppas and cakes next to the river, beside Reading Rowing Club.

Thames Side Promenade, Reading RG1 8BD

07919 186700

### Reading Rowing Club, Reading

One of many waterside clubs on this long stretch of straight Thames. The only non-academic rowing club in Reading.

51.466305, -0.979269

### Reading Slipway, Reading

Slip and launch into the river.

51.466055, -0.978573

### 7 CHRISTCHURCH BRIDGE, READING

A pedestrian and cycle crossing between Reading and Caversham.

51.462483, -0.9702490

### Chapel of St Anne Plaque, Caversham Bridge

Touch the memorial to a long-gone pilgrim site. The Chapel of St Anne once stood on the old Caversham Bridge. The St Mary cult grew in the 12th century, linked to the Thames and its connection to sea and chalk. St Anne was the patron saint of seafarers, protecting them from storms – so it's interesting, then, that her chapel here was built on a bridge over the non-tidal Thames. The chapel was one of the first churches dedicated to her memory in this part of England. Reading, at the time, was largely run by the abbey, which had been built in 1121, and would have been seen in the distance over the river from the chapel on the bridge.
The chapel fell into decline after the 16th century.

51.460720, -0.967980

Christchurch Bridge

## Reading Bridge, Reading

Providing easy access to Christchurch Meadows, the bridge opened in 1923 with a span of 55m (180ft) – the longest in the UK at the time. There are two side arches for FPs.

51.460944, -0.967913

## Christchurch Meadows, Lower Caversham

Find the avenue of Lombardy poplars edges on the E boundary. The meadows are a cycling hub: a metalled FP and cycleway runs along the riverbank as an alternative to the TP.

51.463683, -0.968665

## Reading, Berkshire

Reading is a town on the Kennet, not on the Thames. It never quite reaches the Thames – as if the clever town planners tried to give the riverbank a little breathing space... for the people of Reading.

51.456535, -0.969944

## Caversham Lock, Caversham

Cross the river over the three islands that form the lock and weir. Caversham Lock is on De Bohun Island (commonly known as Lock Island). A FB, known as The Clappers, connects Lower Caversham to Reading, passing over the weir and islands. The lock is just S of Christchurch Meadow.

51.461164, -0.965158

Caversham Lock

Thames Lido

## Caversham Lock fish pass, Caversham
Find the fish pass and salmon ladder.

51.461671, -0.964078

## Thames Lido swimming baths, Reading
This fabulous lido was once an Edwardian outdoor swimming pool. Today it has a bar, a restaurant, hot baths and a pool. The water supply was originally fed from the nearby Thames at a place where white Loddon lilies grew.

In 1879 Reading Corporation (now Reading Borough Council) built the largest pool in the S of England, 80m × 24m (260ft × 80ft) for men only. It's not cheap, but the experience is well worth it. The swim and dine experiences are fun. www.thameslido.com

51.460167, -0.965334

## King's Meadow Steps, Reading
Find steel steps down to the water under an elder tree and large maple, at the end of King's Meadow Rd.

51.460480, -0.965993

## Caversham Path, Caversham
A riverbank stretch known as the Golden Mile. The town has a riverbank path and cycle track from Caversham Bridge to Heron Island.

51.465231, -0.967675

Horseshoe Bridge

### View Island, Caversham
Find the path over the weir and onto the uninhabited island. Wildflower meadows and grasses are surrounded by pollarded willows. The banks are steep and the river currents are dangerous; no fishing or dogs.

51.461946, -0.963073

### Heron Island, Caversham
Connected by FP to View Island.

51.463026, -0.961690

### Kennet and Avon Canal, Berkshire
Explore 87 miles of navigable chalk stream and canal. Starting in Bristol the waterway traces the River Avon's natural course to Bath, then continues via canal links to join the River Kennet at Newbury, eventually reaching Reading on the Thames. There are 105 locks along the navigation.

51.459000, -0.949500

### BRUNEL BRIDGE, READING
A red-brick railway bridge at Kennet Mouth – the point where the river meets the Thames. Brunel built the wooden bridge in 1891, alongside the Great Western Railway bridge, so horses towing barges along the Thames could cross the Kennet. Because of its shape, it's known as the Horseshoe Bridge.

51.458666, -0.949810

# → DETOUR - CYCLING 180M (590FT) – 100 MILES W

## Blakes Lock, Newtown

Administered as a Thames Lock. Operated manually but no key required. Located on the L bank. Canoe portage available up the weir stream.

> **Find** the towpath that joins the TP (51.458827, -0.949395) and follow SW.

51.45582, -0.95506

## Kennet and Avon Canal, Berkshire

Cycle for more than 100 miles along the towpath to Bath.

51.455272, -0.957495

## Thames and Kennet Marina, Reading

The entrance to Thames and Kennet Marina is on the opposite bank to the TP.

51.459208, -0.945993

## Marina Corner FP, Reading

Start of wooded FP.

51.467175, -0.928675

## The Broken Brow, Reading

This area was isolated from Reading by the railway and gravel pits. It became a place known for betting and other illegal proceedings. The Dreadnought Pub is now owned by the University of Reading and used as an administrative centre by its rowing club. Many of their boats can be seen in the former pub garden.

51.459722, -0.943481

## Caversham Lakes, Reading

Open swimming, walking and people-watching. Explore this entire complex for a whole day – ideally by packraft.

51.462852, -0.946099

## Waterside Woodland, Eye and Dusden

More than ½ mile of dense broadleaf wet woodland to explore and shelter from bad weather. Beware dangerous currents and underwater spikes and branches.

> **Find** the riverbank by kayak or punt on the opposite side to the TP, along the NW and N riverbank.

51.468011, -0.929752

###  Marsh Island, Eye and Dusden

Lots of trees to hide and shelter under – and back channels to explore. Tides and currents are a danger.

51.467846, -0.927669

###  Breach's Ait, Eye and Dusden

Tides and currents are a danger, if you're going to explore.

51.467387, -0.924914

###  The Wood Island, Eye and Dusden

An island created, in part, by the creation of The Redgrave and Pinsent Rowing Lake.

51.468730, -0.921685

Waterside Woodland south of Sonning

Sonning Lock

### Holme Park, Sonning
This towpath is a good place to shelter from sun and rain under the beech trees. The tallest trees of Holme Park rise up behind the church.

51.471494, -0.917939

### Holme Park Wood, Sonning
Birds roost in these woods. Listen to owls at dusk. A ghost is supposed to inhabit the park.

51.469502, -0.920471

Sonning Bridge

## Sonning Lock, Sonning

The lock house was built in the 1820s. James Sadler, a beekeeper, served as the lock keeper in the mid-1800s. He was known for his poems about the river and the village of Sonning. Sonning Regatta is held annually in May, while Reading and Thames Valley Park Regattas take place in June.

➤ **Access** from Sonning Bridge and via a FP from St Andrew's Church.

51.473185, -0.917658

## ⑨ SONNING MILL, SONNING

The river widens into a lagoon of several islands, home to the only dinner theatre in the UK.

51.476113, -0.916464

### THE BULL INN

A timber-framed pub and hotel with seven boutique bedrooms. Famously featured in *Three Men in a Boat*, which Jerome described as the 'veritable picture of an old country inn'.

High St, Sonning, Reading, RG4 6UP

www.bullinnsonning.co.uk

01189 693901

## Sonning Weir, Sonning

A beautiful place to sit on the W bank to look over the broad weir and pool. Kingfishers are sometimes seen fishing in the weir.

51.473785, -0.919180

## St Andrew's Church, Sonning

One of the Thames' most beautiful churches, inside and out. This place gets overlooked because the bridge, lock and weir were favoured by artists and poets. St Andrew's Church stands on what was once an Anglo-Saxon cathedral. The graveyard is huge, surrounded by a red-brick wall.

51.474122, -0.913165

## Sonning Archimedes screw 2020, Sonning hydroelectric plant

It's quite an impressive sight, at the weir.

51.473785, -0.919180

## Sonning, Berkshire

Roses grow all along by the Thames but nowhere quite as well as they do at Sonning. These gardens have attracted visitors for centuries.

51.474707, -0.912317

## → DETOUR - WALKING 1½ – 3 MILES

## St Patrick Bridge, Nr Charvil

**Find the chalk stream.**
➤ **Find** the FP that leaves the TP at Sonning Bridge (51.656522, -1.982299) and walk E 1½ miles.

51.485906, -0.898046

## Milestone Avenue, Nr Charvil

**A lost Ln to Charvil from St Patrick Bridge.**

51.484076, -0.896486

## Charvil Lakes, Charvil

Flooded gravel pits within 1 mile of the Thames. Listen to black caps in summer, the closest any bird gets to sounding like a nightingale. Kingfishers, herons and cormorants fish here.

51.469162, -0.872199

## Loddon Nature Reserve, Twyford

A bird nesting site beside the River Loddon. Swans, terns and geese use the offshore islands for nests.

51.476226, -0.870609

### St Patrick's Stream, Nr Charvil

The water is clear, and the riverbank is wild. The stream is rare in that it flows out of the Thames rather than into it, at this place.

51.486675, -0.899782

### St Patrick's Bridge W Bank, Nr Shiplake

Look for the snake's head fritillary flowers that bloom here in spring.

51.486675, -0.899782

### Loddon Drive Bridge, Charvil

A 1-mile lost Ln to Charvil and Loddon Nature Reserve. The highlight, though, is probably looking over the water of St Patrick's Stream from the bridge.

51.491854, -0.888253

### Marsh Stream, Charvil

The end of the 2½ mile walk finishes where you must put in a packraft to glide back.

51.493026, -0.887205

### St Patrick's (chalk) Stream, TP

Launch your packraft and paddle across to the chalk stream mouth. Best in September on a sunny day just before leaves turn brown. The current runs from Thames to Loddon, defining it as 'Thames Water' and navigable to public rather than private. Despite more than 400 years of protest, various landowners have failed to get the courts and Parliament to restrict public access by declassifying the water as 'Thames'. St Patrick's Stream takes its name from the Irish saint who according to folklore performed miracles with nature, most notably eradicating Ireland of snakes, and his use of the three-leafed shamrock in stories. The name 'St Patrick's' relates to what is an anomaly in nature. St Patrick's is considered one of the rarest waterways on the Thames – because the water flows from the Thames, upstream to the River Loddon, rather than downstream.

➤ **Find** where the TP and riverbank face St Patrick's Stream W entrance.

51.486949, -0.898725

### Berry Brook, Nr Shiplake

Find the brook as it enters the River Thames at Hallsmead Ait. The backwater flows through farmland owned by Phillimore estate.

51.491716, -0.896730

The Lynch riverbank

### Hallsmead Ait, Nr Shiplake

Explore by packraft but some care is needed because of eddies and currents.

51.491396, -0.895105

### THE LYNCH, NR SHIPLAKE

An uninhabited island full of birds, dragonflies and nettles, surrounded by tree-covered moorings on all sides.

51.493637, -0.894194

### Shiplake, Henley-on-Thames

The jewel in the Reading crown – famous for chalk streams and the Loddon lily. Victorian naturalists noted how the river here was unique for species of fish attracted to the chalk waters.

51.496717, -0.894506

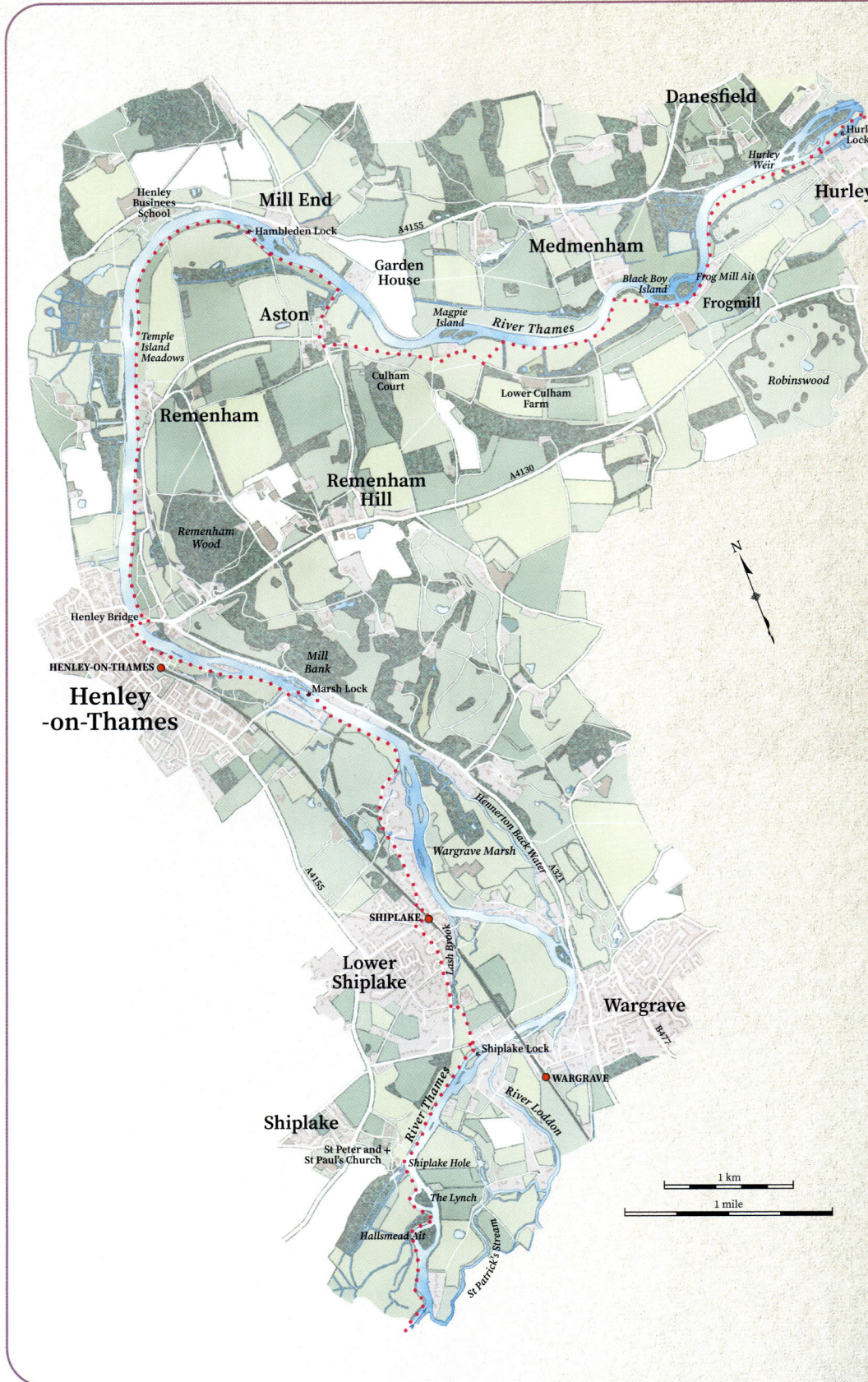

Danesfield

Hurley Lock

Hurley Weir

Hurley

Henley Business School

Mill End

A4155

Hambleden Lock

Garden House

Medmenham

Black Boy Island

Frog Mill Ait

Frogmill

Magpie Island

River Thames

Aston

Temple Island Meadows

Culham Court

Lower Culham Farm

Robinswood

Remenham

Remenham Hill

A4130

Remenham Wood

N

Henley Bridge

HENLEY-ON-THAMES

Henley -on-Thames

Mill Bank

Marsh Lock

Hennerton Back Water

A321

Wargrave Marsh

A4155

SHIPLAKE

Lower Shiplake

Lash Brook

Wargrave

B477

Shiplake Lock

Shiplake

River Thames

WARGRAVE

River Loddon

St Peter and St Paul's Church

Shiplake Hole

The Lynch

Hallsmead Ait

St Patrick's Stream

1 km

1 mile

# 11. SHIPLAKE TO HURLEY

Hurley Lock

## CHALK

This section is washed in white and green – chalk stream and Loddon lily in the shade of ivory towers and Hurley yew. Possibly the widest and most accessible section of chalk in the world. Calcium carbonate fossils hang from the edges of sunshine and mist, bubble up from the springs, and fall into the water from 30m (100ft) milky cliffs.

## 10 STEPPING STONES

Shiplake College Boathouse
Shiplake Lock
Marsh Lock
Henley Bridge
St Mary & St Nicholas Church
Hambleden Lock
Aston Ferry Ln
Culham Court Steps
Frog Mill Ait
Danesfield Chalk Cliffs

###  SHIPLAKE COLLEGE BOATHOUSE, SHIPLAKE

Look for Lodden lilies around the tiny natural harbour. A path leads up to the church.

51.496540, -0.894717

###  St Peter's & St Paul's Church, Shiplake

Touch the shaft of the cross monument in the churchyard. The cross memorialises the Phillimore family and their claim to the land.

51.497837, -0.896010

###  Phillimore's Island, Shiplake

George Orwell and his friends fished here for roach and pike. The island is named after the Phillimore family, who were once owners of Shiplake House.

51.498604, -0.890697

Wargrave

## → DETOUR – PACKRAFTING 35M (115FT) – ½ MILE SE

### Marsh Stream, Wargrave
Stream opposite Phillimore's Island on the S bank. Beware the wooden signs and posts.
→ **Find** the riverbank where it meets the TP (51.644408, -1.855094), just after Phillimore's Island and paddle SE to the marsh stream on the facing bank.

51.498327, -0.889517

### Borough Lake, Wargrave
A large lagoon lies between St Patrick's Stream and the Thames.

51.498161, -0.889437

### St Patrick's Stream Wood, Charvil
This three-way junction of water and wet woodland is one of the finest beauty spots of the backwater Thames.

51.492932, -0.887092

## ② SHIPLAKE LOCK, SHIPLAKE
A lock and weir sit just above the confluence of the River Loddon and the Thames. In 1891 the City of London Corporation purchased Shiplake Lock Island 'to preserve its use for camping and bathing'. The island was later managed by the Thames Conservancy and its successor organisations, which permitted huts to be built there. Their use was restricted to cooking only – overnight stays were not allowed.
In 2022 the Environment Agency declined to renew the leases for the camp plots.

51.502464, -0.883231

## → DETOUR – WALKING 275M (900FT) – 1 MILE E AND N

### Viaduct Green Way, Henley-on-Thames
Find where the BW leaves the TP (51.502539, -0.882840) and walk E.

51.503017, -0.878549

### Lash Brook Greenway, Shiplake
Walk the lost Ln that leads to the old Ferry crossing to N Wargrave. The PRoW access still exists on the opposite side at two locations.

51.503570, -0.870996

### Towpath detour, Shiplake

Launch a kayak or punt towards the backwaters and the Thames reach.

51.502120, -0.881602

### ➔ DETOUR– PACKRAFTING 45M (150FT) – 2 MILES E AND N

### River Loddon Chalk Stream, Wargrave

Best experienced in morning mist, before it gives way to the sun. Willows wet with dew gleam as the sunlight breaks through.
➤ **Find** the riverbank on the opposite side to Wargrave (51.502120, -0.881602) and launch your kayak.

51.501602, -0.880034

### Bushnell Marine Services Ltd, Wargrave

Moorings and boat services are located just E of the railway line.

51.501918, -0.876294

### Heron's Creek, Wargrave

A former waterway once led up to St Mary's Church, now severed from the river. Explore the wooded maze. Visit at dusk in late June or early July, when the riverbanks can be lit up with glowworms.

51.501821, -0.872104

### St Mary's Church, Wargrave

Find the 15-century font carved from chalk. It was restored in the early 20th century. The previous church dates from the 13th century, but it was burnt down by suffragettes in 1914.
➤ **No** river access – walk in from Ferry Ln (see below).

51.499698, -0.873671

### Ferry Ln riverside, Wargrave

An important public access to the water via a PRoW. A beautiful little Ln bends at a right angle down to the waterside past several houses and parked cars.

51.502223, -0.871173

### Henley Rd riverside, Wargrave

Wooded public access to the water via a PRoW. A narrow alley between houses and garages leads down to a pretty part of the river. The PRoW notice is sometimes missing, but locals are always friendly and happy to give directions.

51.503036, -0.870246

## High Street riverside, Wargrave

An important public access to the water via PRoW.
This old ford or ferry crossing is the only river crossing along 9 miles of river between Henley and Sonning. Without this crossing, walkers lose access to one of the most important backwater detours on the entire walk: Henning Water.

51.503689, -0.869954

## Wargrave, Henley-on-Thames

Once a famous stopover for stagecoaches travelling between Henley-on-Thames and Reading, High St used to have seven pubs. Most of them have now gone.

51.502966, -0.869410

## Camps Pool, Wargrave

A chalk stream backwater leading to Iósaf Ait that runs into and out of Hennerton Backwater.

51.505552, -0.869565

## Iósaf Ait, Wargrave

A wooded islet marking the start of the Hennerton Chalk Stream. Celtic axes, flints and other remains were found here in the mid-18th century. It is thought to be an ancient sacred site.

51.505969, -0.870696

## Hennerton Chalk Stream, Wargrave

The area is mostly ash, sycamore and alder. Look for places to shelter, rest and hide.

51.505690, -0.869623

## The Backwater, Hennerton

Look for pike and Canada geese.
➤ **Hennerton** Backwater leaves the Thames at Iósaf Ait, passes through Willow Marina and rejoins just below Ferry Eyot. It's navigable for small boats from the downstream end for much of its length.
➤ **Fiddler's** Bridge, on Willow Ln, spans the upstream end but has very limited clearance, restricting passage to canoes and small dinghies only.

51.519141, -0.874390

## Willow Ln Bridge, Wargrave

Look out across the backwater – the only place a PRoW exists for those on foot.

51.507643, -0.869792

## Willow Ln, Wargrave

A historic FP and the only crossing over Wargrave Marsh, leading down to the towpath on the opposite bank to Shiplake Station. Look for glowworms after dusk in late June and early July.

51.510078, -0.873422

## Wargrave Marsh, Lower Shiplake

The best access is by boat. Look for kingfishers around fen and wet meadow. The fen is slowly being overtaken by scrub, but that's true rewilding. To the E, the chalk hills force the Thames on its long loop past Henley.

51.514689, -0.880188

## Siobhán Eyot, Hennerton

A tiny islet that floods in winter, where coots and swans nest.

51.515546, -0.871780

## The Backwater, Hennerton

A 1-mile-long waterway. After a good deal of litigation in the past, the only obstacles now – to kayakers, punters and paddle boarders – should be fallen trees. Nothing more sinister. The wooded Rd between Wargrave and Henley skirts the chalk stream.

➤ **Walk** in from Wargrave on Henley Rd or kayak.

51.507655, -0.869736

## Johnson's Bridge, Henley-on-Thames

The site of the old ford across The Backwater onto Wargrave Marsh, visible from the waterway. Plumes of reeds and reedmace, reaching up to 8ft high, give the area a tropical feel.

51.519629, -0.874604

## Wargrave Marsh, Lower Shiplake

Look for Loddon lilies from mid-March. The island was formed by the backwater loop that connects to the Thames at both ends. Sheltered and calm, it's at its best – quiet and most colourful – before dusk at the end of September. The weeds and riverbank bathe in the still-warm sunlight.

51.514641, -0.880044

## Lashbrook Eyot, Lower Shiplake

The premises of Henley Sailing Club. The islet is no longer distinctive, as its channel has grown over. Its W bank features the towpath and overlooks several other islands. Look for Loddon lilies.

51.511005, -0.880057

###  Wargrave Marsh Island, Wargrave

A crystal-clear backwater, spliced with wooden humpback bridges. Saved from silting and theft by Henderson Blackwater Association, the island is reminiscent of Romney Marsh.

51.522032, -0.877893

###  Conway's Bridge, Henley-on-Thames

Touch the stones of the ruined Reading Abbey. This bridge, designed by Humphrey Gainsborough (brother of the artist Thomas Gainsborough), was built using stones reclaimed from the abbey.

51.526400, -0.880800

###  Handbuck Eyot, Shiplake

A thin, wooded island on the eastern edge of Shiplake, Oxfordshire. It's only accessible by boat.

51.515077, -0.880838

###  Poplar Eyot, Lower Shiplake

A small, secluded island of willow.

51.518224, -0.879088

North Shiplake Path

## Ferry Eyot, Lower Shiplake

This uninhabited island is named after the Bolney ferry, which once carried barge horses across to the towpath on the opposite side.

51.520724, -0.879132

## Wargrave Marsh Tip, Nr Lower Shiplake

The heart of darkness. A wild stretch of water, populated with more species of tree, plant and bird than almost anywhere else on this section of river. A must-visit, if you can find a way here.
➤ **The** easiest access is by boat across from the TP ⅔ of a mile S of Marsh Weir or 1 mile N of Shiplake Station. It's a 2¼-mile walk from Wargrave.

51.522271, -0.877833

## ➔ DETOUR – PACKRAFTING

## Hennerton Backwater N Mouth, Hennerton

A Thames backwater, from the northern entrance. Bring warm clothes and camo.

51.522446, -0.877685

## Shiplake Railway, Shiplake

Wrought-iron plate girders rest on cast-iron cylinders filled with concrete. The bridge was built in 1897.

51.511648, -0.882664

## Island Bank, Nr Lower Shiplake

A shallow riverbed ideal for launching into the surrounding backwaters.

51.522003, -0.879403

## MARSH LOCK, HENNERTON

A lock close to the entrance of Hennerton Backwater, Wargrave Marsh and water meadows.
➤ **These** two islands are among the most beautiful sites today, circled by Thames waters with a backdrop of wooded hills. The lock bridge is often closed because of the Environment Agency's ongoing repairs.

51.528030, -0.887100

### Park Place, Henley-on-Thames

The chalk cliffs reflect their glowing light off beech trees in sunshine and cloud. The best views are from the end of Mill Ln, looking across to the riverbank on the other side.

➤ **Watch** shoals of fish leap out of the water when being chased by pike.

51.529308, -0.887941

### Newton Lock N, Henley-on-Thames

Find and touch ash trees – Constable's favourite. He most admired their pale olive-grey bark.

In spring the gentle lime keys contrast with the dead flowers that stubbornly cling from previous years.

51.529274, -0.887696

### Rod Eyot, Henley-on-Thames

The largest of a series of islets here that flood. Cottages are built on stilts. Accessible by boat and best after rainfall. Beware of strong currents.

51.532317, -0.893335

### Marsh Meadows, Henley-on-Thames

Listen to wintering tufted duck, pochard and goosander. A quieter meadow in summertime.

51.530853, -0.892018

## Eyot Centre, Henley-on-Thames

Home of The Henley Canoe Club and The Henley Dragon Boat Club, it's now a directly licensed centre for the Duke of Edinburgh Awards.

51.534870, -0.896123

## E Eyot, Henley-on-Thames

A thin wooded islet that is uninhabited and can be submerged in water in winter. It's a good habitat for birds and is known locally as Bird Island.

51.534438, -0.897501

## Public Landing Henley, Henley-on-Thames

A convenient parking spot for kayaks and punts when shopping or taking a break.

51.536713, -0.900725

Remenham

## Boathouse Reach, Henley-on-Thames

Watch people move about moored boats under wooded hills – beautiful in sunshine or rain.

51.535593, -0.899947

## Remenham Creek, Henley-on-Thames

Find the creek nestled between overhanging maple trees and boat moorings.

51.536483, -0.899435

## HENLEY BRIDGE, HENLEY-ON-THAMES

This iconic bridge with five stone arches, built in 1786, offers good views of the river. It famously served as the finish line for the inaugural Oxford–Cambridge boat race in 1829. The Leander Club, one of the oldest rowing clubs in the world, is located on the Berkshire side. Nearby, the path marks the boundary where Oxfordshire ends.

The Romans used this crossing in 43 AD to pursue the armies of the Britons.

51.537636, -0.901078

## The Angel on the bridge, Henley-on-Thames

Look for sculptures of Isis and Tamesis by Anne Seymour Damer either side of the central arch.  Tamesis faces N; Isis faces S. Models can be seen at the River and Rowing Museum.

51.537508, -0.900149

## Phyllis Court Opp Bank, Remenham

A narrow harbour and one of the three great houses on the Henley Reach, alongside Greenlands and Fawley Court.

▶ **Phyllis** Court is a private club located on the R bank at the Henley Royal Regatta finish.

51.541416, -0.899033

## Remenham Wood, Remenham

Look for goldcrests, and listen to ravens that roost here.

51.543255, -0.893691

## Remenham Access land, Remenham

Remenham means 'home of the ravens'.  It could also mean 'home of the Remi', an old Celtic tribe once based here.

51.541436, -0.894815

## Remenham Church FP, Remenham

Dewy cobwebs hang heavy at dawn around the churchyard. They are most beautiful in August, when seen from the FP wall.

51.551959, -0.890451

---

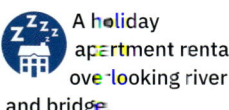
### THE BOATHOUSE HENLEY-ON-THAMES

A holiday apartment rental overlooking river and bridge.

Stonebridge Henley Bridge, Henley-on-Thames, RG9 2LN

www.theboathousehenley.co.uk

07747 037123

### EMBERS CAMPING – HENLEY CAMPSITE

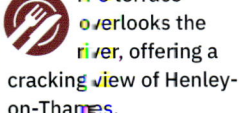
Dog-free camping that allows fires.

Marlow Rd, Henley-on-Thames, RG9 3AP

www.emberscamping.co.uk/campsites/henley-oxfordshire

03452 572267

### BISTRO AT THE BOATHOUSE

The terrace overlooks the river, offering a cracking view of Henley-on-Thames.

Station Rd, Henley-on-Thames, RG9 1AZ

www.bistroattheboathouse.co.uk

01491 577937

### THE ANCHOR INN

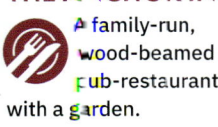
A family-run, wood-beamed pub-restaurant with a garden.

58 Friday St, Henley-on-Thames, RG9 1AH

www.anchorhenley.co.uk

07734 713591

**⑤ ST MARY & ST NICHOLAS CHURCH, REMENHAM**

Look for the windows in the apse, which depict St John the Baptist, the Crucifixion and St Nicholas. They were designed by Charles Eamer Kempe, a renowned Victorian stained-glass artist. Fragments of the original church survive, including the chalk window near the pulpit and sections of the N wall, dating back to around 1320. Kempe's signature motif, a psychedelic golden wheatsheaf, can be seen in the windows.

The church is dedicated to St Nicholas, who was born in the 3rd century in what is now Turkey. Known for giving away his inheritance to help the poor, sick and suffering, he became the bishop of Myra and was known for his love of children, generosity and care for sailors.

51.551189, -0.889836

 ## Fawley Court, Fawley

Find the Thames inlet under a low FB. Fawley Court, a country house on the W bank of the river, sits on historic grounds. After the Norman Conquest, Fawley Manor was granted to Walter Giffard, one of the Domesday Book's compilers.

51.551600, -0.897800

 ## Temple Island, Remenham

An 18th-century folly known as Fawley Temple dominates the island view, surrounded by manicured garden and weeping willow. The owner of Fawley Court built this Grecian-style temple to host all-night fishing parties and banquets. Its design was inspired by discoveries made at Pompeii.

51.556740, -0.888229

 ## Falelie Water, Hambleden

A Saxon common of chalk stream and springs. The open water is connected to the Thames. Navigation is difficult due to thick greenery. Though the surrounding meadow is no longer common land, its historic status is partially preserved by an old PRoW between Hambleden, Great Wood and Henley. Downgraded to a FP more than 400 years ago, it's still worthy of the 3-mile walk from Henley to Hambleden.

51.560446, -0.886809

 ## Greenlands, Hambleden

Look out for heron and lapwing flying over the inland ponds. This site was once the home of W.H. Smith, later becoming the Imperial Staff College. Today it's home to Henley Business School, part of the University of Reading, and the Henley Greenlands Hotel. The Greenlands campus is set in its own 30 acres.

51.561787, -0.879597

### Hambleden Valley, Hambleden

A Chiltern beech woodland full of red kites.

51.561787, -0.879597

### Hambleden Mill, Hambleden

They used to catch 1,000 eels a year here. Hambleden Mill, once the best-known watermill on the Thames, stopped operating in 1959 and was later converted into flats. It still retains some of its charm. The site, nestled in the foot of a Chilterns valley, also includes the remains of a Roman villa.

51.558892, -0.869756

### HAMBLEDEN LOCK, HAMBLEDEN

Balance over a beautiful lock, with a weir that connects to both sides of the river. Hambleden Mill on the other side is worth crossing the river for. There is access to one of two chalk streams feeding into the Thames (51.562016, -0.868066).

51.558601, -0.870158

### Hambleden Weir Crossing, Hambleden

Walk the weir if you like waterfalls. It's like a tumbling carpet at a fairground, shaking every sense in your body.

51.559128, -0.871576

Hambleden Lock chalk stream

Aston Ferry Lane

## Hamble Brook, Chalk Stream, Hambleden Marina

A peaceful chalk stream follows the riotous crossing at the lock; a lovely place to sit and rest.

51.558500, -0.869500

## St Mary the Virgin Church, Hambleden

A church beside the Hamble Brook chalk stream, where a carved Saxon font sits near the S door.
W.H. Smith, once a churchwarden here, is buried in the churchyard.
➤ **A** 1-mile detour from the old mill.

51.572848, -0.870210

## Lock Wood, Hambleden

Listen to warblers in summer that feed around the marsh willows and alder.

51.557078, -0.872380

## ⑦ ASTON FERRY LN, ASTON

Children and adults sometimes swim here in summer, although there's no indication it's safe. Launch a boat to reach a towpath on the opposite bank. The removal of the towpath to the other side was thanks to a friendship between George III and the then-owners of the Culham Court estate.
➤ **Paddle** across the front of Hambleden Place opposite to find the towpath, or continue on to Magpie Eyot.
➤ **Directly** opposite Aston Ferry Ln is Ferry Ln on the other side. Find the grassy Ln that leads down to the river from Aston and Remenham Hill, where the towpath changes sides.

51.553913, -0.866597

## Ferry Ln, Hambleden

The best access is via Hambleden Lock by bike along Westfields and then Ferry Ln. A historic and worthy route to pedal, especially if you can carry a packraft. This route still functions as a portage.

51.553089, -0.864329

## Aston, Henley-on-Thames

Red kites roost in the trees either side of Aston.

51.550621, -0.870313

## CULHAM COURT STEPS, REMENHAM

If you do nothing else on this journey, make it a point to moor either your boots or boat as a 'thank you' to Viscount Hambleden. This stretch of the Thames estate is gently sloping chalk hill that meets the riverbank. The original estate owners once secured laws banning access and navigation here, rewarding George III with free stays at the estate. In 1895 Viscount Hambleden, grandson of the second W.H. Smith, purchased the Culham estate. He overturned these earlier restrictions and placed protective covenants on land along both sides of the river, gifting them to the National Trust and safeguarding public access forever.

51.548266, -0.862583

## Magpie Eyot, Nr Aston

Touch the water while sliding down from the sloping bank by packraft – beware the currents. This is a favourite place for herons and fish, and it offers good shelter from the sun.
➤ **Like** most Thames 'islands', it is divided into two or three parts by streams that periodically close then reopen over time. Explore the edges, shallows and the entrances.

51.546463, -0.851666

Culham Court

## Medmenham Slip, Medmenham

A slipway on the right bank at the end of Ferry Ln off A4155 (public access).

➤ **While** the S bank slipway has been lost, access to climb onto that bank remains, and a greenway is still in place.

51.546805, -0.839323

## Black Boy Island, Hurley

An uninhabited island lies beside the small hamlet of Frogmill on the southern side of the river. It floods whenever the Thames rises. There is a beautiful manicured green and two benches in front of the houses looking onto the island. Carpeted in a sea of white ransoms, the wooded island offers a peaceful spot to land and picnic outside the nesting season.

➤ **Heavily** wooded, the island sits where Black Boy Ln meets the Thames.

51.544958, -0.831418

Black Boy Island

Frogmill Slip

## → DETOUR – CYCLING 90M (295FT) – 2 MILES S

### Frogmill Farm Ln, Hurley

There's a cycle way and BW up to Ashley Hill Forest.
➤ **Find** the lost name that joins the TP (51.544360, -0.832976) and follow S.

51.541569, -0.832589

## 9 FROG MILL AIT, HURLEY

Frog Mill Ait takes its name from the mill that once stood on the bank. There's a name tied to the place: Poisson Deux. It's said to come from the fish ducts or traps that once dotted the river here. The current still moves past, so care is needed when exploring by boat.

51.544389, -0.833127

## DANESFIELD HOUSE HOTEL & SPA

 The hotel occupies the ancient earthworks of a Bronze Age hillfort, set across 65 acres of grounds and gardens with uninterrupted views of the river. Neolithic finds have also been discovered on the site, known as Danesfield Camp. During World War II, the RAF requisitioned the house for the Joint Service Imagery Intelligence (IMINT) Unit.

Henley Rd, Marlow-On-Thames, SL7 2EY

www.danesfieldhouse.co.uk

01628 891010

Giant Plane Tree

## Ashley Hill Forest

This wooded escape lies along a lost Ln past Frogmill Farm. Only helpful if you carry or push a bike.

➤ **Find** the lost Ln ⅓ of a mile up to Henley Rd, where chicanes lead left and right into a BW. The BW forks 1½ miles ahead into two woodlands: Ashley Hill Forest to the E and Bowsey Hill to the W, both part of the Chiltern Way.

51.522867, -0.813045

## Frogmill Farm Ln, Hurley

Steps down to the riverbank from the lane provide access for walkers and boaters.

51.541569, -0.832589

## DANESFIELD CHALK CLIFFS

The tallest cliffs on the Thames rise more than 30m (100ft) above the river. A cliffside chapel designed by the Westminster architect Pugin once stood here but was demolished around 1900 to make way for Danesfield House. In the 18th century, archeologists named the cliff Danesfield after mistakenly believing the hill fort had been settled by Danes.

The true prehistoric nature of the cliff settlement was only recently uncovered during the construction of a car park next to Danesfield House. Excavations revealed more than 70 flint artefacts, showing that the cliffs were inhabited through the Bronze and Iron ages.

51.551386, -0.818235

## Hurley Lock, Hurley

Lock at the centre of a cluster of seven wooded islands separated by narrow channels – all uninhabited.

51.551325, -0.808773

Hurley Lock East

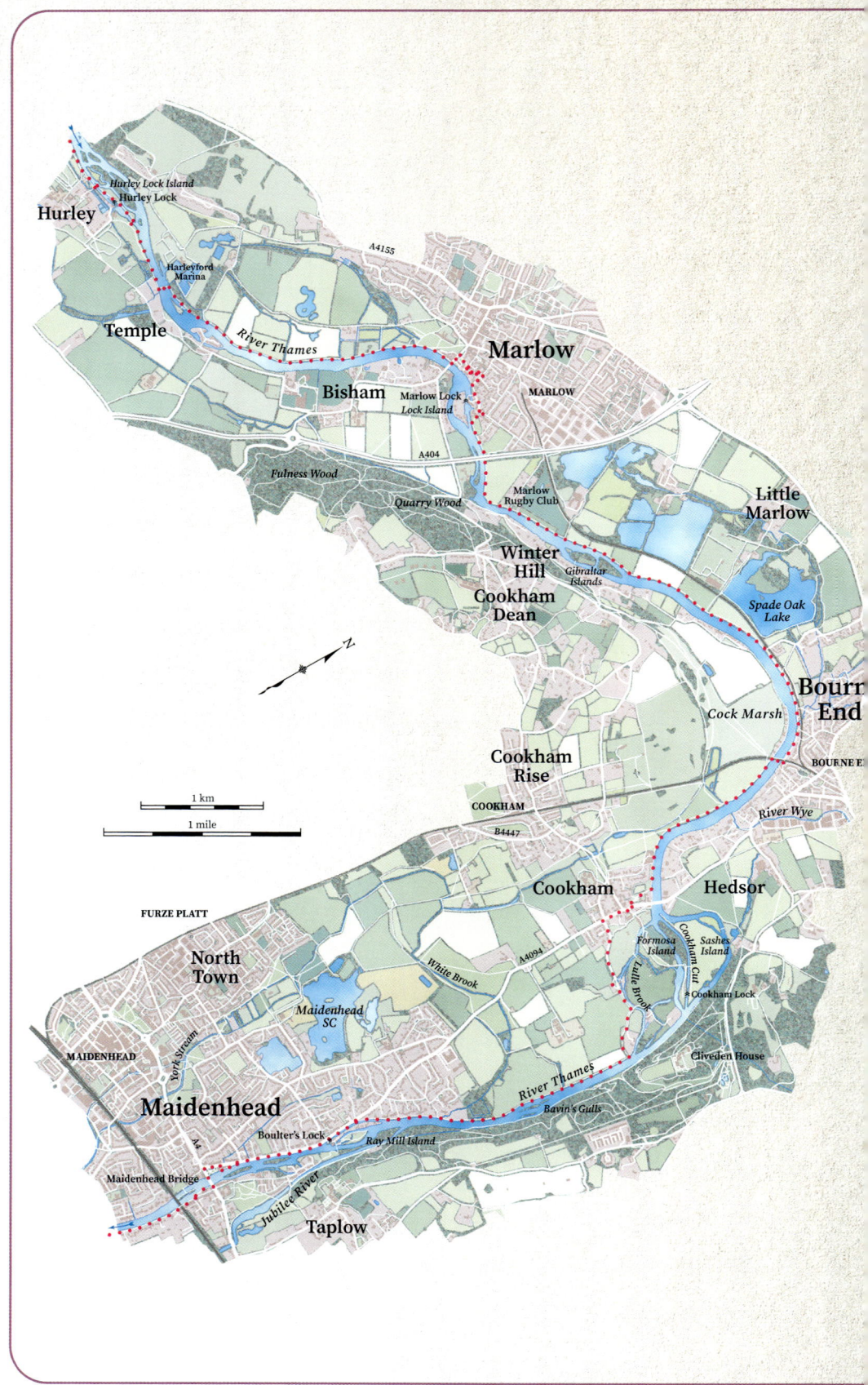

# 12. HURLEY TO MAIDENHEAD BRIDGE

Bridge to Cock Marsh

## DREAMS

This is enchanted forest. Trees fall to riverbank, where pixies and fairies furl for fun.

The Celts and their predecessors cherished Cliveden for its deceptive, warm feel in winter.

If you prefer spring, beech trees start to unfurl their leaves in late April.

## 10 STEPPING STONES

Temple Lock
Church of All Saints
Marlow Cemetery
Plane Tree Avenue
Bourne End
Cock Marsh
Cliveden Deep Corner
Battlemead Common (Woodland Path)
Boulter's Lock
Guards Club Island

## Hurley Weir, Hurley

Move over the river in a packraft. Care is needed around the weir. It's a popular summer spot for kayakers and often busy on weekends. The standing wave here is ideal for freestyle kayaking. Hurley hosts the annual Hurley Classic, a rodeo competition for kayakers.

51.551113, -0.809237

## Hurley Weir N Bank, Hurley

Listen to the rush of falling water. Spirals and waves form where the river leaves the weir. The canal cuts are calm, grassy islands of picnic tables, slow movement and boats.

51.551752, -0.805939

## Harleyford Manor, Marlow

Some of this area is limited for FPs, but there's plenty to see by boat: inlets and little sandy bays. There's a nice boathouse, with a stream running through it. A large plane tree hangs over the water.

51.551308, -0.799974

### THE OLDE BELL (BEST WESTERN)

Outstanding service, food and rooms – all a five-minute walk from the river. One of the oldest inns in the UK.

High St, Maidenhead, SL6 5LX

www.theoldebell.co.uk

01628 969790

### CRAZY FOX HOUSE

Bit different. Stylish rooms in a laid-back B&B.

High St, Hurley, SL6 5NB

www.crazyfoxhurley.com

02045 870948

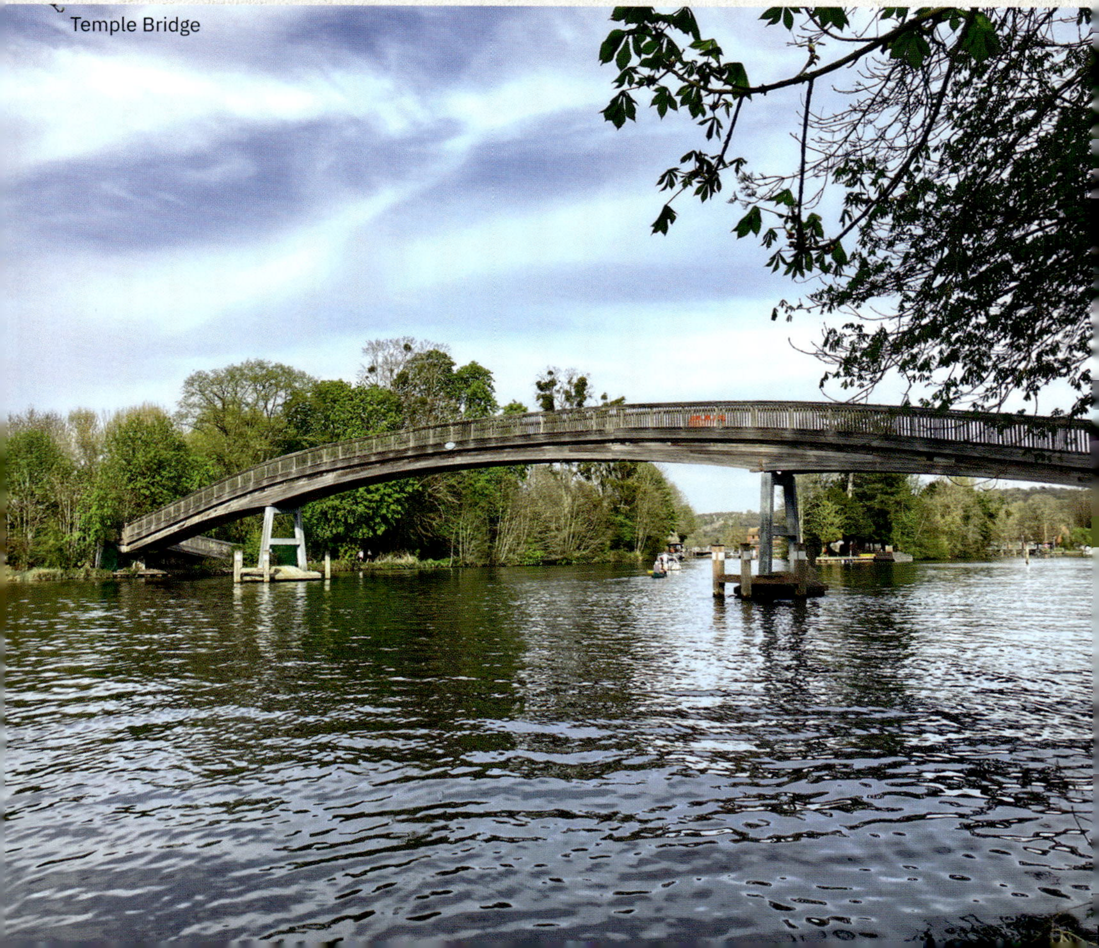

Temple Bridge

## Home Copse, Harleyford Park E, Marlow

The park falls into two parts. The N park is mostly golf course, while the E park has been restored to pasture as parkland.

51.555896, -0.803534

## Harleyford Marina, Marlow

There's a lot of moorings along this beautiful stretch of river, opposite the wooded towpath to Temple Bridge.

51.551979, -0.798622

## Temple FB, Marlow/Hurley

The bridge, which was built in 1989 at the crossing of the former ferry, was installed following a local campaign for better road safety. Sadly its repair/open status is as unreliable as pub opening hours in an apocalypse. Bring a packraft.

51.552132, -0.797082

## Temple Lock Island, Marlow

A small, wooded island with lawns, flowerbeds and the backdrop of Foulness Wood.

51.552554, -0.789333

## Temple Mill Island, Marlow

Named after the Knights Templars, who once owned the surrounding Bisham estate. The old mill became a foundry for converting copper into brass. It's believed the Templars converted or even created mills for the working of copper.

51.552554, -0.789333

## TEMPLE LOCK, MARLOW

Accessible only by foot, this man-made bridge leads to one of the Thames' most vegetated islands. A working weir and lock make this a special place.

51.552143, -0.793944

## Harleyford Ln, Marlow

A lost Ln 1½ miles from riverbank beside Temple Lock to Marlow. It also survives as a FP.

51.552903, -0.791605

## Bondig Bank, Bisham

Perfect views of the abbey can be enjoyed from the opposite bank, where the wild riverside is full of alders, hawthorns and nettles.

51.555406, -0.785067

Church of All Saints, The Causeway

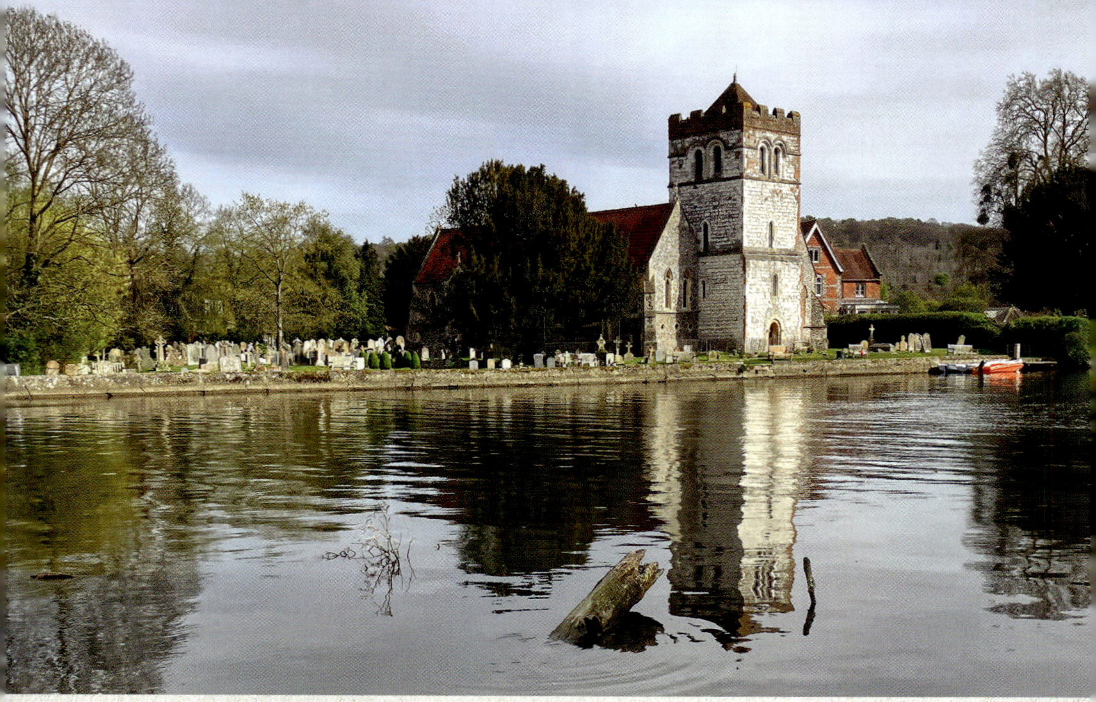

## Bisham Woods, Bisham

Expansive vast beech and yew woods on chalk terrain offer numerous walking and cycling paths, along with great views of the Thames.

51.554321, -0.769452

## CHURCH OF ALL SAINTS, THE CAUSEWAY

An Anglo-Saxon church that sits across the river from Thames path, beside Bisham Abbey. Tall trees and gravestones hang over the river. It's much like Marlow cemetery, but perhaps not quite as dramatic and busy. Touch the stone bowl font, decorated with crosses and set on a base with marble shafts.

51.561535, -0.777967

## Higginson Creek

A beautiful backwater, surrounded by plane and beech trees.

51.565772, -0.777168

## Higginson Park, Marlow

Walk barefoot over the park's lawn, surrounded by flowerbeds, trees and a maze. Formerly gifted by William the Conqueror to his wife, it's been a public park for just over 100 years.

51.566602, -0.776448

### MACDONALD COMPLEAT ANGLER

A riverside hotel nestled among willow-fringed banks of the Thames, offering views of the river and lock. The 18th-century building is a short walk from the town centre.

Marlow Bridge, Bisham, Marlow, SL7 1RG

www.macdonaldhotels.co.uk/compleat-angler

03448 799128

## THE TWO BREWERS

British pub grub in a historic red brick building, a short walk from the river. One of the oldest pubs in Marlow.

St Peter St, Marlow, SL7 1NQ

www.twobrewers-marlow.co.uk

02081 437 43

## Marlow High St Bridge, Marlow

A suspension bridge designed by William Tierney Clark, opened in 1832. The bridge is a bit busy with people and cars for standing about to admire the views, but it's nice to hang around either end.

51.567600 -0.773328

## → DETOUR - CYCLING ⅔ – 1 MILE W

### Cookham BW Circuit, Bisham

There are 3 miles of cycle and BW between Winter Hill and Inmkydown Wood.

➤ **Find** the S bank of Marlow Bridge (51.567068, -0.773099) and move S, forking SE towards Quarry Wood.

51.563433 -0.759251

### Fultness Wood, Maidenhead

Look for spring orchids in broadleaf and conifer woodland.

51.553876 -0.769590

Path into South Marlow

### ③ MARLOW CEMETERY, MARLOW

The graveyard next to Marlow's suspension bridge seems to hang over the river. One of the most impressive church sites in England – not situated on a hill. Look out for the Victorian stained-glass windows, mostly by Burlisson and Grylls.

51.567940, -0.772726

### Marlow Slipway, St Peter's St

Take in the river views and Quarry Wood hills. A wonderful Ln leads down to the riverside with a ramp and bench.

51.567968, -0.771949

### Marlow Lock Island, Marlow

Listen to the sound of falling water, while looking over Quarry Wood.

51.567063, -0.768691

St Peter Street Ramp, Marlow

### Marlow Lock and Mill, Marlow

A secluded place out to relax, which contrasts nicely with the bustle of Marlow Bridge. There's no access to the mill area for walkers, but the views across the riverfront are pretty. The best way to explore the mill riverside is by boat.

51.5673, -0.768812

### Pergola Wood, Marlow

Small woodland that marks the spot where path returns to water.

51.566972, -0.766789

### Marlow Bypass Bridge, Marlow

This bypass carries the A404 E of the town. It was built in 1972. The area underneath the bridge is used for boat storage.

51.566492, -0.761723

### Bridge Eyot, Marlow

An uninhabited island where people in boats sometimes picnic between trees and grassland.

51.566095, -0.762357

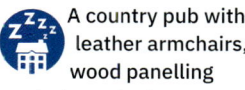

## THE SPADE OAK

A country pub with leather armchairs, wood panelling and a beer garden.

Coldmoorholme Ln, Bourne End, SL8 5PS

www.thespadeoak.co.uk

01628 520090

### Shakespeare Way Naze, Bisham

Grassy riverbank with views across river and hills of Quarry Wood.

51.565241, -0.757298

### Shakespeare Way Naze, Bisham

Packraft to Lost Ln on the opposite riverbank. The river path is lined in cherry laurel. It's best in autumn.

51.564541, -0.756890

### Quarry Woods, Bisham

Beech, larch and yew woodland. It's best in early spring when bluebells are out. The beautiful greens and mauves seem unique to this chalky wood in morning mist.

51.557563, -0.766253

### Marlow Aits, Bisham

A complete archipelago of islets. The riverbank is full of primroses, hyacinths and forget-me-nots.

51.557563, -0.766253

### Riverwoods, Marlow

A wooded beauty spot for shelter and shade.

51.567612, -0.752667

### Gibraltar Islands, Marlow

Look for small fruit trees in late summer. Some houses occupy the islands, which are thickly wooded around the perimeter, with some grassland in the centre.

51.570698, -0.745503

### PLANE TREE AVENUE, MARLOW

Look for mistletoe in the giant London plane trees, which are planted in rows across the wide grass green.

51.567852, -0.751875

### Coldmoorholme Ln, Bourne End

Popular with local families who come here to kayak. The W side of the riverbank has public access. E side, leading into Bourne End, has been enclosed by town planners who have allowed riverbank to be sold and contained behind 2m (6ft) high fences. We humans sacrifice long-term common sense on the altar of short-term financial gain – even here on the Thames.

51.578068, -0.726128

### Spade Oak Meadow, Bourne End

A large flood meadow that is almost impassable on foot in winter. The bank looks out onto a large river pool from a low sandy shore. Good for launching a packraft.

51.582819, -0.726386

### Cook Marsh – tie in with Coldmore Ln, Bourne End

Travel by packraft to the S FP and marsh burials. Look for marsh arrowgrass and water violets across 150 acres of marsh and sloping chalk grassland.

51.577272, -0.722538

Path between Marlow and Bourne End

# Round Barrow Cemetery, Cookham

Find a Bronze Age site of burial mounds (tumuli). Four burials were excavated between 1874 and 1877. The mounds were built in the early Bronze Age and later used by the Saxons. Only the largest mound remains.

➤ **Find** Spade Oak car park (51.580118, -0.725815) and walk 140m (460ft) S to the riverbank. Facing the river, turn left and walk ⅔ of a mile E to the railway bridge across the river.

51.575351, -0.722144

# Wharf Ln Marina, Bourne End

A busy marina and waterside, with lots of public access and views.

51.577475, -0.716862

# Ford Shoal, Bourne End

A shoal about 90m (295ft) in length. The water can become shallow at different times of year depending on rainfall and season.

51.577359, -0.716401

# BOURNE END, WOOBURN

A riverside village between cornfields and woodland.

51.576925, -0.710782

# Bourne End Railway Bridge, Wooburn Green

Good views along the Thames, as the path crosses from E to the W bank.

➤ **The** walk from Bourne End into the open grass and scrub on the E bank is a nice urban-to-rural contrast.

51.575439, -0.713682

# COCK MARSH E, COOKHAM

A rare fruit grows here: brown galingale. The plant is a small sedge with brown-purple flower spikes. The spikes become a brown nut-like fruit. The fruit was used in folklore as a medicine. This common land is unique in that it was protected from enclosure by local people at Cookham who bought and gifted it to the National Trust, who manage the site on their behalf.

51.571938, -0.712895

# River Wye Chalk Stream, Bourne End

Listen to nightingales where the River Wye empties into the Thames close to Bourne End.

➤ **The** River Wye is one of six chalk streams in Buckinghamshire. The Wye runs through the Chiltern Hills to the Thames. The Wye is on the E bank, opposite the path. Packraft across for access.

51.570183, -0.711078

## FERRY COOKHAM

The pub is located on the banks of the Thames, next to the hustle and bustle of a boat ramp.

Sutton Rd, Cookham, Maidenhead, SL6 9SN

www.theferry.co.uk

01628 525123

### Strand Water FP, Cookham

There are lots of dragonflies because of the chalk stream opposite.

51.570011, -0.712413

### Holy Trinity Church, Cookham

Bursting with yellow primroses and yew flowers in late March, this spot features an 11th-century church next to the towpath. The Trinity tower dominates the town skyline.

51.561493, -0.707496

### Cookham Bridge, Cookham

This was once a ford. Two Neolithic flint knives have been found here. Other finds include a bronze dagger sheath, a spearhead, a bronze sword and a collection of bronze spearheads.

51.562309, -0.705952

### Cookham Slipway, Cookham

A public slipway beside the Ferry Inn.

51.561847, -0.705751

### Lulle Brook, Cookham

The stream down to the mill on the Cookham side is picturesque.

51.557217, -0.700103

Holy Trinity Church, Cookham

###  Cookham Weir, Cookham

You'll be alone at the end of this Ln, so it's worth the visit. The Environment Agency closed the bridge access to the weir during the Covid pandemic and has yet to reopen it. The closure means there's no access to the PRoW on the other side unless you arrive on the island by boat. Like all weirs, this is a hazardous place, so be careful.

51.561905, -0.702860

###  Cookham Lock, Cookham

A former mill surrounded by meadows and wild grasslands interspersed with little tracks. The lock was created by a human-made cut that flows through several islands, including Sashes Island and Mill Island, and is surrounded by woods. The TP bypasses the lock, and the Environment Agency blocked public access to the PRoW after two children drowned in June 2020.

51.558276, -0.706392

###  Mill Ln, Cookham

The remarkable people of this town successfully defended themselves against enclosure – most notably at Odney Common, where legislators and owners tried to ban access and stop people swimming in the Thames.
Local finds include a Bronze Age axe head that dates to 3500 BC.

51.558276, -0.706392

###  Sashes Island, Hedsor Water, Hedsor Cookham

Listen along one of the quietest parts of the Thames. This is an excellent place to see shoveler and overwintering smew.

51.565558, -0.699143

###  Cookham Moor, Cookham

Smell cowslips and cuckoo flowers around the grassy edges of pond at the centre of the moor. Cycle the green Ln at the S end of the moor to Maidenhead.

51.562679, -0.714926

###  Odney Common Ln Bridge

Boat or boot. The bridge leads over onto Odney Island. The southern section is all open-access land. Fill your boots.

51.560626, -0.704154

###  Odney Common Bridge, Cookham

Walk the wooded path between Cookham and Cookham Lock's steel arch bridge.

51.560334, -0.700632

###  The Drey, Cookham

A lost Ln, Mill Ln, of ivy, maple and beech. The TP diverts from the Ln around this little woodland.

51.556634, -0.700121

Cookham

### 7 CLIVEDEN DEEP CORNER, CLIVEDEN

Where Thames meets Cliveden is beautiful. The Cliveden slopes on the opposite bank close to pedestrians after dark.

51.555234, -0.691807

 ### Cliveden Spring, Cliveden

Spring empties into the Thames at the foot of Cliveden Wood.

51.551951, -0.690822

 ### Yew Tree Walk, Taplow

The Cliveden estate is a highlight... though it's a bit of a long detour, so perhaps it's somewhere to see on a return visit.

51.555419, -0.690366

 ### Slow Grove Islands, Taplow

There are three eyots that divide the river in the middle of the reach into four streams.

51.547517, -0.692134

 ### 8 BATTLEMEAD COMMON, MAIDENHEAD

More than 100 acres of wet marsh and common land. A 'dog-proof' path links the common to the TP here, N of Maidenhead, and the TP N of Hurley. That's 5 miles as the crow flies, cutting across the peninsula via Widbrook Common and Quarry Wood. The common provides some of the best views of the surrounding tree-lined hills.

Some public access has been restricted for conservation.

51.545944, -0.692790

Slow Grove Islands

**THE BOATHOUSE AT BOULTERS LOCK**

Situated on its very own island, with al fresco dining and drinking, and perhaps the best view in Maidenhead.

Boulters Lock Island, Maidenhead, SL6 8PE

www.boathouseboulters lock.cc.uk

01628 621291

## Whitebrook Wood, Battlemead Common (summer only), Maidenhead

Smell leaf after rain along some of the best woodland on both sides of the river.

51.543122 -0.693934

## Widbrook Common, Maidenhead

Find bullrushes around White Brook stream. Red kites and kestrel hunt here too.

51.543122 -0.693934

## → DETOUR - PACKRAFT 180M (590FT)

### Jubilee River, Taplow

A tree-lined backwater stretches ½ mile into Taplow Mills. River barriers allow canoes and small craft to pass.

➤ **Look** for gaps in the stolen mooring and riverbank where it meets the TP (51.644408, -1.855094) and paddle E towards the mouth of the Jubilee River.

51.538195 -0.697000

### Jubilee Creek, Taplow

Look for oyster mushrooms in this wide, willow-lined water hideaway. The area is wet and full of dead trees.

51.537447 -0.696218

### Taplow River Bank, Taplow

Explore the riverbank where church once led down to water.

51.530865 -0.697427

## Boulter's Weir, Maidenhead

Look for kingfishers darting along the millstream on the Buckinghamshire side of the river. The stream runs down the left side, beyond which lies the lock island and the human-made cut. The area is dotted with interesting statues and artwork. At Boulter's Weir, the salmon ladder, opened in 2000 by the Duke of Wellington, was part of a wider initiative to help restore salmon migration along the Thames. The last recorded salmon caught at Boulter's Weir, in 1993, weighed 14lbs and was 97cm long.

51.536673 -0.699485

## BOULTER'S LOCK, MAIDENHEAD

One of the most popular whitewater freestyle kayaking areas on the Thames. The area has become a favourite for kayakers, as its design minimises disruption to other river users.

➤ **Access** to the lock is easy.

51.536673 -0.699485

The Boathouse at Boulter's Lock

### Boulter's Bridge, Maidenhead
Perfect views down the Thames.

51.533258, -0.698331

### Ray Mill Island, Boat Ramp, Maidenhead
A wooded, open area to picnic or hire boats. Beside Taplow Bridge, the island gets busy in summer. It's a lovely park for kids, with lots to see and do.

51.534664, -0.698565

### Taplow Bridge, Taplow
A pedestrian and cycle bridge linking Taplow with Maidenhead across the River Thames; it's sadly not open at night.

51.533258, -0.698331

### Grass Eyot, Maidenhead
Some of the tallest poplars on the Thames.

51.528669, -0.700507

### Grosvenor Island, Maidenhead
A tiny central island between Bridge Eyot and Grass Eyot, opposite Grosvenor Drive.

51.527637, -0.701098

### Dunloie Island, Maidenhead
A narrow strip of land between Bridge Eyot to halfway up Grass Eyot. There's a FB over the water, surrounded by moorings.

51.527949, -0.700271

###  Bridge Eyot, Maidenhead

Human skull and deer bones have been found buried in the riverbank. The wooded island is uninhabited with some moored houseboats. One of many islands through Maidenhead.

51.526081, -0.701629

###  GUARDS CLUB ISLAND, MAIDENHEAD

The island is situated under Maidenhead Bridge and connects to Maidenhead by FB. There's limited access when birds are nesting between June to December.

51.521748, -0.701906

###  Maidenhead Bridge, Maidenhead

Views of Cliveden and Windsor Castle. Its 13 arches are made from Portland stone.

51.523938, -0.701953

Boulter's Lock

# 13. MAIDENHEAD BRIDGE TO OLD WINDSOR

Albert Bridge

## BRIDGES

Isambard Kingdom Brunel has two bridges along this route. It's interesting how his engineering blends with nature.

Brunel must have had ideas we can steal. I'm sure he won't mind.

He learnt Euclidean geometry by eight. His philosophy and work ethic challenge everything here, from Eton and Windsor to rotten sewage farms and struggling businesses.

He seemed to work from nature, and for nature, as much as he worked for us.

## 10 STEPPING STONES

Brunel Railway Arch
Bray Lock
The Maidenhead Waterways
Dorney Lake
St Mary Magdalene Church
Boveney Lock
The Brocas
Windsor Castle
Romney Lock
Old Windsor Lock

Thames Riviera Hotel, Maidenhead Bridge

## Guards Club Island, Maidenhead

Nesting sites for swans, moorhens and coots lie just upstream of the Maidenhead Railway Bridge.

Within the boundary of Maidenhead town, there's a group of eight islands and other small islands that contain both the longest island on the river and one of the smallest.

51.522497, -0.701989

## Maidenhead Rowing Club, Maidenhead

Concrete ramps reach down into the shallows, where canoe hulls hang over water from racks.

51.523076, -0.701587

## Chapel Arches, York Stream

A 1-mile detour to York Stream. This was once an important part of the river network around the town.

51.523122, -0.716959

## BRUNEL RAILWAY ARCH, MAIDENHEAD

Brunel predicted he would design the flattest, widest arch ever seen. And he did. His Thames bridge at Maidenhead contains two of the flattest arches ever constructed in brickwork.
The foundations were sunk into hard gravel, overlying chalk. Completed in 1838, the arch design was so controversial that some engineers predicted the bridge would collapse under the weight of the first train.

51.521262, -0.701051

 ## FB to Bucks Ait, Maidenhead

Look for the crossing just past the railway bridge. The island is uninhabited and tree covered. The island was named after eels because so many were caught in the bucks and traps here.
The European eel has declined by more than 95% in the Thames in the last 20 years. Pollution, the overfishing of elvers from the Sargasso Sea and eel parasites all seem to be the problem.
The Thames River Trust are doing lots of good work to help them return.
www.the-ies.org/analysis/eels-river-thames
Go to www.thamesriverstrust.org.uk and look up 'eels' using their search bar.

51.520694, -0.701690

Maidenhead Railway Bridge

Bray Lock

### The Fisher, Maidenhead
A tiny island after the railway bridge.

51.520694, -0.701690

### Railway Steps, Maidenhead
Large concrete steps lead down to the waterside from a sloping grass bank.

51.520309, -0.700985

### Bray Pennyroyal Field, Bray
Look for the creeping mint, which grows around the edges of ponds here. The smell of pennyroyal is stronger than common mint. The ancients used it as a remedy for colds and flu.

51.509239, -0.699277

### Bray Slip, Bray
A pretty ramp fringed in evergreen and willow.

51.509239, -0.699277

### Headpile Eyot, Bray
A small island of horse chestnut and oak. Bronze Age finds have been discovered.

51.509851, -0.694841

## AMERDEN CARAVAN PARK

A family-run caravan and motorhome site at the side of the Thames, alongside the towpath. The site welcomes caravans, motorhomes and small campervans.

Old Marsh Ln, Taplow, Maidenhead, SL6 0DZ

www.amerdencaravan park.com

07514 765856

## ② BRAY LOCK, BRAY

This wooded island once had an ancient mill.
The lock and weir were rebuilt in 1885 after Charles Dickens described them as 'rotten and dangerous'.
Many houses in the reach above the lock are owned by British celebrities. The lock is just above the M4 Bridge and opposite Bray. The lock keeper's cottage is on Parting Eyot, between the lock and the weir.

51.509556, -0.690240

## St Michael's Church, Bray

Find the old church sculptures including the Sheela na Gig. They are thought to be the last remnants of what was an older church. This one dates from 1293, replacing a Saxon church at Water Oakley.

51.509142, -0.702155

## Pigeonhill Eyot, Bray

A thick tree-covered island. Bronze Age artefacts have been found. Look for the red 'light' of early spring. The male catkins of alder start to form before the leaves. They give the tree a red-like flush in morning mist.
Alder was used in folklore remedies. Leaves were rubbed into shoes and feet to help with aches and tiredness. Fresh leaves were also rubbed onto feet and legs to repel insects. The weir is at its upstream tip next to Bray Loch Island.

51.508000, -0.688400

Oakley Court

## MONKEY ISLAND ESTATE

Nestled on a charming private island, this elegant hotel has welcomed monarchs, aristocrats and artists. At its heart are two Grade-I listed heritage pavilions, built in 1723 for the third Duke of Marlborough as a peaceful fishing retreat.

Bray, Maidenhead, SL6 2EE

www.monkeyislandestate.co.uk

01628 623400

## Jubilee River Cycle Path, Taplow

A ½ mile detour via a BW. Explore more than 8 miles of cycle path from Taplow to where the river rejoins the Thames when it loops around Eton.

51.510679, -0.676802

## M4 Bridge, Taplow

A small, wooded islet close to the W riverbank. A great place to shelter. There are one or two crab apple trees in the thickets. Crab apples were a sacred symbol to the ancients. The five-pointed star was used in rituals when the core was sliced open. The ancients associated the star with the five elements: earth, air, fire, water and wood.

51.506348, -0.685798

## Monkey Island Riverbank, Bray

A large island of walnut and chestnut trees and near tame rabbits. The downstream tip is almost impenetrable. Eton boys of old partied on the island.

51.503017, -0.682243

Monkey Island

## MEDITERRANEVM AT BRAY

Mediterranean food with Thames views.

Marina, Horrabray, Monkey Island Ln, Bray, Windsor, SL6 2EB

www.mediterranevm.co.uk

01628 633512

Summerleaze Bridge

## Summerleaze FB, Bray

A wonderful pedestrian and cycle link between the Berkshire and Buckinghamshire banks of the Thames. Originally built in the 1990s, the bridge acted as a conveyor belt that transported gravel for the construction of the new Eton College (Dorney) Olympic rowing course. It was later converted to a public access point after completion.

51.499769, -0.681579

## ❸ YORK STREAM, MAIDENHEAD WATERWAYS

Walk and paddle York Stream, a waterway regeneration that has improved and even created river access in and out of the town centre.

51.517963, -0.712736

## Bray Marina, Bray

A 400-berth marina that provides courses, a small chandlery, engineering services, brokerage and fuel.

51.497630, -0.681850

## Queen's Eyot, Bray

Densely wooded island with a large central lawn overlooking the clubhouse that belongs to Eton College. A nice mixture of wilderness and gardens at either end.

➤ **Beware** of shallows and currents on the downstream point.

51.496447, -0.678838

## Windsor Marina Opposite Bank, Windsor

A pretty marina, in a garden-like setting, featuring a large river frontage and lots of moorings.

51.487093, -0.661337

## DORNEY LAKE, DORNEY

Cormorants and swans fly over the still water. Olympic rowing events were held here during the London 2012 games.

➤ **The** entire lake can be cycled or walked.

51.487309, -0.654257

## Sutherland Grange, Dorney

A hay meadow is a short walk from the Thames across the cut grass and park.

51.487450, -0.648667

## Ruddles Pool, Windsor

A sometimes-hazardous river bends above Boveney Lock. Boats coming downstream occasionally cut the corner.

51.485270, -0.652379

## The Willows, WIndsor

Osiers blanket this swampy, wet woodland.

51.485270, -0.652379

## ST MARY MAGDALENE CHURCH, BOVENEY

Look for bats at dusk near the riverside pews with access to the water. Touch the old oak doors and medieval tiles in this riverside church. The 12th-century building was built to serve the bargemen working on the Thames; there was a quay alongside the church but there's no sign of it today.

51.489876, -0.647532

## Bush Ait, Boveney

A small, wooded island at the entrance to Clewer Mill Stream, which bypasses Boveney Lock.

➤ **The** stream is navigable for several hundred metres into the marina. This island is separated from the racecourse by the stream.

51.487396, -0.648419

## Clewer Mill Stream, Boveney

A wooded waterway entrance to Racecourse Marina, stretching more than ½ mile to the marina entrance and almost 2 miles before meeting the Thames on the other side. Along the way, there are lots of places to explore and find shelter.

51.487310, -0.646868

St Mary Magdalene Church

## 6 BOVENEY LOCK, BOVENEY

A kayak/canoe portage that's always fun to sit and watch. It's best visited in school holidays when river traffic is busiest. The lock is located opposite Windsor Racecourse and close to Eton Wick.

➤**Find** the towpath along the river and follow it to Eton Wick.

51.489959, -0.641250

## Windsor Racecourse Marina, Windsor

**Moorings, shop and advice.**

➤ **Access** Racecourse Marina either by the millstream 500 yards above Boveney lock or by Rd from the M4, M25, M3 and M40.

51.488157, -0.637943

## Boveney Ditch FB, Eton Wick

Look for the barbel and chub that come to spawn in spring. The Environment Agency has added gravel to the riverbed to encourage a greater variety of fish species. Watercress grows here. The L fork of the ditch is called Cress Brook.

51.492928, -0.634180

 ## St John the Baptist, Eton Wick

A 19th-century red brick church full of yew. Look inside for a wooden board above the sanctuary arch, inscribed with a Gothic-script text beginning 'Glory to God', etc.

51.495950, -0.630206

 ## Windsor Slipway, Clewer

A boat-launch behind Windsor Leisure Centre, immediately downstream of the Queen Elizabeth Bridge (Royal Windsor Way bridge).

51.486561, -0.622677

 ## Clewer Village Church, Clewer

There is a FP on the E side of a bridge that you can get to via packraft.

51.485643, -0.624575

 ## Cuckoo Weir Wood, Eton

Smell the nutty scent of blackthorn flowers in March and early April.

51.487529, -0.620675

 ## Cuckoo Weir Island, Eton

A treatment centre for injured swans. It includes indoor and outdoor pens, a decontamination unit and cygnet enclosures.

51.487966, -0.627202

 ## Clewer Mill Stream, Queen Elizabeth Bridge, Clewer

A narrow twisting backwater between Bush Ait and Queen Elizabeth Bridge. Navigate 1½ miles. It takes its name from the old watermill.

51.487000, -0.624000

 ## Baths Island, Windsor

A public open space that was once the town's swimming baths.

51.486400, -0.618500

## Windsor Railway Bridge, Windsor

Brunel's famous 'bowstring' bridge is the oldest wrought iron bridge still in use today, carrying the Great Western Railway on the branch line between Slough and Windsor.

Nearby stands one of the longest brick viaducts anywhere in the world, originally constructed in wood when the railway first opened in 1849. A plaque on Baths Island beside the bridge provides historical details.

51.486806, -0.617917

## Deadwater Ait, Windsor

Thames views from a large uninhabited island. Look for Windsor Castle and Brunel's railway bridge. Swans, geese and a small number of coots all live on this island.

➤ **The** island is reached by a FB from the Windsor bank.

51.485000, -0.613400

## THE BROCAS FP W, ETON

Walk the vast meadows, commons and fields that span the academic urban edges.

The view of Windsor from the Brocas is one of the best on the River. It's best in late September when warm autumn light casts red colour over the trees.

51.487282, -0.618079

## Eton, Windsor

The College was founded by Henry VI in 1440. The Gothic chapel contains rare Flemish style paintings.

51.491280, -0.609071

## Fireworks Ait, Windsor

Willow, swamp cypress and wild rose cover this beautiful, wooded island – one of the smallest on the Thames. It takes its name from the poet and writer Percy Bysshe Shelley, who would hold firework parties on the island during his time at Eton in the early 19th century. Shelley had a bad reputation at Eton and was considered eccentric. He was known for using gunpowder to blow up tree stumps along the Thames and for practising occult rituals on the island.

51.485200, -0.610400

## Windsor Bridge, Windsor

This bridge connects the towns of Windsor and Eton in the English county of Berkshire. It carries pedestrians, cyclists and vehicles just above Romney Lock.

51.485867, -0.608412

## Lime Avenue, Windsor

Travel the N path or paddle the Thames. The S side is closed for security reasons.

51.483875, -0.586677

### → DETOUR – WALKING 90M (295FT) – 2½ MILES

### ⑧ WINDSOR CASTLE, WINDSOR

The N wall lies less than 180m (590ft) from the Thames, just across Windsor Bridge. Explore the curve of the wall: the towers and turrets seem to rise from the shore with some grandeur.
➤ **Find** where Windsor bridge (S) leaves the TP (51.485736, -0.608215) and follow S to the castle wall.

51.484425, -0.607309

Windsor Castle

Romney Lock

### St John the Baptist Church, Windsor

Explore the churchyard where many interesting people are buried. Two of the three Protestant Windsor Martyrs, who were burnt at the stake in 1543, were associated with this church. The church itself was rebuilt in Gothic Revival style in 1822.

51.481886, -0.606371

### The Long Walk

Walk the 2½-mile avenue of trees. It's one of the most impressive landmarks along the path. Finish at the copper statue of King George III and his horse.

51.481886, -0.606371

### The Copper Horse, Windsor

The view from the statue of King George III and his horse down the avenue is as impressive as the view from below, looking up at statue against sky.

51.445056, -0.609245

 ### Romney Weir, WIndsor

This thickly wooded FP runs along the island. Look for flowering hawthorn on warm days in early May – long known in folklore for improving circulation and heart conditions.

51.490616, -0.604909

 ### ROMNEY LOCK, WINDSOR

The lock sits ½ a mile downstream from Windsor Bridge, on the Windsor side of the river. The lock was last rebuilt in 1980, with the weir also being relocated in the early 20th century.

51.491741, -0.603707

Windsor riverside

### Romney Eyot, Windsor

A £100,000 fish tunnel here allows migratory salmon, trout and eels to bypass the hydroelectric system installed in 2011. The 200kW generation station was installed to supply electricity to Windsor Castle, alongside the uninhabited islands known collectively as the Romneys.

51.491741, -0.603707

### Cutler's Ait, Eton

Find the deep-water lagoons to watch fish feeding on warm days. Sit on one of the wooden humpback bridges that connects this island to the riverbank.

➤ **The** tree-covered island looks over Romney Island.

51.489444, -0.606111

### Black Potts Ait, Eton

A vast peninsula of wet woodland created by the Jubilee River extension. This island was once a favourite area for fishing for Charles II, Henry Wotton and John Hales. It was particularly famous for eel traps; the remains can still be seen close to the bridge.

➤ **A** tree-covered triangle at the mouth of the Jubilee River.

51.491417, -0.594720

###  Railway Island, Eton

Explore an eyot of ancient woodland. The best access is by boat via the N-shore backwater.

51.493225, -0.598005

###  Jubilee River, Datchet

Kayak or cycle along this artificial flood-relief channel constructed in the late 1990s and early 2000s. It was designed to stop the Thames flooding Maidenhead and Windsor. Portage around weirs.

➤ **A** cycle lane follows the riverbank for 6 miles from Taplow to Eton.

51.491000, -0.593000

###  Victoria Bridge, Datchet

This bridge connects Windsor with the village of Datchet. There is a second bridge, a mile downstream – the Albert Bridge.

51.487873, -0.590911

Datchet Riverside

### Sumptermead Ait, Datchet

An uninhabited wooded island that follows the Thames riverbank. A new riverside path was created here in 1955 for the diverted TP. The island is named after the meadow behind it, which is now a golf course.

51.484311, -0.585172

### Datchet Ford, Datchet

Come here in summer to find the old ford. There are good views of Windsor Castle and Home Park on the skyline.

➤ **Private** moorings have occupied the site, but walk to the R, facing the water onto the grass beside the trees and down to the water.

51.482121, -0.582271

### Southlea Farm Woods, Datchet

Sit back on a coat of (sticky) soft cleaver from March in the shade of white poplar and willow.

➤ **Packraft** here for the best free access to Windsor Castle. Find the shallow parts around the riverbank that allow feet to be grounded on the Windsor side.

51.474797, -0.583395

### Lion Wood, Datchet

More than three acres of riverside woodland, with plenty of overhanging trees for hiding and shelter.

51.469785, -0.581260

### Lion Island, Windsor

A thickly wooded island that floods in winter, with a secluded backwater running along its northern bank. The island is owned by the Crown Estate.

51.469424, -0.579515

Albert Bridge

Datchet Wood

## Ham Island

One of the largest Thames islands is open fields, unkept scrubland and a sewage works. Ham was created by a cut that diverted the Thames in 1822. The work reduced the distance around the Thames bend by about a third.

51.468532, -0.576446

## Ham Bridge, Old Windsor

A narrow steel bridge offers good views up and down the river. There are steps down to the waterside on the E bank.

51.466412, -0.572870

## OLD WINDSOR LOCK, OLD WINDSOR

This lock is like a gateway to Windsor Castle and the commons of Eton College. A FB provides access to the island nearby. The site has a rich history, dating back to the 18th century, with the lock itself last rebuilt in 1957.

➤ **Access** is available from the TP, which links to Ham Ln and a FP leading to The Manor and The Priory.

51.463263, -0.569121

Old Windsor

Wraysbury

*New Cut*

Old Windsor Lock

*Friary Field*

A308

A308

*River Thames*

Runnymede House

A328

*Magna Carta Island Ankerwyke Yew*

*Runnymede*

A308

Runnymede

Bell Weir Lock

A30

B376

Hythe End

*Colne Brook*

M25

Church Lamas

*Queensmead Lake*

A30

B376

*River Colne*

Staines -upon- Thames

Egham

A308

Staines Bridge

STAINES

B3376

Egham Hythe

Knowle Green

A320

B376

N

Penton Hook Lock

*Penton Hook Island*

Manor Lake

*Fleet Lake*

*Penton Hook Marina*

B377

Thorpe Park

Penton Hook

Laleham

*Abbey Lake*

B376

*Laleham Park*

*Abbey River*

M3

Chertsey    Chertsey Lock

Chertsey Bridge    *Dumsey Meadow*

*River Thames*

B375

*Chertsey Meads*

*The Bourne*

Towpath

*Pharaoh's Island*    Shepperton Lo

*Lock Island*

Hamm Court

*Hamhaugh Island*

*River Wey*

A3050

Weybridge

1 km

1 mile

# 14. OLD WINDSOR TO SHEPPERTON LOCK

Old Windsor

## YEW

The yew grove in English culture is like the Old Bailey. It has something to do with justice, responsibility and rights. Like golf club etiquette for national leaders.

One of the most important trees in the world thrives here. The Ankerwycke Yew, at Runnymede, is more than 2,000 years old. The only thing still living to witness Magna Carta in 1215.

Witness to the writ in water: that no free man shall be seized or imprisoned.

## 10 STEPPING STONES

Old Windsor Church FP
Bells of Ouzely
Ankerwycke Yew
Bell Weir Lock
Holm Island
The London Stone
St Peter's Church
Penton Hook Lock
Laleham Abbey
Shepperton Lock

## Old Windsor Lock, Old Windsor

Walk the FB onto the island. Saxon kings held court at Old Windsor. Windsor Castle's towers rise on the horizon; the trees of Windsor Great Park are behind.

➤ **There** are path links to Ham Ln, and the FP leads to the manor and priory.

51.463468, -0.568979

## Friday Island, Old Windsor

The island supposedly got its name because it resembles Man Friday's footprint. Willow shrubs and trees line the water's edge.
➤ **Find** the woodland just below Windsor Lock. The island is on the the R bank, close to the lock.

51.462418, -0.569349

## Kingswood Creek, Wraysbury

Much of this creek and bank have been occupied, so explore from path or punt.

51.462867, -0.567955

## Friary Island, Wraysbury

An island on the reach above Bell Weir Lock. There was a friary here. There are about 40 houses, all accessible by Rd bridge. Gardens front the water's edge.

51.458000, -0.573000

## Old Windsor Church Graveyard, Old Windsor

Smell the growth of new yew around the old church. The churchyard contains the grave of celebrated Georgian actress Mary 'Perdita' Robinson. She was a Shakespearean actress and the alleged mistress of King George IV. Perdita was the Shakespeare character in *Winter's Tale*. Her tomb is often overgrown with nettles.

51.463669, -0.569394

## ST PETER AND ANDREW'S CHURCH, OLD WINDSOR CHURCH

Look for the wall paintings inside. The church was rebuilt in 1218, soon after King John was required to sign and seal Magna Carta in 1215. The original wooden church was destroyed by mercenary French soldiers.

51.462216, -0.572598

## Old Ferry Ln FP, Wraysbury

Walk the lost Ln into the woodland of an old, royal hunting lodge.
➤ **Find** the riverbank and the TP opposite Old Ferry N PRoW (51.460797, -0.571362).

51.460363, -0.570782

St Peter and Andrew's Church, Old Windsor

### Windsor Great Park, Windsor
A 5,000-acre park of oak, hornbeam and beech towards Virginia Water.
➤ **A** 1-mile detour from the TP but somewhere to spend a few hours.

51.452786, -0.608257

### St Peter's Creek, Windsor
A beautiful narrow creek draped in weeping willow and shadow. The creek follows the line of the old church FP. Moorings are now at the end of Church Rd.

51.460229, -0.572769

### Thames Common bank, Old Windsor
Too much of the Old Windsor riverbank is gated and fenced. There are one or two gaps between gates. This is one of them. There is another one nearby.

51.455196, -0.574392

## Whard Rd Riverbank, Wraysbury

## Whard Rd Riverbank, Wraysbury

The trick to navigating is finding a PRoW. This 100m (350ft) FP provides precious access to a riverfront. It's a beautiful thing.

51.455261, -0.573453

## Ousely Island, Wraysbury

The backwater stream is only navigable for smaller boats, so explore. There is a FB to the R bank.

51.453651, -0.573158

## BELLS OF OUZELY

A mock Tudor Harvester stands on the site of what was once a ford and ferry crossing. The original 'Bells of Osney Abbey' were brought here after the Dissolution of the Monasteries in 1538 – and somehow got 'lost' in the mud (no doubt recovered when everyone had gone home). The 'Ouzely' name refers to Osney, the abbey outside Oxford that vanished. The bells were highly regarded and said to possess a magic ring.

51.452238, -0.574146

## Pat's Croft, Wraysbury

A heavily wooded, private island. There is a bridge to the Wraysbury bank.

51.449, -0.5658

---

### DE VERE BEAUMONT ESTATE

A 40-acre estate with a hotel. The site is a 15-minute walk from historic Runnymede and the Magna Carta monument. Windsor Castle is 3.2 miles away. The grounds include a 14th-century chapel.

Burfield Rd, Old Windsor, Windsor, SL4 2JJ

www.devere.co.uk/beaumont-estate

01753 640000

Bells of Ouzely

## MAGNA CARTA TEA ROOM

A National Trust cafe on the Old Windsor side of Runnymede.

Windsor Rd, Englefield Green, Egham. TW20 0AE

www.nationaltrust.org.uk/
visit/surrey/runnymede-
and-ankerwycke

01784 432891

Runnymede

## → DETOUR - PACKRAFT 45M (150FT) – 1 MILE E

### Runnymede House, Wraysbury

Where Henry VIII wooed Anne Boleyn. The entrance to the Magna Carta site is guarded by willows and the kindness of fishermen.

➤ **Find** the riverbank where it meets the TP (51.441959, -0.557223) and paddle E to the island bank and permissive FP.

51.441739, -0.555199

### Magna Carta Memorial, Windsor Rd, Nr Old Windsor

A monument surrounded by woods. The Magna Carta is supposed to have been signed by King John in June 1215. King John is thought to have hidden at Windsor Castle in 1215, as the power of the barons had become stronger leading up to the signing. The island is midway between Runnymede and Ankerwycke. It's difficult to reach from the mainland, as the long path crosses several wild and remote fields.

51.444439, -0.566043

Ankerwycke Yew

## ANKERWYCKE YEW, RUNNYMEDE

Touch a very old tree with an 8m (26ft) girth. The ruins of a Benedictine nunnery are nearby. The meadows of Runnymede are opposite.

51.445448, -0.561526

## St Andrew's Church, Wraysbury

Find the FP from church to yew. There's something special about walking that path.

51.455609, -0.560276

## Cooper's Hill, Englefield Green

Explore 87 acres of broad-leaved wood, which offer good views over the Thames and Runnymede. Look out for oaks, noctule bats and bluebells. Some of the steeper climbs have steps and handrails.

51.439391, -0.564789

## Writ in Water, Englefield Green

A beautiful and clever piece of art by Mark Wallinger celebrates the justice enshrined in Magna Carta. Wallinger took the line from John Keats' gravestone and combined it with clause 39 of Magna Carta. He installed the words upside down inside the bathtub's rim so you can read them in the reflection: that no free man shall be seized or imprisoned.

51.442069, -0.564094

## The Island (Hythe End Island), Hythe End

A residential island just above Bell Weir Lock. It takes its name from its connecting Rd, Hythe End Rd. A hythe was a landing place or wharf.

51.442229, -0.547367

## ④ BELL WEIR LOCK, EGHAM

Originally called Egham Lock, it was renamed in honor of Charlie Bell, the founder of the nearby Anglers Retreat Inn.

51.438440, -0.537871

## Colne Brook, Hythe End

The river empties into the Thames just below Bell Weir Lock in Hythe End.

51.4379, -0.5352

## M25 Runnymede Bridge, Egham

A Bronze Age site built over by motorway. There's also an A-Rd, pedestrian and cycle bridge, built in the 1960s and 1980s. This is one of three bridges that carry motorways across the Thames, the others being the M3, Chertsey Bridge and the M4 Thames Bridge, Maidenhead. The Queen Elizabeth II Bridge, at the Dartford Crossing, is not considered part of the M25.

51.437302, -0.535387

## Church Island, Egham

A private, wooded island. The Staines Swimming Club had its headquarters on Church Island in the early 1900s. The island is connected to the N bank by a FB.

51.437302, -0.535387

Runnymede East

###  ⑤ HOLM ISLAND, NR STAINES-UPON-THAMES

An island with lots of fruit trees. It was here that King Edward, then the Duke of Windsor, spent time with Wallis Simpson during their controversial relationship.

51.436292, -0.528492

###  Hollyhock Island, Nr Staines-upon-Thames

A tiny R-bank island that sits inside Holm Island. Although the island is separate, it doesn't appear so, as most of the backwaters have overgrown. The area has lots of trees and waterlogged ditches.

51.436249, -0.527639

###  Staines Wood, Staines-upon-Thames

Taste chestnuts in autumn. The woodland is beside the M25.

51.436447, -0.534151

###  Staines Bridge, Staines-upon-Thames

Move across on to the N bank via one of the river's most impressive bridges. This was once the upper limit of the tidal reach. Good for fishing as water is deep. The bridge takes its name from the Saxon word stana, or stone.

51.433273, -0.516867

Bell Weir Lock

Bell Weir Lock view of M25

### 6 THE LONDON STONE, STAINES-UPON-THAMES

Touch the landmark that signals the jurisdiction of the City of London over the river navigation. On top of the original stone, the inscription 'God preserve the City of London, A.D. 1280' is still legible. A replica was placed here in 1986. Richard I granted the Corporation of London control and rights.

51.432513, -0.513502

### St Peter's Church, Staines-upon-Thames

Founded in 1873 by the Vicar of St Mary's, Staines, it was originally known as St Peter's Mission Chapel.

51.428604, -0.509308

### Church Island, Staines-upon-Thames

This traffic-free island is connected by FB. Houses clustered around the largest church of St Mary's, from which the island gets its name. The London Stone sits just behind the island on the N bank of the river.

51.432513, -0.513502

### Staines-upon-Thames

A market town 17 miles W of central London. Inigo Jones (1573–1652) – the architect credited with introducing the classical Rome and the Italian Renaissance design to England – lived here. He is believed to have designed the tower of the church.

51.433293, -0.512466

**SUNDAY LONDON STAINES-UPON-THAMES HEATHROW T5**

 A hotel on the banks of the Thames in a cottage-style building – 6 miles from Windsor Castle.

Thames St, Staines, TW18 4SJ

www.oyorooms.com/gb/291294

01784 464433

 ## River Colne, Hertfordshire

The river marks the boundary between Buckinghamshire and the London Borough of Hillingdon. The confluence with the Thames is on the Staines reach (above Penton Hook Lock).

51.432900, -0.515200

## ⑦ ST PETER'S CHURCH, STAINES-UPON-THAMES

Look for the life-size statues of St Peter (centre) St John the Baptist (L) and St James (R) in pilgrim's garb and holding a thick staff.

The church was founded by Sir Edward Clarke, former Conservative MP for Southwark and then, later, Plymouth. He was solicitor-general from 1886 to 1892. Sir Edward famously defended Oscar Wilde in court for no fee. He decided to found a riverside church because his wife, Lady Clarke, admired Buckfast Abbey, overlooking the River Dart.

51.428556, -0.509278

 ## Truss's Island and Slipway, Egham Hythe

A wooded island and riverside park with a public slipway to the Thames. There's a fishing platform for the disabled.

51.419212, -0.513332

 ## Riverbank Apartments, Staines-upon-Thames

A sloping grass bank is somewhere to relax and river watch in the sunshine. It's private and fenced, but the gardens are the start of the riverbank verges with good river access.

51.417347, -0.511521

 ## Thames Side Green, Staines-upon-Thames

Explore the wooded riverbank, shaded by willow and London plane trees. Fish feed in the shallows.

51.417347, -0.511521

## ⑧ PENTON HOOK LOCK, STAINES-UPON-THAMES

One of the longest locks on the river – at 81m (266ft).

➤ **Access** to Penton Hook Lock is available on foot or by bike from Blacksmiths N, Riverside or Penton Hook Rd. It can also be reached by boat from Thorpe. A camper's association was formed here in 1903. The club lasted for some years, but it's long gone.

51.413527, -0.501423

## Penton Hook Island Stream, Staines-upon-Thames
Look for fish and fry in the stream that runs through the island. It's been used as a spawning ground for thousands of years. Birds include herons, parakeets, kingfishers and grey waterfowl.

51.412356, -0 501911

## All Saints' Church, Laleham
The English Matthew Arnold is buried in the churchyard. He was famous for his 1853 poem, 'The Scholar-Gipsy'.

➤ **Find** the large painting by George Henry Harlow in 1810 – one of England's greatest artists at the time. The image shows Jesus walking on the water to save Peter before he sinks beneath the waves. The painting is at the N end of the W wall. Parts of the church building date back over 800 years. The nave contains 12th-century pillars made from clunch (a form of chalk). The W wall at the back of the church dates back to the 12th century.

51.409317, -0.489961

## Laleham Slipway, Laleham
A small slipway for canoes and boats. No parking. There is no slipway on the opposite bank, although this may have been a summer ford in the ancient past.

51.405846, -0.492391

## Laleham Ferry Ln BW, Laleham
Dead straight path from the riverbank to St Peter's Church, Chertsey. Ferry Ln runs for a mile, across the M3, and was the old crossing between Laleham and Chertsey.

➤ **The** BW has no access from the TP, so cross the river at Chertsey Bridge and find St Peter's Church, in Windsor Street (51.392650, -0.503735).

51.405056, -0.493430

## Queen Mary Reservoir, Laleham
Once the largest reservoir in the world. Queen Mary Reservoir, just N of the M3 motorway, stores water from the River Thames and supplies western London and Surrey. It's a popular place for watersports.

51.417461, -0.461032

## LALEHAM ABBEY, LALEHAM
The former Laleham Abbey was built for the Earl of Lucan between 1803 and 1806.

When the Lucan family left the village, the 70 acres of abbey grounds were given for public use.

51.404146, -0.490889

Chertsey Bridge

## Abbey River, Laleham

A small stream that once provided Chertsey monastery with water.

51.397000, -0.488000

## Chertsey Weir, Chertsey

Deep water that flows into Abbey River.

51.391315, -0.486471

## M3 Bridge, Chertsey

M3 Bridge – a place to be thankful... that you're not in a car.

51.394020, -0.485846

## Chertsey Lock, Chertsey

Boats grounded on the shallow 'Laleham Gulls' until the lock was built. Lord Lucan, who owned the nearby Laleham Manor, insisted the lock was built out of earshot and would not ruin his views. The lock was built in 1813 and then lengthened in 1913. Chertsey Bridge is 180m (590ft) downstream.

51.391315, -0.486471

## Chertsey Bridge, Chertsey

The Tate holds a pencil sketch of Chertsey Bridge by the artist J.M.W. Turner. The bridge connects the town of Chertsey on the S bank of the river (sometimes known as the 'Surrey bank') to the village of Laleham.

51.388855, -0.485735

###  Chertsey Abbey, Chertsey

Chertsey Abbey was founded in 666 AD. The mention of Chertsey town is by Bede in around 750.

51.388856, -0.485762

###  Chertsey Meads, Chertsey

Smell the flowers in spring around the flood meadow, where many public access points invite you to explore.

51.387227, -0.483241

###  Chertsey Marina, Chertsey

Boat trips, boat hire and repairs.

51.386669, -0.481262

###  Dumsey Meadow, Chertsey

Trees, meadows and parakeets. A grazing meadow that has never been ploughed, allowing a variety of flowers to thrive. The last undeveloped water meadow that remains unfenced, below Caversham. Everything else from here has been enclosed or stolen.

51.389686, -0.479472

Dumsey Meadows

### Dumsey Eyot, Shepperton

A wooded naze opposite Dumsey Meadow. A wonderful place to explore around the riverbank. Look for the ash trees and their keys. The young leaves can be used for tea.

➤ **A** 1-mile detour on the S bank FP. Cross Chertsey Bridge and walk SE along the river.

51.390608, -0.477689

### Docket Eddy N, Shepperton

Inhale the scent of wet willow and oak woodland. There is a quiet boreen into the lock that is worth finding and walking.

51.385891, -0.469703

### Pharoah's Island, Shepperton

Presented to Admiral Lord Nelson after the Battle of the Nile. Many of the homes here today have Egyptian-inspired names. Admiral Nelson accepted the island in 1798 in recognition of his victory. Nelson enjoyed fishing the Thames, and particularly the island which he used as a fishing retreat. A central pathway leads down to a large green that islanders use for various events.

51.382387, -0.464986

### Hamhaugh Island, Weybridge

A large island full of fruit trees. Follow the path onto the island. It can be illusive. Cross over the gates at Shipton Lock, and find the tree-lined path across a weir.

51.378919, -0.459355

## Shepperton Weir, Shepperton

One of the biggest weirs on the Thames – a favourite place for kayakers. There are 10 vertical sluices in a row, which, in perfect conditions can produce a bowl-shaped green wave. The Shepperton wave is regarded as one of the best 'play' waves in Europe. The white waters and slaloms are not for beginners or intermediates.

51.382377, -0.458328

## Shepperton Island, Shepperton

Home of the Shepperton Canoe Club and lock. The club introduces people to canoes and slalom kayaking. The W end island is thickly wooded.

51.381747, -0.458695

## SHEPPERTON LOCK, SHEPPERTON

The lock sits beside a stream known as Stoner's Gut. There is a pedestrian ferry to Weybridge 100m E. Cross the river by packraft when the ferry is not running. The S bank has fewer Rds, so better than N.

Shepperton Lock featured in Charles Dickens' *Our Mutual Friend* and H.G. Wells' *The War of the Worlds*. It was also the filming location for the 1987 film *Hope and Glory*. High trees and lots of wildlife, including water voles.

51.382377, -0.458328

Shepperton Lock

# 15. SHEPPERTON LOCK TO KINGSTON BRIDGE

Hampton Court (from south shore)

## ISLANDS

There are more than 1,000 islands along the Thames from source to estuary. A chain of chalk pearls you'll barely notice – even as you cross them.

The Thames archipelago is an island-cluster of woods, ruins and fresh air.

Hampton Gardens has free public access a couple of weekends a year. For all that, it's the 10 miles of riverside cycle paths and public slipways that make this section of islets and aits so accessible

## 10 STEPPING STONES

Shepperton Ferry Slipway
St Nichola Church, Shepperton
Halliford Isle
Walton Bridge
Sunbury Lock
Molesey Lock
Hampton Court
Thames Ditton Island
Raven's Ait
Kingston Bridge

## Shepperton Lock, Shepperton

Paddle across the river to the towpath on the Middlesex side. Barge horses were ferried across. There's strong currents, so care is needed. Voles live here, between the roots of tall trees and riverbanks. The waters by Lock Island are used for whitewater and slalom canoeing.

51.382377, -0.458328

## → DETOUR - PACKRAFTING 365M (1,200FT) – ½ MILE S

## Weybridge Point Slipway, Weybridge

Walk the long concrete slipway – it enters the water under a hawthorn tree surrounded by unkept grass. Ideal for launching or landing a small boat.

➤ **You'll** find it just off Walton Ln where it meets Thames Street, facing a weir.

51.380606, -0.456943

## River Bourne, Chertsey

The River Bourne (or Chertsey Bourne) runs from its source in Windsor Great Park and Swinley Forest through to the River Thames.

51.378500, -0.463800

## Hamhaugh Island (L bank), Weybridge

Look for fruit trees on this large island. The old Thames loop runs to its S – the river here was bypassed by the cut. Apples, pears, peaches and several varieties of plums still grow wild. Access can be tricky.

51.380706, -0.460634

## Wey and Godalming Navigations, Weybridge

More than 20 miles of navigable water from Thames to Godalming, via Guildford. The River Wey Navigation connects to the Basingstoke Canal at West Byfleet, and the Godalming Navigation to the Wey and Arun Canal near Shalford – a combination of human-made canal and natural river.

51.380400, -0.457000

## D'Oyly Carte Island, Weybridge

This island was once known as Swan Ait because the big white bird liked to make its nests here. It's also a favourite place for anglers who fish for chub, perch and pike.

51.382878, -0.454331

## D'OYLY'S

An island eatery with a café, bar and creperie at the E end of the island. One pontoon is available on a first-come, first-serve basis. Dog friendly.

D'Oyly Carte Island, Walton Ln, Weybridge, KT13 8LX

www.doylycarteisland.com/doylys

07850 586017

## Shepperton, Old River

The original course of the old river can be navigated by avoiding Desborough Cut. Now it's no more than a backwater; it's all the better for that.

51.383803, -0.450655

## ① SHEPPERTON FERRY SLIPWAY, SHEPPERTON

Free unlimited use of the slipway during office hours, seven days a week. It's based on the R bank of the Shepperton side.
An ancient ferry ran here in the 14th century.

51.382727, -0 456971

## ② ST NICHOLA CHURCH, SHEPPERTON

A church by the river under ancient chestnuts and elms. The site sits above an old ford. Novelist George Eliot was associated with the church. There are references to King Richard III having stayed at the Rectory on the eve of the Battle of Bosworth Field. But it's unclear why.

51.388200, -0.453695

Shepperton Ferry Point

## Las Palmas Estate Wood, Shepperton

Wooded water's edge and brick wall are the start of the Desborough Cut. Barges park on the grassy knoll. A beautiful stretch of water where woodland is fed by underground springs. The place has a luminous look, best at dawn.

51.387963, -0.449059

## Halliford Ford, Shepperton

The old ford site can be seen from the tip of Desborough Island, where the peaty ground slopes into the water. On the other side, the riverbed is so shallow that a small island emerges in dry weather.

51.390000, -0.443982

## HALLIFORD ISLE, LOWER HALLIFORD

Once part of the ford that gives the town its name, Shepperton is a low-lying area, which is prone to flooding after extreme rainfall.

51.389812, -0.443873

## Silent Pool, Shepperton

A pretty backwater close to the church.

51.387286, -0.454809

## Desborough Playing Field, Weybridge

A sloping woodland down to the riverbank – once the site of a public ford crossing. It's hard to believe now, as dredging has made the river channel so much deeper.

51.389400, -0.442822

## Thames Meadows, Lower Halliford

Open-access land, private Rds, muddy laybys and willow trees.

51.387948, -0.432298

### → DETOUR - WALKING ½ – 2 MILES W

## Walton Slipway, Walton-on-Thames

Tread the riverbank where Julius Caesar may have first crossed the Thames in 65 BC. Caesar rested and made a camp at Walton. This is supposed to be one of the few places the Thames could be crossed on foot, as the river was then 1.8m (6ft). He was greeted by a Briton army that pushed stakes into the bank to defend it. The place is sometimes known as 'Conway Stakes'.

51.384536, -0.432357

### Conway Stake, Walton-on-Thames

Strabo described the Britons here as wearing long dark garments, long hair and beards. Herodotus and Pliny speak of the Britons as puncturing and staining their bodies with the juice of herbs. Caesar notes that they were 'clad with skins; all the Britons stain themselves with woad, which gives a blue colour, and imparts a ferocious aspect in battle; they have long flowing hair, and do not shave the upper lip'.

51.384536, -0.432357

### Engine River, Walton-on-Thames

The river feeds into Walton Marina. The 'Engine River' is a local name for the Wey River, near an old engine plant.

51.385368, -0.430433

### Desborough Cut, Walton-on-Thames

The Desborough Cut was built after 1935 to help reduce flooding and improve navigation. Lord Desborough, formerly W.H. Grenfell, was chairman of the Thames Conservancy when a decision was made to change the river's course. Desborough swam and punted on the river.

51.384000, -0.436000

### Desborough Island, Walton-on-Thames

Sandy meadows and riverbeds. Popular with dog walkers – especially on sunny days.

51.385012, -0.444661

## THE ANGLERS WALTON ON THAMES

British pub grub is served in a large-windowed dining room or at Thames-side outdoor tables.

Riverside Cottages, Manor Rd, Walton-on-Thames, KT12 2PF

www.heritagepubs.co.uk/anglers-walton-on-thames

019322 23996

## St Mary's Church, Walton on Thames

An iron 'scold's bridle' was once kept at the church. Bridles were once forced onto women who were considered outspoken and critical. The bridle was presented to the church by a Mr Chester in 1723, who claimed he had lost his estate because of a 'gossiping, lying woman'.

The bridle was 'stolen' in 1965, and a replica placed in a vestry cabinet, with the inscription 'Chester presents Walton with a bridle, to curb women's tongues that talk too idle.' The bridle was later donated to a Chester museum as 'inappropriate' for a church.

51.387036, -0.417719

## 4 WALTON BRIDGE, LOWER HALLIFORD

The original wooden bridge was described as 'the most beautiful' in the world. Turner was so inspired, he painted it three times in 1805. Still pretty, it's the first and last Thames bridge outside of Greater London.

51.387364, -0.431246

## Walton Bridge Marina, Walton-on-Thames

Boat hire and café, with parking.

51.387926, -0.427557

## Felix Rd Recreation Ground, Walton-on-Thanes

Find the slipway down from the steps, albeit it's more of a portage than a true slipway. Elevated green leads up to Walton Sea Scouts. Step up or down to reach the river. This old site opposite the weir on the facing bank was once a common.

51.393711, -0.419089

## Beasley Ait, Sunbury

A 5.4m (18ft) canoe made of hollow tree trunk was found in the mud at Beasley Island in October 1966. Dated to 1 AD, canoes were first used in the Stone Age. This one is on display in the Reading Museum.

51.394952, -0.418977

## River Ash, Surrey

The River Ash is a small, shallow river that runs for 6 miles. It enters the Thames at Sunbury beside the Ln called The Creek. A good place to explore by punt.

51.397232, -0.419056

**WEIR HOTEL**

This hotel and pub is within a 3-mile walk of Hampton Court via the TP.

The Weir Hotel Towpath, Waterside Dr, Walton-on-Thames, KT12 2JB

www.weir-hotel.co.uk

01932 784530

### Wheatley's Ait, Sunbury

A traffic-free island with FB across to the Sudbury Lock Wheel that is closed to the public. A 30cm-long bronze spearhead and a middle Bronze Age rapier were found on the island in June 1907. The island was used by the Thames Camping and Boating Association, who became tenants in 1927.

➤ **Foot** access is available on the N side of the island called the Creek, which is a natural waterway whose source is Tumbling Bay.

51.396068, -0.418357

### **⑤ SUNBURY LOCK, SUNBURY**

An oasis of islands near Walton-on-Thames. The lock complex includes rollers and a slope for portaging small boats. Popular for kayaking, with the weir stream providing freestyle paddling.

51.405082, -0.406401

### Sunbury Lock Ait, Sunbury

Neolithic remains were found during the excavation of the lock, which is surrounded by wilderness and some small hills. St Mary's Church is directly opposite on the Middlesex bank.

51.405082, -0.406401

### River Mead Island, Sunbury-on-Thames

Touch the most enormous London plane trees on this wooded island, which also features sandy beaches and a small park of open grassland. The island was called Swimming Pool Island in the 1950s as it had a large open-air pool, which closed in 1980. The island is former common land.

51.407000, -0.401000

### Sunbury Court Island, Sunbury-on-Thames

Owned by the Salvation Army since 1921, this island was developed for housing.

51.408889, -0.395833

### Swan's Rest and Rivermead Island, Sunbury-on-Thames

A grassy plateau, running along by the water's edge and overhung by willows.

51.407325, -0.400846

### Rivermead Island, Sunbury-on-Thames

Graceful swans, noisy geese and waterside benches. The gated park is open to the public on the opposite bank to the path.

51.406789, -0.402119

### Grand Junction Island, Sunbury-on-Thames

This island is owned and managed by the Environment Agency and is connected to the reservoir below.

➤ **Surrounding** waters are good for pike, perch and roach fishing. Explore the backwater if you can – but note that the island is private and has no foot access.

51.409959, -0.388540

### Reservoir Wood/cycle path, W Molesey

Touch water around the wooded shallows. This wood is halfway along 9 miles of cycle path from Weybridge to Kingston via Hampton Court.

51.408502, -0.384944

### Molesey Reservoirs, Molesey

There's no access to these old reservoirs at the moment, but they are nature reserves in the making. Plenty to see behind the walls, rail fences and grass bunds even before the naturalists move in. The reservoirs were established in 1872 and taken out of use in 1999. The land was then used for gravel extraction, and it will eventually be converted into a wetland reserve.

51.407357, -0.397624

Garrick Island

St Mary's Church, Hampton

###  Platt's Eyot, Hampton

A raised island of willow, ash and oak. Designated a 'conservation area' at the end of 1990 after waste spoil was dumped here from the excavation of the Middlesex filter beds. You'll have to climb up a steep incline to reach the western part of the island if you land by kayak. Inland grasses are peppered with red sheep sorrel and oxeye daisies in summer.

51.409713, -0.371939

###  Benn's Eyot, Hampton

Home of the Hampton Sailing Club. The clubhouse, built in 1962, is the main feature. It's one of the smallest islands on the Thames to be named on public maps.

➤ **The** backwater between the island and the near bank is quite shallow and only navigable for small vessels.

51.412222, -0.363333

###  Garrick Island Path, Molesey

David Garrick (1717–1779) was an English actor and playwright, who most famously brought Shakespeare to contemporary audiences. He created a temple to Shakespeare and a house on the Hampton bank. He was also famously painted by Thomas Gainsborough.

➤ **Both** the house and temple are best seen from water. The temple is sometimes open to the public during the summer. During dredging in 1970, flints dating from around 8000 BC were found nearby, revealing the area's much earlier history.

51.411308, -0.360895

### St Mary's Church, Hampton

The first church was built of flint and stone more than 600 years ago. This entire site was a former Celtic mission.

➤ **Find** the pyramidal tomb of John Greg (1716–1795), a Dominican plantation owner.

51.413008, -0.361596

Hurst Park

### Hurst Park, Molesey

A meadow that hosts the oldest ferry on the Thames and is known for good fishing. From here, you get lovely views of Hampton on the other side of the Thames.

Hurst Park Racecourse, once located nearby, held its last race in 1962. It was also the site of an arson attack by Kitty Marion and Clara Elizabeth Giveen. The two suffragettes took action after the death of Emily Davison at the 1913 Derby.

51.410708, -0.362076

### Hurst Park Small Boat Launching, Molesey

A concrete-edged quay where small boats can be launched. The slipway stops abruptly at the water's edge, so don't fall in!

51.411151, -0.358191

### Ducks Ait, E Molesey

A tiny island of weeping willow above Tagg's Island – popular with ducks, geese and songbirds as people like to picnic here.

51.410392, -0.355702

### Tagg's Island, E Molesey

The largest of several islands upstream of Ash Island. It has a reputation for hosting and entertaining celebrities and stars.

51.408889, -0.352222

### Trowlock Island, Teddington

There is a large lagoon or small lake at the centre of this 5-acre island.

51.424586, -0.308858

 ### Ash Island, E Molesey

A privately owned community of more than 30 houseboats. Walk across the long FB between Molesey Lock and Ash Island. Look out for nesting waterfowl and hedgehogs.

51.406937, -0.350392

 ### MOLESEY LOCK, E MOLESEY

The second longest lock on the Thames near Hampton Court Palace. Originally opened in 1815 and rebuilt in 1906, it offers good views of the palace through the arches of Hampton Court Bridge.

➤ **The** lock has foot and bike access. The area is home to numerous rowing and sailing clubs, with regattas such as Molesey Regatta and Sunbury Amateur Regatta held annually.

51.405256, -0.346810

 ### St Paul's Church, E Molesey

A gothic-style 19th-century church of Kentish ragstone rubble. Look for the war memorial in the N aisle: a painted canvas showing St George rescuing a maiden of Flanders, with smaller scenes showing the White Cliffs of Dover and a ruined town.

51.404946, -0.353987

Ash Island

## Hampton Court Bridge, E Molesey

Designed to match the style of Hampton Court Palace designed by Sir Christopher Wren. Wren's blue-plaqued house faces the roundabout just N of the bridge and palace gate.

51.403748, -0.342456

## Cigarette Island Park, E Molesey

A public park on L bank below the bridge. The name comes from a houseboat called *Cigarette* that used to be moored here. It was originally known as Secret Island – though it's not strictly an island, as it's bound by the Thames, the River Mole and Hampton Court Railway Station on the third side.

51.401753, -0.340379

## Hampton Court Palace, E Molesey

Built by Cardinal Woolsey during the reign of Henry VIII on the Middlesex side of the Thames. You can pay to go inside, but there's plenty to see outside for free.

51.403748, -0.342456

## Hampton Court Gardens, Hampton Wick

The gardens extend from the river to the public parts of Bushy Park. They link to Home Park, with trees, deer and lakes. The terrace-walk passes in front of the palace.

51.411083, -0.334701

Molesey

Hampton Court Bridge

 **7** ### HAMPTON COURT, HERON POND
Find the grassland on the N side for the wilder parts – the beautiful avenues of trees, deer and wildflower meadows.
➤ **Find** the entrance close to the TP off Hampton Court Rd, at the Kingston Bridge end.

51.413803, -0.327352

 ### Bushy Park, Teddington
Red and fallow deer graze. Henry VIII hunted here. The park is linked to Hampton Court but is less ornate and managed. It's best in spring when bluebells fill the wooded areas.

51.417716, -0.350272

 ### Longford River, Hampton Court Palace
The Longford River is an artificial waterway, designed to hydrate Bushey Park. It diverts water 12 miles from the River Colne at Longford near Colnbrook.

51.401300, -0.338300

 ### River Mole, E Molesey
Listen and look for water voles. The River Mole gives its name to the Surrey district of Mole Valley.

51.401200, -0.339300

 ### Rivers Mole and Ember, Thames Ditton
The union of a numerous series of small streams and brooks, which rise in Sussex and Surrey.

51.401192, -0.339420

River Mole

## THAMES DITTON ISLAND, THAMES DITTON

Famous for hosting Thames picnic parties in the Victorian era.
➤ **An** all-night suspension FB connects the island to the Surrey bank. It has tollgates, to which the inhabitants have keys. The church contains some remarkable tombs.

51.394405, -0.330429

## The Rythe, Thames Ditton

A tributary between Thames Ditton and Long Ditton. Its longest branch is the Arbrook, which drains Arbrook Common, a woodland area of Esher Commons.

51.391100, -0.326000

## Ditton Reach Slipway, Thames Ditton

A slipway at the end of Ditton Reach Ln under maple trees. Ferry Ln appears to have no slipway.

51.391086, -0.324035

## RAVEN'S AIT, KINGSTON UPON THAMES

Neolithic picks used for felling trees have been found on submerged land off Raven's Ait. A disagreement over whether the island was private or common land was lost in 2008, when eco-protesters arrived in a barge. The island is now private. There are areas for walking and cycling along the W side.

51.400077, -0.310291

## Queen's Promenade, Kingston upon Thames

A wide and spacious walkway – best enjoyed at sunset.

51.401201, -0.308454

## BILL'S KINGSTON

Breakfast, brunch, lunch and dinner on the riverfront.

2 Riverside Walk, Kingston upon Thames, KT1 1QN

www.bills-website.co.uk

02080 545400

## THE WHITE HART HOTEL HAMPTON WICK

A Tudor-style pub with rooms, a short walk from the path.

1 High St, Hampton Wick, Kingston upon Thames, KT1 4DA

www.whitehoteluk.co.uk

02089 771786

## Hogsmill River/chalk stream, Surbiton

The chalk stream rises in Ewell and flows into the Thames less than 180m (590ft) from Kingstone's All Saints Church.
A FP follows the river inland more than ½ mile to the Metal Bolt Sculpture.

51.409300, -0.308500

## Coronation Stone (The King's Stone), Kingston upon Thames

The stone used to stand near the church-door and was regarded as the place where Wessex's Saxon Kings were inaugurated, in keeping with Teutonic custom.

51.408401, -0.306800

## All Saints Church, Kingston upon Thames

Look for brass monuments in this 15th-century church.

51.410454, -0.306344

## KINGSTON BRIDGE, KINGSTON UPON THAMES

The bridge links Kingston to Hampton Court Park – but more famous as the reach above Teddington Lock. There has been a crossing here since Anglo-Saxon times. The bridge was widened in 2000 to include two cycle lanes.

51.411216, -0.308160

Kingston

**Hammersmith**

Hammersm Bridge

A315

A4

Chiswick Reach

B350

Chiswick Eyot

Leg o' Mutton Reservoir

**Chiswick**

M4

A4

A306

**Brentford**

Brentford Ait

Kew Bridge

KEW BRIDGE

**CHISWICK**

Dukes Meadows

Chiswick Ground

BRENTFORD

A3002

A315

Lot's Ait

Kew Green

A205

Mortlake Reach

**Barnes**

Grand Union Canal

Brentford Dock Marina

**Kew**

Dukes Meadows

Barnes Bridge

B349

Royal Botanic Gardens Kew

KEW GARDENS

Chiswick Bridge

River Thames

BARNES BRIDGE

The Lake

A307

North Sheen Cemetery

Mortlake Cemetery

A3003

BARNES

Syon Park

Syon Reach

**North Sheen**

**Mortlake**

MORTLAKE

Royal Mid-Surrey Golf Club

NORTH SHEEN

A305

Isleworth Ait

A310

A3004

River Crane

A316

Richmond Lock

RICHMOND

**Richmond**

Twickenham Bridge

**St Margarets**

ST MARGARETS

A3004

B321

Petersham Meadows

N

Marble Hill Park

A307

**Twickenham**

TWICKENHAM

Hammerton's Ferry

**Petersham**

A305

Eel Pie Island

**Strawberry Hill**

A310

H a m   L a n d s

Ham Lake

**Ham**

Ham Common

STRAWBERRY HILL

A309

Teddington Lock

River Thames

**Teddington**

TEDDINGTON

A310

1 km

1 mile

A302

Canbury Gardens

**Hampton Wick**

HAMPTON WICK

KINGSTON

Kingston Bridge

A308

**Kingston upon Thames**

# 16. KINGSTON BRIDGE TO HAMMERSMITH BRIDGE, SOUTH BANK

## STORIES

The stories of men and women who have walked these banks. You'll feel them everywhere.

The writing's on the wall: Darwin, Churchill, Joseph Dalton Hooker, kings and queens, Roman Celts, Gainsborough, Hogarth, William Morris and even, still, Boris.

And then there's The National Archives.

## 10 STEPPING STONES

Half Mile Tree
Teddington Lock
Eel Pie Island
Buccleuch Gardens
Richmond Lock FB
Kew Gardens
Gainsborough's Tomb
The National Archives
Chiswick Eyot
Hammersmith Bridge

## THE BOATERS INN

A riverside beer garden next to the park.

Canbury Gardens, Lower Ham Rd, Kingston Upon Thames, KT2 5AU

www.boaterskingston.com

02085 414672

Canbury Gardens West

## Kingston Bridge, Kingston upon Thames

Links Kingston to Hampton Court Park.

51.411168, -0.308814

## All Saints Church, Kingston upon Thames

People come here for the stained-glass windows. The church is thought to be the place where Saxon kings and queens had their coronations.

Kingston celebrated the 1,100th anniversary of the crowning of King Athelstan as the first king of a united England in 2025. He was grandson of Alfred the Great – the King of Wessex. Kingston Council funded six months of celebrations to mark the event.

51.410530, -0.306213

## Railway Bridge, Kingston upon Thames

Links Kingston and Hampton Wick stations.

51.413513, -0.307956

## Canbury Gardens, Norbiton, Kingston upon Thames

Touch trees along the Kingston riverside.

51.415005, -0.307479

## Stevens Eyot, Kingston upon Thames

The island was the site of Kingston's first public swimming area in 1872. It's now home to lots of geese, ducks and the Small Boat Club. It's busiest from April until October.

➤ **An** on-demand ferry service operates for members and guests. The ait sits on the reach above Teddington Lock, just downstream from the Kingston Rowing Club.

51.419856, -0.306089

## THE LENSBURY

Rooms, food and drink set within 25 acres of riverside grounds. The Lensbury Club was first formed in 1920 as the sports and social club for employees of the Dutch petroleum giant Shell, close to Teddington Lock. It was acquired by London & Regional Hotels in 2019.

The Lensbury, Broom Rd, Teddington, TW11 9NU

www.lensbury.com

02086 146400

### ① HALF MILE TREE, TEDDINGTON

Find the Halfway Tree. It was once a large elm – a giant horse chestnut today. Nothing stays the same. It marks the halfway point between Kingston town centre and Teddington Lock. Good for fishing.

51.424440, -0.306947

### Wood Cycle Lane, Ham

A 1-mile cycle path from Kingston to Ham.

51.425488, -0.308142

### Trowlock Island, Teddington

An island set into a bend, privately owned by its residents. The downstream end is semi-wild, surrounded by lots of houseboats. There are gardens close to a building that houses the Royal Canoe Club, formed in July 1866.

51.426525, -0.311616

### ② TEDDINGTON LOCK, TEDDINGTON

Walk about the place. Explore every nook, corner, bridge and walkway. Get your bearings. The lock is a complex hydraulic river system between Ham and Teddington, built in 1810. It marks the point where the tidal Thames ends and the freshwater Thames beings – or vice versa, depending on your direction.

➤ **The** lock system and large weir were designed to reduce flooding and make navigation easier. FBs provide pedestrians and cyclist access to the lock complex. Teddington takes its name from 'Tide End Town'.

51.431975, -0.323834

Teddington Lock

### Teddington Weir, Teddington

Listen and feel the fall of water over the weir. Fish ladders were introduced in 1864. The weir is good fishing for barbel.
Trout return from the sea to the freshwater Thames each year to spawn. These fish bypass 20 Thames weirs and 17 more on the Kennet to reach their breeding grounds.

51.431975, -0.323834

### Teddington Lock Ait, Teddington

A long, narrow island that used to be called Crow Heights until it was added to Teddington Lock.

51.431975, -0.323834

### Angler's Ait, Ham

Look for the small shingle beach close to the whirlpool in the weir bay.

51.431975, -0.323834

Ham Lands Woods

Ham Riverside Meadow

###  Ham Lands Nature Reserve, Ham

A flood meadow full of rare wildflowers and plants in spring –
bee and pyramidal orchids, meadow saxifrage, yellow vetchling
and hoary silver cinquefoil.

51.435921, -0.327462

###  Thames Young Mariners Lake, Ham

A 10-acre lake, connected to the Thames by lock gates. The lake
is a flooded gravel pit now used as an activity centre. Courses
are recognised by the Royal Yachting Association and the British
Canoe Union. Fishing is also allowed.

51.437763, -0.328688

###  Ham Lands Bend, Ham

A mass of woodland and ivy for hide and shelter.

51.441532, -0.329866

Eel Pie Island and path beach

### ③ EEL PIE ISLAND, TWICKENHAM

Watch sand martins and bats over the river and island – a good summer view from the path. An artificial sand cliff has been built at the SW end of the island for the martins. The Rolling Stones played 14 concerts here in 1963.

51.443580, -0.327339

### Petersham FP, Petersham

Hay meadows where cattle still graze beside the Thames.

51.447723, -0.307823

### → DETOUR - WALKING ⅔ – 2 MILES E

### Richmond Park, Sawyers Hill Gate

Good views of the Thames and London. Richmond Park is a must-visit from the Thames: a 2,500-acre park of ancient woodland on grass. More than 40 species of grass grow here, grazed by vast herds or red and fallow deer.

The park embraces conflicting ideas: an enclosed and walled space with 24/7 public, pedestrian access (except during culling season) and the introduction of non-native plants such as azaleas and rhododendrons. These so-called 'invasive plants' are prolific. Almost 100 years after their introduction, they still complement harebells, snowdrops and bluebells.

➤ **Find** where Nightingale Ln links to the TP (51.451709, -0.301110) and follow Rds E and then S ⅔ mile to the park entrance.

51.450059, -0.296197

###  River Ln, Petersham

A lovely Ln down to the river beside fields that lead to Richmond Park's SW tip.

51.448700, -0.305800

###  Sudbrook (stream), Petersham

Sudbrook empties here, just N of Kingston.

51.448700, -0.305800

###  Glover's Island, Richmond

Best seen from the Richmond hills but otherwise walk the gardens. Roach, dace and other small fish spawn in the gravel shallows. The island was named after the Richmond waterman Joseph Glover, who paid £70 for it in 1872 and then tried to make a large profit on its sale.
Max Waechter, who lived in Terrace House, Richmond Hill, bought Glover's Island in 1900 and then sold it to the Council for an undisclosed sum.

51.449667, -0.305925

###  Richmond Hill, E Twickenham

The best view of the Thames and Glover's Island has been celebrated by poets and artists including Pope, Wordsworth and Turner. Turner painted the view over Petersham Meadow, in which Glover's Island appears as a thin strip of grassland. The view includes Highgate, Hampstead Hill and Harrow-on-the-Hill.

51.449674, -0.305820

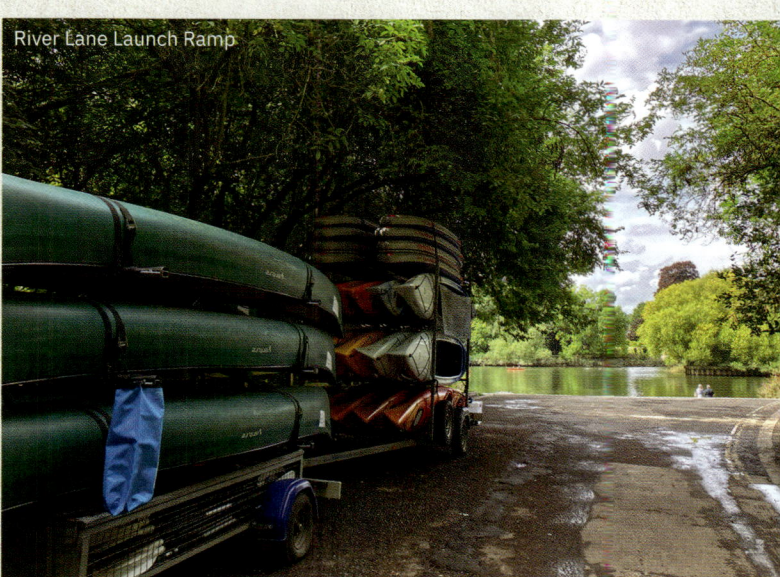
River Lane Launch Ramp

## THE WHITE CROSS

This pub dates back to 1780 when it was called the Waterman's Arms. It was built on the site of a Franciscan friary dissolved by Henry VIII in 1534. Today the remains of the friary are now used as cellars. The menu features favourites such as beer-battered fish and chips, sausage and mash, homemade pies and burgers.

Riverside House, Water Ln, Richmond, TW9 1NR

www.thewhitecross richmond.com

02089 406 844

### Petersham Meadows, Petersham

Some of the best views on this section of path. A place to star watch too.

51.449684, -0.302552

### ④ BUCCLEUCH GARDENS, PETERSHAM

Inhale the sunsets over Glover's Island and Richmond Bridge.

51.451675, -0.302003

### Richmond Bridge, Richmond

A lagoon full of boats, people and the reflections of limes, greens and blues under Surrey hills. Best on a hot bank holiday in May.

51.457405, -0.306945

### Water Ln, Richmond

Steps down to waterside – a beautiful place to sit and watch at the edge of the park and pubs.

51.458814, -0.308078

Richmond Bridge

Kew Riverbank

## ⑤ RICHMOND LOCK FB, RICHMOND

The first or last of the Thames' 45 locks. It was built to deepen the shallow water at low tide.

➤ **A** FB links Richmond and St Margaret's but closes at night. Pedestrians paid a toll when the FB first opened. The toll booths and turnstiles are still visible. The lock also includes slipways for small boats, which allow kayaks and rowing boats to bypass the sluices.

51.462208, -0.317216

## Obelisk, Old Deer Park, Kew/Richmond

Eroded and defaced, this small obelisk lies on the original Meridian Line that ran through the King's Observatory in the Old Deer Park. The clocks in the Houses of Parliament used to be set in time with this Meridian Line, until Greenwich Mean Time took over as the timekeeping benchmark in the 1880s.

51.464492, -0.314617

## Kew Corner, Kew

One of the best views on the river is from the staircase down into the water.

51.470993, -0.317660

## Kew Gardens Wood, Kew

A vast wood, part of one of the largest botanical garden collections in the world. A plant-inspired zone of smells, colours and sounds. Water, sand and treetop walks are a change from the semi-wild edges of the feral Thames.

51.482354, -0.298543

## THE SHIP

A pub beside an old, cobbled ramp down to the stony foreshore, overlooking the London Boat Race finishing line. It's best visited at high tide when the waters lap up to the Rd.

The Ship, Mortlake, 10 Thames Bank, London, SW14 7QR

www.greeneking.co.uk/ pubs/greater-london/ship

02088 761439

## THE WHITE HART

Wonderful sunsets. Built in 1662 (and rebuilt in 1899) on the banks of the river, this pub features trees, terraced balconies, foreshore and steps down to the water.

The White Hart, The Terrace, Mortlake, Richmond, SW13 0NR

www.whitehartbarnes. co.uk

02088 765177

# KEW GARDENS, KEW

Somewhere to learn and to be in awe of nature. There's a wildlife observatory in the SW corner. The park spans 300 acres and is home to more than 20,000 plant species .

51.484337, -0.294067

# Kew Palace, Kew

A royal palace within the grounds of Kew Gardens on the banks of the Thames. Originally larger than today, a few walls survive. The Gardens and Palace were once the exclusive property of the Crown until Queen Victoria changed their status to public.

51.484337, -0.294067

# The Dutch House, Kew

A palace used by King Charles to host a dinner to celebrate the Queen's 80th birthday in 2006. Open to the public.

51.484337, -0.294067

# Queen Charlotte's Cottage, Kew

Queen Victoria gave both the cottage and Kew Palace to the public in 1898, to commemorate her diamond jubilee the following year. The gift of the cottage was conditional upon the grounds being left in an uncultivated state.

51.483891, -0.287785

# St Anne's Church, Kew Green Church

St Anne's Church was built in 1714 on land given by Queen Anne. ➤ **The** church stands on the W side of the green. Its graveyard contains the graves of several famous people, including Gainsborough.

51.483891, -0.287785

# GAINSBOROUGH'S TOMB, KEW GREEN

Gainsborough's name is cut into a stone here. It reads: 'Thomas Gainsborough, Esq, died August 2nd, 1788, aged 61 years.' Gainsborough is beside the grave of his old friend Joshua Kirby (1716–74), author of *The Perspective of Architecture*. Kirby was a painter and topographer from Suffolk. He was encouraged by William Hogarth to become a specialist in perspective – particularly in architecture. J.M.W. Turner studied the book and used its ideas in his work.

51.483891, -0.287785

### THE BULLS HEAD

This pub serves great value food with views from the river path over Kew Railway Bridge.

373 Lonsdale Rd, Barnes, London SW13 9PY

www.chefandbrewer.com/pubs/greater-london/bulls-head

02089 741204

### Olivers Ait, Richmond

Cormorant and herons fish on this small gravel island, just upstream of Kew Railway Bridge. The island was used for building and repairing barges in the 19th century. The smithy was demolished in 1990.

51.484974, -0.280972

### THE NATIONAL ARCHIVES, KEW

Taste one of the Thames' greatest national treasures. The coffee is good. The dust in the archive is uniquely uplifting too.

51.481104, -0.280768

### Chiswick Bridge, Mortlake

Busiest during the annual Oxford and Cambridge University Boat Race. Best seen at night when lit up by the special effect lights.

51.470624, -0.264109

### Duke's Hollow, Barnes

A wild shoreline, swamp and reeds on the way to Chiswick Eyot, between Barnes Railway Bridge and Chiswick Bridge.

51.472315, -0.253313

### Duke's Meadow, Barnes

Japanese Knotweed mixes with flowers. On a still day in early summer, it sprouts so fast the little clicks of growth can be heard. It takes intensive work to suppress – and even then will almost certainly return. Some London restaurants are cooking this stuff as it's so tasty and nutritious (but not from here – as it might have been contaminated). Why are we not using it to feed the world?

51.472315, -0.253313

### Leg O'Mutton Reservoir BW, Barnes

Look for turtles sunning themselves. The site is famous for birds that nest on floating rafts, but like any attractive homestead, invaders have moved in. The invasive turtles love E London sunshine as much as local fowl. A good place to see bats – over the disused reservoir, along the ½-mile stretch of riverfront. Also known as Lonsdale Rd Reservoir.

51.485556, -0.246019

## Chiswick Eyot Causeway, Chiswick

Find the low-tide stone path. The stones can get scattered about by the high tide, but it's fun attempting to track a path. Beware sinking mud and returning tide. Don't go alone.

51.486596, -0.247603

## CHISWICK EYOT

Listen for reed warblers chirping: 'Chiswick Eyot! Chiswick Eyot!' The 4-acre island is thick with willow osiers or withies. London traders once made and sold baskets and other wicker utensils from here.

Huge yellow marsh-marigolds bloom here in spring, alongside yellow chamomile, comfrey and ragged robin. It can flood on a high tide.

51.486539, -0.244441

## Hogarth's Tomb, Chiswick Old Cemetery

The monument was erected by Hogarth's friends, and the epitaph was written by Garrick:

---

Farewell! great painter of mankind,
Who reach'd the noblest point of art;
Whose pictured morals charm the mind,
And throngh the eye correct the heart.
If genius fire thee, reader, stay;
If nature touch thee, drop a tear;
If neither move thee, turn away,
For Hogarth's honour'd dust lies here.

---

Hogarth lived, died and was buried in Chiswick.

51.483788, -0.253582

## HAMMERSMITH BRIDGE, HAMMERSMITH

One of the best viewing galleries on the Thames – much like the old London Bridge, constantly closing over fears it'll collapse under the strain of people and traffic.

51.487712, -0.230966

# 16. KINGSTON BRIDGE TO HAMMERSMITH BRIDGE, NORTH BANK

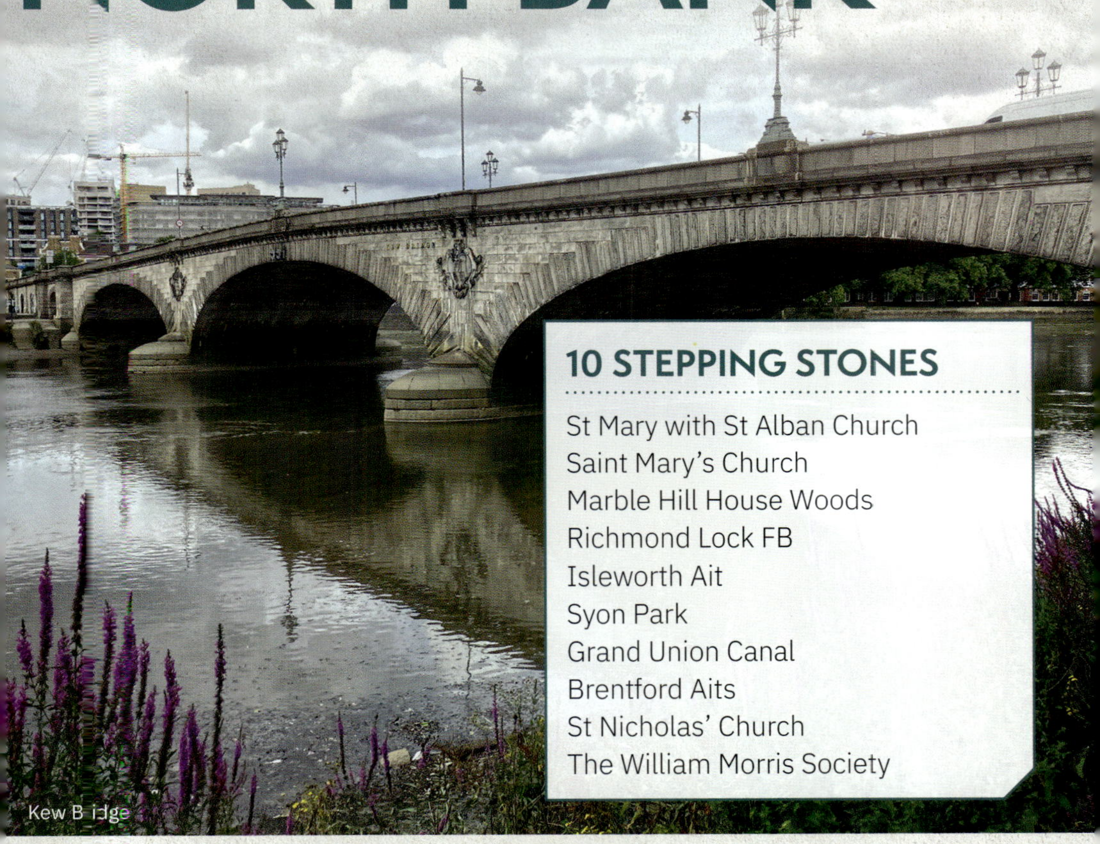

Kew Bridge

## 10 STEPPING STONES

St Mary with St Alban Church
Saint Mary's Church
Marble Hill House Woods
Richmond Lock FB
Isleworth Ait
Syon Park
Grand Union Canal
Brentford Aits
St Nicholas' Church
The William Morris Society

## Tidal Teddington Lock, Ham, Richmond-upon-Thames

The Tidal TP starts and ends at the gateway to the greatest city in the world. London is a forager's paradise. Nuts, greens, berries and unlimited freshwater between the ancient trees – tidal cuisine. A complex of three locks in the London Borough of Richmond marks the coming together of fresh and tidal Thames.
➤ **Find** where the river path meets Riverside Dr, Richmond, TW10 7RP. Just before the parked cars, follow the hard path 400 yards down to the Thames. The Teddington Lock FB can be crossed to the other side of the river.

51.430090, -0.322110

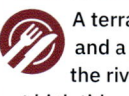
 # ST MARY WITH ST ALBAN CHURCH, TEDDINGTON

The church at the top of Ferry Ln is home to beautiful stained-glass windows depicting Madonna and Child, by Goddard and Biggs. The church's most famous vicar was the Reverend Stephen Hales (1677–1761), a scientist who studied plant physiology and the chemistry of air. Hales invented the 'pneumatic trough', a device to collect gases over water. Hales also experimented with ways of distilling freshwater from seawater; and preserving water and meat on sea-voyages. He is buried next to the church's tower.

51.428535, -0.325359

 ## Swan Island, Strawberry Hill

A Gothic mansion built by Horace Walpole in Strawberry Hill.

51.439077, -0.330928

 ## Pope's Villa, Strawberry Hill

Pope dug a tunnel beneath the Rd that became 'the grotto' after he filled it with spas from the springs he discovered. Pope's own words in 1725 were that he had found a spring of the 'clearest water, which falls in a perpetual Rill, that echoes thru the Cavern day and night'. Pope's Villa was later demolished.

51.442017, -0.331347

 ## Champions Wharf, Twickenham

Church Ln is the communal brick platform under the shadow of Saint Mary's. Explore the low tide beach. These modest squares, sometimes still with their old cobble floors, often have more character when there's no pub.

51.446717, -0.324701

 # SAINT MARY'S CHURCH, TWICKENHAM

Find the small garden that honours the work of Alexander Pope. This Georgian church has a surviving medieval ragstone tower that looks over the Thames.

51.446929, -0.325129

### MARBLE HILL HOUSE WOODS, E TWICKENHAM

Stand under the UK's oldest black walnut tree – planted in the early 18th century. The symmetrical park and lawns were designed in the Palladian style by Henrietta Howard. Alexander Pope helped with the design of the gardens, which were used to entertain rich and famous neighbours like Horace Walpole. An Act of Parliament passed in 1902 to protect public access to both the property, the park and the views from Richmond Hill. Entry is free. Walk through ⅓ mile of tree-lined path. Then walk down to the marina and, facing the water, turn L along the wooded foreshore.

51.449165, -0.308056

 ### Riverside, Twickenham

Find the gravel beaches between large river houses at the end of Ferry Ln. There are two ramps for canoes or small boats wedged between houses and other buildings – remnants of an enlightened era when public access and private residence were of equal importance.

51.446843, -0.320708

 ### Meadowbank, E Twickenham

Glorious, shabby walk along avenues of trees either side; willows dipping into the river and London planes and broadleaf trees lining the green path.

51.450569, -0.305544

 ### Corporation Island, E Twickenham

Huge trees tower over the water. It's best visited in autumn to see colours of red, yellow and brown. Home to herons, coots, moorhens and floods on a high-spring tide.

51.458057, -0.308889

 ### Willoughby Rd, Twickenham

Ramp down to the waterside.

51.457926, -0.309750

 ### Flowerpot Islands, Twickenham

Look for the heronries on both islands. These wooded aits are between Richmond rail and Rd bridges. Collectively known as the Two Tree Islands until the 1950s, when the name was adopted by another island with two trees, downstream between Southend and Castle Point.

51.458129, -0.309018

Richmond Bridge

### Richmond Railway Bridge, Twickenham

A ferry once crossed here from Richmond Recreation Ground. Generations of developers and landowners have attempted to steal more and more of this riverbank, but the local planners have done much work to keep public access to as much riverbank as possible.

51.460090, -0.313421

### Twickenham Bridge, Twickenham

A lovely view of the working lock below. The bridge is next to Old Deer Park and a short walk downstream from Richmond town centre.

51.460510, -0.314181

### RICHMOND LOCK FB, RICHMOND

Watching people and their boats navigating the lock is never boring.

51.462208, -0.317216

### River Crane, Richmond

Where the river empties into the Thames. The Crane passes through three London boroughs: Hillingdon, Hounslow and Richmond upon Thames.

51.465400, -0.321500

### The King's Observatory, Richmond

Sir William Chambers (1726–96) designed the observatory which was built in the Old Deer Park in Richmond. The building was to watch Venus, on 3 June 1769, cross in front of the sun – an event that would not repeat for 105 years.

King George III, a keen amateur astronomer, told his friend Dr. Stephen Demainbray that he wanted to see the event. Although the royal summer residence in Kew had an observatory, it was no longer usable, so a new one was built.

51.469203, -0.314612

### ISLEWORTH AIT S, ISLEWORTH

You must visit at low tide. An uninhabited island of escapees from Kew Gardens. Giant trees include ash, willow, swamp cypress, black poplar and a rare dawn redwood. The 10 acres flood on the tide, but they are a good place to see kingfishers, herons and great crested grebes. There are two rare species of mollusks that live in the tidal waters here. There was once a pool at the centre of the island that was used by local schools, but it's not clear whether it was tidal or fresh. It's been filled in.
➤ **The** island foreshore can be visited by packraft or the island itself by contacting the London Wildlife Trust.

51.468773, -0.320635

### Duke of Northumberland's River, Isleworth

A human-made watercourse to drive the old Isleworth Mill. A sluice underneath Mill Plat feeds the main lake in Syon Park.

51.470400, -0.321200

### Church Street Ramp, Isleworth

Follow the cobbled ramp down to the stone foreshore beside Isleworth Ait. A beautiful junction between land and water, which can be mesmerising in sunshine.

51.471275, -0.319911

### All Saints' Church, Isleworth

Watch tidal bats over the river, while standing in the graveyard at dusk. All Saints' Church is the oldest parish church in Isleworth. The 14th-century Kentish ragstone tower and foundations are all that's left of the pre-20th-century builds.

51.471627, -0.319854

### Syon Reach, Richmond

One of the best views of the Thames, with the gardens of Kew on the L and a wild piece of London riverbank at Syon Park on the R.

51.476338, -0.306834

### Syon Marsh N, Brentford

An everglade of channels, greens and fallen trees. Explore and find shade when you have lots of time.

51.4755534, -0.308336

### Syon Marsh S, Brentford

Gravel beach and sinking mud. More native than the Mississippi. Somewhere to hide, with attention for the incoming tide.

51.4738478, -0.311737

### 6 SYON PARK, BRENTFORD

It's all a bit 'park like' and enclosed, but it's pretty – especially with over 200 species of rare trees.

There are 40 acres of garden across the 200-acre estate and park. Check out the trout fishery.

51.476737, -0.310424

### Brentford Marina, Brentford

More than 50 berths on lit pontoons. Centrally heated showers and toilet facilities. There's no residential moorings but visiting boats are welcome.

51.481887, -0.302203

### River Brent/Grand Union Canal, Brentford

Where Thames meets canal.

51.481564, -0.312494

### River Brent, Brentford

Where the river empties into the Thames. The Brent rises in Barnet and flows almost 18 miles to the tide.

51.483, -0.3

### 7 GRAND UNION CANAL, BRENTFORD

The main waterway between London and the Midlands can't rival the Thames for its 185-mile length. It does, though, offer the option of travelling to the N, rather than E to W.

➤ **One** arm runs to Leicester, the other 137 miles to Birmingham. The latter has 166 locks and several branches that fork off to other towns: Slough, Aylesbury, Wendover and Northampton. The Leicester line has two short arms of its own – to Market Harborough and Welford.

51.483000, -0.300000

### River Brent/Grand Union Canal Marina, Brentford

Sit and watch the tide ebb and flood over 12 hours. This first section from the Thames to the double Thames Lock is very tide dependent. Look out for seabirds and shellfish.

51.481918, -0.302107

### Liquidity, Ferry Point

A stainless-steel sculpture beside the entrance to Grand Union Canal. Three waves are engraved with shoals of fish. Sunlight shines through the steel like a lantern. It was erected in 2002 by Simon Packard.

51.484456, -0.298659

### Lot's Ait, Brentford

Once known as Barbel Island because so many fish spawned and were caught here. Poplars dominate the S end, willows the N. The island was used for scenes in the 1951 film *The African Queen*, starring Humphrey Bogart and Katharine Hepburn. Bogart won an Oscar for his role.

➤ **It's** best approached by boat as the mud is thick and sinking.

51.484894, -0.298476

### Waterman's Park, Brentford

Look for the channel between park and river, where there are lots of ducks.

51.486735, -0.295324

### BRENTFORD AITS, BRENTFORD

Come here at low tide. Crack willow, giant plane trees and poplars. Colonies of bats thrive here. A huge heronry looms. Green trees, purple flowers and grey gravel in sunshine light up like reflections in a jacuzzi. It. Is. Breathtaking. Snipe, dunlin and sandpipers feed at low tide.

➤ **There** was a notorious pub here in the 18th century called the Swan. The old pub steps lead down to the river at the E end of the long and narrow riverside park, Waterman's Park. Trees were planted in the 1920s to block out Brentford's gasworks from ruining the Kew Gardens view.

51.486629, -0.292633

Kew Bridge

### Kew Hard, Strand-on the-Green

Hard ground and trees either side of the bridge at low tide.
There are lots of places to fish or go mudlarking.

51.488024, -0.287264

### Kew Bridge, Kew

The largest area of tidal mud on the upper Thames. Waders feed
on the flatworms and shrimps.

51.487417, -0.286488

### Oliver's Eyot, Richmond

Oliver Cromwell came here. Touch the stream that reveals itself
between the riverbank and the island at low tide.
Most of the island is wooded. There are three Joanne Lombardi
poplars in the centre of the island – with dogwood, cherry
and bamboo in the lower canopy. Look for the rare pink
water speedwell.

51.484974, -0.280972

### THE BELL & CROWN

Riverside pub, licensed as the Bell & Crown in 1787. Peaceful benches right by the water.

11–13 Thames Rd, Strand on the Green, London, W4 3PL

www.bell-and-crown.co.uk

02089 944164

## Railway Bridge, Strand-on the-Green

Explore old cottages and pubs dating back to the 18th century. Many of them have steps up to the doors to prevent flood waters entering.

51.484694, -0.278761

## Strand on the Green, Grove Park Rd

A boat ramp by scrub woodland – best at low tide.

51.483353, -0.276787

## Hartington Steps, Chiswick

Walk 18 steps down to a low-tide stone beach. A good place to mudlark.

51.480999, -0.275217

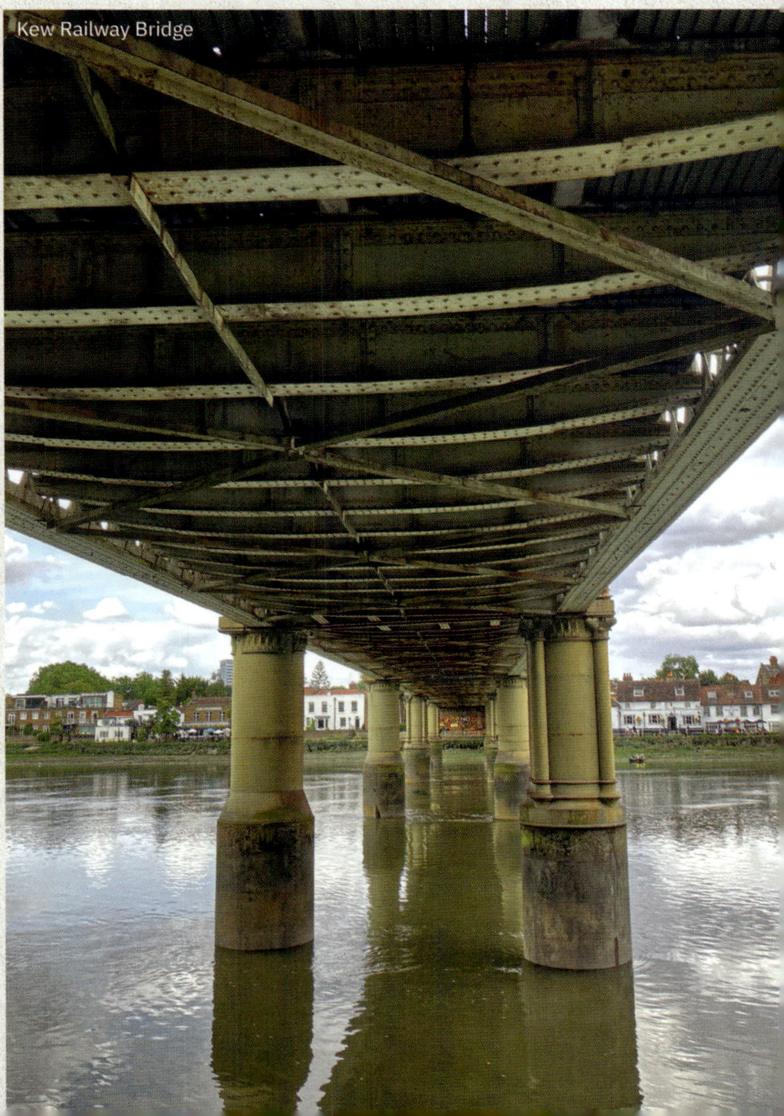

Kew Railway Bridge

## Chiswick Marina, Chiswick

Walk along the riverbank at low tide between the marina and Chiswick Bridge.

51.475764, -0.271328

## Dan Mason Drive, Chiswick

An unmade avenue of lime, alder and willow between the riverbank and Dukes Meadows Golf Course.

51.471910, -0.264590

## Duke Meadows Canoe Launch, Chiswick

A stone beach and ramp. The local canoe club has been here on the Thames since 1957. Club members have represented Great Britain every year since 1984.

51.473072, -0.268064

## Dukes Hollow, Chiswick

London plane and willow woodland on the riverbank.

51.473105, -0.255312

## ST NICHOLAS' CHURCH, CHISWICK

A graveyard of treasures. William Hogarth 1697–1764 is buried here. Hogarth was an English painter, engraver and social critic famous for The Rakes Progress. He lived in Leicester Square but also had a summer house in Chiswick, a few minutes' walk from the church.

51.485989, -0.250305

## Chiswick Draw Dock, Chiswick

A hard slope down to the river, shaped now by a long public ramp, surrounded by pollarded willow.

51.485439, -0.249046

## Chiswick Launch, Chiswick

One of the most beautiful sites – the river flooding the Rd at high tide. Profoundly beautiful in sunshine, especially if you can take your shoes and socks off at the SW edge of Chiswick Eyot.

51.488071, -0.249569

## Chiswick Eyot Edge, Chiswick

On the riverbank opposite the tip of the island is a remarkable edge, where wild riverbank bleeds into spiked, gated gardens and houses, underneath a single, defiant oak tree with attitude.

51.486937, -0.248293

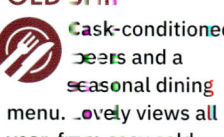

### OLD SHIP

Cask-conditioned beers and a seasonal dining menu. Lovely views all year, from cosy cold days in front of the fires to summer days on the terrace. A short walk from Ravenscourt Park, Stamford Brook and Hammersmith Underground stations.

25 Upper Mall, Hammersmith, W6 9TD

www.oldship hammersmith.co.uk

02087 482593

## Chiswick Eyot, Chiswick

There is a sand and shingle beach here. Beautiful views are found downstream towards Hammersmith and back upstream towards Kew. The island is full of willow, and basket makers still come here to cut rods for their craft.

51.487502, -0.246121

## Alexander Pope Blue Plaque, Chiswick Ln S

Find the plaque at 112 Chiswick Ln S, Chiswick, London W4 2QA.

51.488071, -0.249569

## Upper Mall, Hammersmith

Willow trees rooted into the riverbanks arch over the old brickwork and Rd.

51.490444, -0.236483

## THE WILLIAM MORRIS SOCIETY, HAMMERSMITH

Magical. Why Morris was here – mud, canal, magic. You'll find a small museum in the basement rooms and Coach House of Kelmscott House, William Morris's Hammersmith home on the Thames. The museum guides are highly knowledgeable.
Open to society members 2–5pm on Thursdays and Saturdays.

51.490502, -0.235502

## Stamford Brook, Hammersmith

It may be a corruption of 'stony ford', for a crossing by King Street. It has given its name to the surrounding area between Hammersmith and Chiswick, and to the local London Underground station, Stamford Brook.

51.490300 -0.234100

## Hammersmith Bridge, Hammersmith

Links Hammersmith and Fulham to Richmond upon Thames.

51.487712, -0.230966

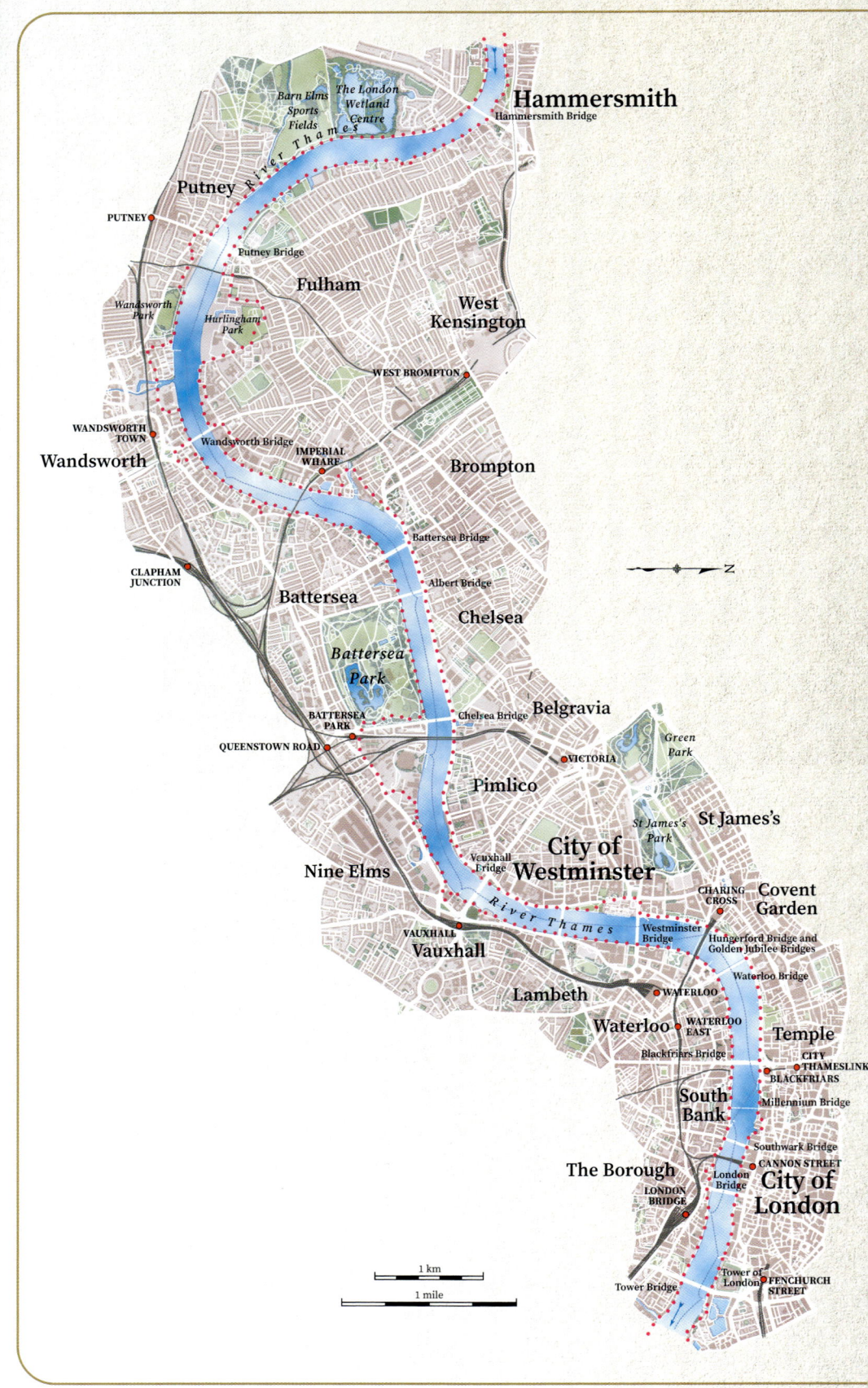

# 17. HAMMERSMITH BRIDGE TO **TOWER BRIDGE,** SOUTH BANK

## ART

Artists come here because of fog, mist and atmosphere. They leave their brushstrokes and ideas everywhere – from Girtin to Vivienne Westwood, Gainsborough to Defoe, Mary Robinson ('Perdita') to Soanes and everything in between.

This is where you will fall in love with London.

## 10 STEPPING STONES

WWT London Wetland Centre
Putney Bridge
River Wandle
St Mary's Church, Battersea
Battersea Park Art
William Blake Mosaics
Westminster Bridge
Tate Modern
Golden Hinde
Tower Bridge

### Hammersmith Bridge, Hammersmith

One of the oldest suspension bridges in the world – it was built in 1887.

51.487712, -0.230966

### Barnes Towpath, WWT London Wetland Centre, Richmond upon Thames

More than 40 black poplars line one of the best wooded sections of the tidal Thames. The trees are thought to be the last remnants of a wild species. DNA tests have shown they are genetically rare. Eleven of the 40 are genetically unique. Many of the trees are female, which is also extremely rare, as only 10 per cent of the UK population is female.

51.477943, -0.226857

### WWT LONDON WETLAND CENTRE, BARNES

Watch bitterns, parakeets, sparrowhawks and sand martins. A wetland over 100 acres of disused reservoirs on a loop in the Thames. Bird hides, plus a café, daily tours and specialist talks. www.wwt.org.uk/wetland-centres/london

51.476261, -0.234601

### Queen Elizabeth Walk, Barnes

A 100-acre disused waterworks reclaimed by nature as acidic grassland, broom and birch. There are six bird hides and almost 180 species of birds, they say, including whistling ducks and geese.

51.476397, -0.226976

### Barnes Common, Barnes

A wilderness of paths between patches of scrub and trees. The middle is like an old cemetery; the NW corner has more formal grass lawns and ponds.

51.476397, -0.226976

### Beverly Brook, Barnes

A stream running along the N side of the common – it comes from Wimbledon and has a FP.

51.476397, -0.226976

### Lagoon, Barnes

A quiet place. People come here to feed birds or read books.

51.476397, -0.226976

**THE DUKE'S HEAD**

This Putney pub sits at the start of the Oxford and Cambridge University Boat Race.

8 Lower Richmond Road, Putney, SW15 1JN

www.dukesheadputney.com

02087 882552

### Beverley Brook Walk FB, Barnes

Edgeland between city and wild river. You'll sense the wild between hogweed, cobbles and splintered benches that haven't seen varnish for a long time. The entrance/exit to the Barnes peninsula is lined with giant London plane trees.

51.471559, -0.223680

### Beverley Brook Foreshore, Barnes

Sit riverside at low tide and inhale the fumes of water and the view of a tree-lined riverbank that is surreal at sunset. Mudlark and look for fossils.

51.471559, -0.223680

### Waterman's Green and boat ramp, Putney

A grass- and tree-lined river access next to Putney Bridge.

51.466459, -0.214875

### ② PUTNEY BRIDGE, PUTNEY

The mecca for Thames boat racing. The story goes... the two churches of Putney and Fulham were built by a pair of angels, who have one mallet between them. They throw it backwards and forwards to each other across the river, and when it arrives they either cry out, 'Put nigh' or 'Full home' – hence the names of the places at either end of the bridge.

51.465996, -0.213980

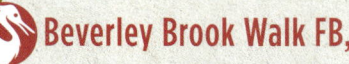

Putney Bridge

## St Mary's Church, Putney

A historic church where, in August 1647, Oliver Cromwell and his New Model Army set up headquarters to hold their first parliamentary conference, known as the Putney Debates.

51.46594, -0.213603

## Brewhouse Slipway, Putney

A public boat ramp at the end of Brewhouse Ln. It opens up onto wide gravel foreshore between Putney and Fulham Railway bridges.

51.465603, -0.212699

## Wandsworth Park E, Wandsworth

Smell the lime in spring. An avenue of 77 lime trees lines the park's northern FP. Not to be outdone, an avenue of 31 London planes lines the waterfront, which are even more impressive. Hundreds of noisy crows shelter in the London plane trees at dawn and dusk. Bats roost in the trees: beech, hornbeam, tulip tree, mountain ash, Indian bean, ginkgo, evergreen oak, yew, horse chestnut, poplar and laburnum.

51.463092, -0.204293

## Wandsworth Park W, Wandsworth

Watch sand martins feeding along the low-tide shore. Many bats hunt here at dusk too: pipistrelles, greater horseshoes, Daubenton's, Leisler's and noctule, roosting in the beech, yew and poplars.

51.463092, -0.204293

Wandsworth Park

Battersea

### Bell Ln Creek, Wandsworth

Walk over chalk and gravel foreshore at low tide. The River Wandle chalk stream empties into the Thames at this creek.

51.461422, -0.194853

### The Spit, Wandsworth

A wooded spit that needs a tidy up – a remarkable place to explore at low tide.

51.461546, -0.194612

## ③ RIVER WANDLE, WANDSWORTH

Where River Wandle meets Thames beside Wandsworth Bridge. Wandsworth takes its name from the chalk stream.
William Morris' mill once produced his wallpaper and fabrics here. The Wandle flows for 9 miles through Croydon, Sutton, Merton and Wandsworth.

51.461391, -0.194062

### Falconbrook, Battersea

The stream rises in Balham and Tooting, then forms the Wandsworth Town border, before emptying into the Thames.

51.468000, -0.180800

### Battersea Reach, Battersea

Bats hunt all along here: pipistrelles, greater horseshoes, Daubenton's, Leisler's and noctule.

51.471550, -0.178202

### Railway Bridge, Battersea

Five iron-arched spans are supported by four stone-faced river piers.

51.472564, -0.177898

## Battersea Church Rd, Battersea

A public boat ramp associated with the church – best used at low tide and dusk when the sun lights up the mud and water as it falls behind the railway bridge. A good place for mudlarking.

51.476205, -0.175963

## ❹ ST MARY'S CHURCH, BATTERSEA

Artist and poet William Blake married Catherine Boucher here on 17 August 1782. J.M.W. Turner painted the river from the vestry window, and this was one of his favourite riverside locations. He painted city landscapes from this church.
The oldest church in Battersea was designed by local architect Joseph Dixon and completed in 1777. Get inside and look closely at the stained glass. The E window in the sanctuary dates from 1379. There are four newer windows associated with William Blake and Turner.

51.476680, -0.175961

## St Mary's Church Crypt, Battersea

Famous as the last resting place of Benedict Arnold – an American military officer who, in 1780 during the American Revolutionary War, defected to the British. He infamously led the British army in battle against the very men he had once commanded as a celebrated hero.
His handler, the British officer John André, was caught and hanged as a spy, while Arnold escaped to England.

51.476680, -0.175961

## Ransome's Dock, Battersea

A rare inlet. This old dock was designed to take barges and coastal steamers because they could all leave on the lowest of tide from this creek.

51.481042, -0.167834

## Battersea Park, Battersea

The 200-acre park on reclaimed flood meadow and marshland. Before the park opened in 1858, the area was known as Battersea fields. It was a popular place for duelling, and the fields were most famous for asparagus known as 'Battersea bunches' – similar to the wild asparagus that grows around Bath. Many surrounding fields were lined with streams and ditches where people grew carrots, melons and lavender. Lavender Hill is nearby.

51.481736, -0.163038

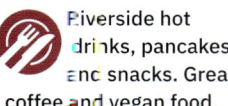

## The London Peace Pagoda, Battersea Park

Symbolic architecture in a serene location, with views over Chelsea Embankment. One of 80 peace pagodas around the world.

51.481980, -0.159067

## 5 BATTERSEA PARK ART, BATTERSEA

Henry Moore's stone sculpture, Three Standing Figures. Moore is best known for his abstract bronze figures. His work can also be seen in The Wallace Collection, a small museum within walking distance of Danebury. (He also has a bronze, Knife Edge Two Piece, beside the Palace of Westminster.)

51.478130, -0.156910

### THE BLACK CAB COFFEE CO

Riverside hot drinks, pancakes and snacks. Great coffee and vegan food.

1 Riverlight Quay, London, SW11 8AU

www.theblackcabcoffee co.com

02074 983760

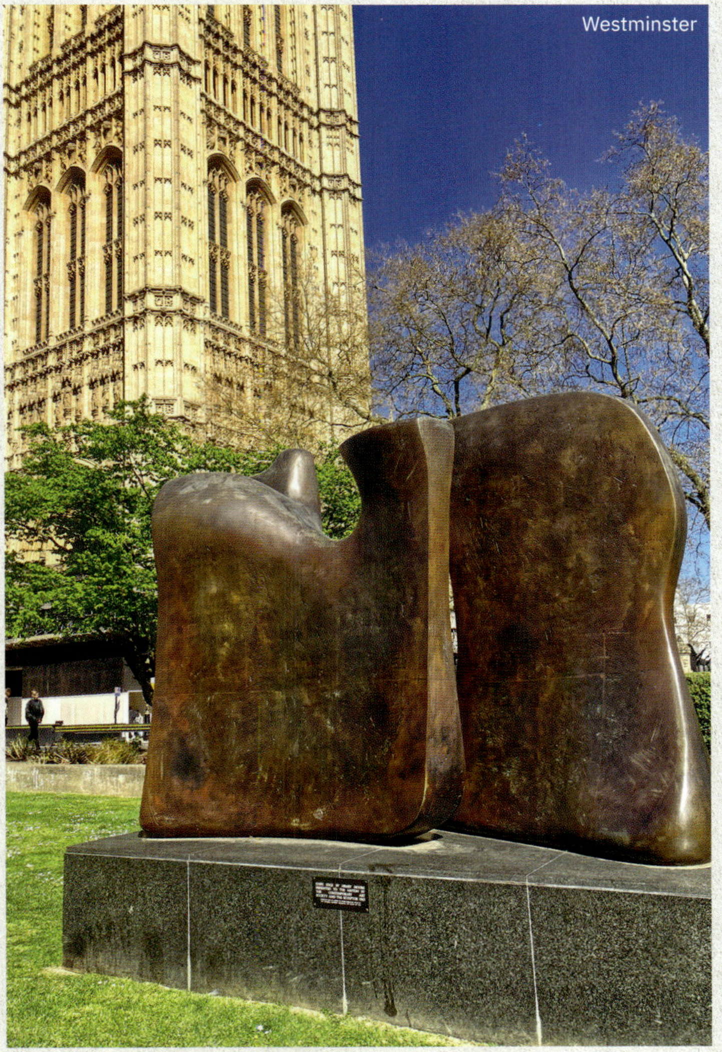

Westminster

## Chelsea Bridge, Battersea

Opened in 1858 by Queen Victoria. The Rd down the eastern edge of the park is called Victoria Rd and is linked to Queens Rd by Victoria Circus (now Queen's Circus). Victoria Rd and Queens Rd later became Queenstown Rd.

51.483669, -0.149690

 ## Battersea Power Station, Nine Elms

Battersea Power Station's four-chimney profile hangs over the Thames like the opening scene to an Orwellian novel. Campaigners argued in 1927 that it would be ugly. They also said it would pollute the air for people, wildlife and... damage priceless paintings in the Tate Gallery across the river. Ministers said it was the perfect site for Londoners, who needed access to 400MW of electricity.

Legislation was introduced to curb pollution. The architect Sir Giles Gilbert Scott was commissioned to remedy the 'ugly' problem. He was most famous for designing red telephone boxes. Now redundant of power, Battersea Power Station remains the world's largest brick building that retains its original Art Deco exterior and interior. Sir Giles' design was so successful that he was asked to design the Bankside power station, which is now home to the Tate Modern 4 miles downstream. Isn't that wonderful?

51.479562, -0.142624

 ## Riverside Gardens, Nine Elms

Huge plane trees and grass hang over chalky foreshore.

51.484735, -0.129059

 ## Vauxhall Bridge, Vauxhall

This bridge replaced a ferry service. No fords were ever available along this part of the Thames. The width of the river at Vauxhall is about 275m (900ft), with a depth at low water of 2.4–3m (8–10ft), and the tide rises about 3.7m (12ft).

51.487494, -0.126862

 ## Bronze Statues, Vauxhall

Four huge bronze statues were erected in late 1907 above the piers. The upstream piers featured Pomeroy's Agriculture, Architecture, Engineering and Pottery. The downstream piers are Drury's Science, Fine Arts, Local Government and Education. Each statue weighs approximately 2 tonnes. None of the statues can be seen by bridge users. They are only visible to walkers on the riverbanks or those on the river.

51.487494, -0.126862

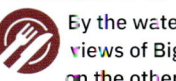

## Vauxhall Foreshore, Vauxhall

Look for a prehistoric bridge crossing. A bridge-like structure dating back to 1550–300 BC was discovered next to Vauxhall Bridge in 1993 during a low-spring tide. Historians claimed two rows of wooden posts would have carried a bridge from the S bank to an island that has now sunk. The island was possibly used for burial of the dead. The posts can still be seen at the lowest spring tides.

51.487494, -0.126862

## Lambeth Bridge, Lambeth

Stairs down to the ferry landing. A horse ferry once linked Lambeth and Westminster. There were very few Thames ferries capable of taking a coach and horses, hence 'Horse Ferry Rd'. Lambeth Bridge was opened by King George V and Queen Mary in 1932.

51.494346, -0.121091

## Lambeth Church, Lambeth

Views of the church with Big Ben and Westminster Palace across the water.

51.495043, -0.120234

## Lambeth Palace Park, Lambeth

Official residence and gardens of the Archbishop of Canterbury, just past Lambeth Bridge.

51.495355, -0.120096

## 6 WILLIAM BLAKE MOSAICS, LAMBETH

Mosaic replicas of William Blake in Waterloo bridges can be found on the exit to Lambeth Park.
Blake was a Lambeth resident. He was a visionary and a rebel, and arguably the most important artist in British history. His legacy is barely recognised in Lambeth – which is strange, as he was at his most productive during his years living there.

51.497849, -0.115230

## 7 WESTMINSTER BRIDGE

Very different by day or night – but equally beautiful, I think. Walk around gothic architecture, with its masonic symbols, and English faux woodland, while tidal waters lap beneath your feet.

51.500787, -0.120030

## TATTERSHALL CASTLE, WESTMINSTER

An old steam ferry converted to a pub, serving fish and chips on the deck. Located opposite the London Eye and between Westminster and Embankment Underground stations.

Victoria Embankment, SW1A 2HR

www.thetattershallcastle.co.uk

02078 39 6548

# Houses of Parliament, Westminster Bridge

Look and listen for peregrines from Westminster Bridge. More than 30 breeding pairs live in London and their favourite hunting ground is Parliament (Tate Modern is also a hotspot). London has the largest urban peregrine falcon population in the world, after New York.

51.500963, -0.123543

# Central Lobby, Palace of Westminster

Any British citizen can enter this place and ask to see their MP. Central Lobby is a rare place in politics: the crossroads of the Palace where corridors from the Lords, Commons and Westminster Hall all meet.

A stone octagon built over an intricately tiled floor marks the spot. There is a mosaic-covered vault inside the lobby and a public reception. This lobby was designed as a public area where constituents can ask at reception to call down their MP to discuss important matters. It's also where MPs and Lords meet to discuss things.

51.500787, -0.120030

# Waterloo Bridge, Waterloo

(See N bank, p344.)

51.507532, -0.116028

# Southbank Boardwalk

A tree-lined avenue overlooking a wide sandy beach. A beautiful place to spend at low tide.

51.508007, -0.113737

# Gabriel's Wharf, Bankside, Southwark

One of the few places past Tilbury where you can find a sandy beach at low tide. Somewhere to either get on the water or shore, or just sit around. The nearest station is Blackfriars Overground.

51.508464, -0.108914

## Blackfriars Bridge, Southwark

This crossing has strange links to pagan and masonic rituals (see N bank, p346). Perhaps it is most famous for the death by hanging of an Italian banker and freemason, Roberto Calvi, in 1982. He was dubbed 'God's Banker' by the press.
Calvi was chairman of the Vatican Bank, Banco Ambrosiano, which collapsed in 1982 in one of Italy's biggest political scandals. The bank was established in 1896. Calvi's death was investigated by two coroners' inquests, an independent investigation, numerous police investigations and the BBC's Panorama.

51.508648, -0.104439

## Millennium Bridge, Thames Embankment
(See N bank, p346.)

51.508648, -0.104439

Art London Bridge

 ## TATE MODERN, BANKSIDE

Look out from the windows over the skyline of City, Shard and Wharf. Like most of London's galleries, it's free to enter. Charges apply for exhibitions.

51.507707, -0.099363

 ## Southwark Bridge, Southwark

Famous for its appearance in many popular films, most notably *Harry Potter and the Order of the Phoenix* and the infamous last scene of *Lock, Stock and Two Smoking Barrels*.

51.508066, -0.094581

 ## *GOLDEN HINDE*, ST MARY OVERIES DOCK

The original was the first English ship to circumnavigate the globe between 1577 and 1580 under Drake's command. This replica was launched in 1973 and has sailed over 140,000 miles, retracing the historic voyages of the original. It's now a floating museum that describes the challenges of 16th-century navigation.

51.507025, -0.090257

 ## London Bridge, Southwark

Watch the sunrise over the greatest river city in the world. This bridge is the link between the City of London and Southwark.

51.506890, -0.088229

## TOWER BRIDGE, SOUTHWARK

A more iconic landmark than the Tower of London because it so dominates the skyline. Officially opened on 30 June 1894, it still prioritises ship traffic, so the bridge is raised about three times a day – or a thousand times a year.

51.505240, -0.075587

## Tower of London

Epitomised by the phrase 'sent to the Tower' its reputation for torture and death is partly based on the execution of seven here. Most deaths took place to the N of the Tower at the equally notorious Tower Hill, where more than 100 people were executed over a 400-year period.

➤ **Sit** under the shade or shelter of trees in the shadow of Tower Bridge. Direct water access is ⅓ mile W along the shore via concrete steps.

51.506904, -0.075556

Tower Bridge

# 17. HAMMERSMITH BRIDGE TO TOWER BRIDGE, NORTH BANK

Thames Rowing Club

## 10 STEPPING STONES

Lancelot 'Capability' Brown
Hurlingham House
Chelsea Creek
Albert Bridge
Tate Britain
Boudiccan Rebellion
Cleopatra's Needle
Blackfriars Bridge
Millennium Bridge
Tower of London

---

## THE BLUE BOAT

An open-plan kitchen for some real theatre of food on the riverside.

Fulham Reach, Distillery Wharf, Parr's Way, Fulham, W6 9GD

www.theblueboat.co.uk

02030 922090

---

 **Hammersmith Bridge, Hammersmith**

(See S bank, p326.)

51.487712, -0.230966

 **① LANCELOT 'CAPABILITY' BROWN, HAMMERSMITH**

A caste bronze of the legendary Georgian garden landscaper, unveiled in 2017 on Distillery Wharf alongside the Thames Walk. Brown lived in Hammersmith.

51.487327, -0.227383

 **Hammersmith and Fulham Foreshore N, Hammersmith**

Wide open sand banks for hiding.

51.483736, -0.225817

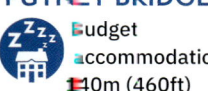
**PREMIER INN,
PUTNEY BRIDGE**

Budget
accommodation
140m (460ft)
from Putney Bridge
Underground station and
70m (230ft) from the
river path.

3 Putney Bridge Approach,
Hurlingham, Fulham,
SW6 3JD

www.premierinn.com

03333 21273

## Hammersmith and Fulham Foreshore S, Fulham

Gravel foreshore for fishing or low tide exploring.

51.479028, -0.224771

## Bishops Park Sculptures, Fulham

Touch the river walk sculptures: Adoration, Protection, Grief and
Leda by sculptor James Wedgwood. They were presented and
placed in the park in 1953 to commemorate the coronation of
Queen Elizabeth II.

51.473137, -0.221062

## Bishop Park, Fulham

Scenes from *The Omen* were shot on location in the park in 1974.
The park was opened in 1893 on land donated by the Church
commissioners. The grass and trees run N of the Thames from
All Saints Church, along a tree-lined avenue to Bishop's Park Rd,
next to Fulham Football club.

51.470833, -0.218258

## All Saints Church, Fulham

Where Henry VIII's doctor was buried.
Sir William Butts played an important role in King Henry's
relations with Thomas Wolsey, while the cardinal lay sick at
Esher in 1529–30. The church was featured in the film *The
Omen.* There's been a church or temple here for more than
1,000 years.

51.468078, -0.212540

## Putney Bridge, Fulham

(See S bank, p327).

51.467082, -0.212909

## Carrara Wharf, Fulham

A small, still water to shelter from bad weather if on water.

51.467322, -0.210835

## HURLINGHAM HOUSE, HURLINGHAM

Walk the gravel foreshore at low tide past one of the most
exclusive private clubs in the world. There's no public access to
the riverbank above the high tide mark.
The Hurlingham Club is a green oasis of tradition set in 42 acres.
The club published the rules of polo in 1873.

51.466525, -0.199278

## Hurlingham House E, Hurlingham

One of the most beautiful parts of riverbank on the Thames at
low tide.

51.465045, -0.201506

## Hurlingham House W, Hurlingham

Almost all private... until the tide goes out. Stunning.

51.464918, -0.198580

## Hurlingham Park, Broomhouse Ln

Boat-launch or walk at low tide under the canopy of trees on the E side of the park. Find the wooded area next to the river and the boat ramp. A stretch of wet woodland and sand.

51.464975, -0.197786

## Imperial Park, Sands End

Sit on grass listening to the poetry of water from the fountain pool. Lime trees smell sweet in late spring.

51.471295, -0.181845

## Chelsea Harbour, Sands End

A 20-acre triangle bounded by the Thames and Counter's Creek to the S and E, and to the W by the W London Line (Overground Network and National Rail) on a viaduct.

51.474735, -0.180266

## ③ CHELSEA CREEK, SANDS END

As upmarket as a waterway in Valderzere. Visit this by kayak. Look for crabs where the creek shallows and empties into the River Thames at Sands End, Fulham.

51.477228, -0.183022

## Cremorne Gardens, Chelsea

James Abbott McNeill Whistler painted Cremorne Gardens by night between 1872 and 1877. He was a resident of Cheyne Walk, a few hundred metres away. The landing stages where visitors arrived by boat are still visible as two attached jetties. The gardens were once much larger.

51.479490, -0.178548

## 118 and 119 Cheyne Walk, Chelsea

The place where J.M.W. Turner spent his last years. He painted from the roof and used the main bedroom as his studio. Turner lived in Chelsea with Sophia Caroline Booth from 1846 until his death in 1851.

The little street has also been home of writer George Eliot, James Bond creator Ian Fleming (his mother lived in Turner's house) and Sir Mick Jagger. King Henry VIII once owned a property here.

51.481285, -0.176809

### Lindsey House (96–101 Cheyne Walk), Chelsea

The home of Brunel and Whistler. Brunel grew up here in the middle section of the house. It's thought to be the oldest house in Kensington and Chelsea.

51.482056, -0.174756

 ### Chelsea Embankment, Chelsea

The Embankment was completed in 1874. Its purpose was to push the river away from riverside houses (like Lindsey Embankment above) because residents complained about the smell of Thames sewage. The Embankment was part of Joseph Bazalgette's groundbreaking plan to create a modern sewage system.

51.482056, -0.174756

 ### Battersea Bridge Gardens, Chelsea

Touch the James McNeill Whistler statue under a poplar tree. There's an old black mulberry that Whistler sat under.

➤ **The** statue stands on the N side of Battersea Bridge on the Cheyne Walk side.

51.482006, -0.173476

 ### Carlyle's House Church, Chelsea

Look for the tribute to Thomas More. He was executed for not agreeing with Henry VIII on his marriage to Anne Boleyn.

51.483068, -0.170927

 ### ④ ALBERT BRIDGE, CHELSEA

London's most beautiful bridge. Best seen from a seat in Albert Bridge Gardens after dark. Watch the water and lights shine off the steel. Built in 1875, the bridge connects Chelsea to Battersea Park westside.

51.483216, -0.167183

 ### A Clockwork Orange, Chelsea

The pedestrian passageway under Albert Bridge was immortalised as the location where Alex is beaten in revenge by a tramp in *A Clockwork Orange*.

51.483216, -0.167183

 ### Memorial to Dante Gabriel Rossetti, Chelsea

A non-functioning water fountain dedicated to the British painter and poet Dante Gabriele Rossetti. Find the 1887 memorial under the trees of Chelsea Embankment Gardens in front of his old home.

51.483673, -0.165846

## Chelsea Embankment Gardens, Chelsea
A thin strip of grass and trees between Battersea and Chelsea, to learn about...not nature, but any of the many statues, and the stories, of those who left some sort of mark, or stain, around London, and beyond.
➤ **Find** S Kensington Underground station (51.494201, -0.174056). Walk just under 1 mile to the river.

51.485471, -0.150597

## The Carabiniers Memorial, Chelsea Embankment
A war memorial to those who died in the Second Boer War (1899–1902) – a red brick, white stone and dark black bronze relief of the 6th Dragoon Guards.

51.485471, -0.150597

## Westminster Boating Base, Pimlico
A youth club in a beautiful small riverside park. Courses from beginner to advanced in canoeing and kayaking. Riverfront balconies are available to hire.
www.westminsterboatingbase.co.uk/activities/kayak-canoe

51.485433, -0.134749

## Pimlico Gardens, Pimlico
Green space and views up and down the river. Continue from here up the pathway to the Houses of Parliament.

51.485541, -0.134074

## St George's Square, Pimlico
A public park full of old trees and a fountain pool. Somewhere to escape in summer or weekends from Westminster crowds.

51.486962, -0.134592

## St Saviour's, Pimlico
A Victorian Gothic church built by the architect Thomas Cundy. Touch the wooden pews and look for the stained-glass arched windows.

51.488581, -0.135439

## TATE BRITAIN, MILLBANK
Known as the National Gallery of British Art from 1897–1932. Founded by Sir Henry Tate, it's home to many of the works of J.M.W. Turner, who bequeathed his collection to the nation.

51.491137, -0.127250

## Parliament Green, Westminster
A lovely place to sit and watch.

51.496787, -0.124428

Boudica

 ## Big Ben, Westminster

**Where British law makers practise the art of governance.**

➤ **Listen** to the architecture of art around Westminster. The traffic, traffic horns, hard office heels across pavement and then... every 15 minutes, Big Ben. Westminster is everything art should be. Offensive, beautiful and alive.

51.496787, -0.124428

 ## ⑥ BOUDICCAN REBELLION, WESTMINSTER BRIDGE

English sculptor Thomas Thornycroft spent 27 years working on the statue until he died in 1885. It was erected at Westminster in 1902. Surrounded by Westminster Palace, London Eye, Big Ben and the Thames, the statue depicts Boudicca – the legendary Celtic queen of the Iceni tribe who led an uprising against the Roman armies in 60 AD.

➤ **Find** Westminster Underground station, Bridge St, SW1A 2JR. Walk 80m (260ft) to Westminster Bridge. The statue stands at the entrance to the bridge with the London Eye on the other side of the river in the foreground.

51.500803, -0.121852

 ## Victoria Embankment Gardens, Whitehall Gardens

Peaceful fountains and seasonal floral displays. Statues and memorials blend history and stories.

51.504797, -0.123418

 ## Hungerford (Charing Cross) Railway Bridge & FBs

Claude Monet painted Charing Cross Bridge in 1901, during the last of three consecutive winter trips here. He was fascinated with the 'golden light' of early morning, which he said filtered through London's smog. The smog has gone, but the golden light remains – as fog. Monet stayed on the sixth floor of the Savoy Hotel, so he could see the railway bridge and the neo-Gothic towers of Westminster.

51.506263, -0.120022

### ⑦ CLEOPATRA'S NEEDLE, VICTORIA EMBANKMENT

One of London's most spectacular monuments.

The Egyptian obelisk from Alexandria is based on the river stairs of the Victoria Thames Embankment. It originally stood at Heliopolis and was carved in honour of Thutmose III, King of Egypt, in about 1500 BC. Mehemet Ali, the Ottoman ruler of Egypt, presented the 20m (68ft) stone pillar to the UK in 1819, as a 'thank you' to the nation for Lord Nelson's victory at the Battle of the Nile. Delivery was not included. The British government initially refused to finance ferrying the giant monolith across the Bay of Biscay, so it stayed buried on its side in sand at Alexandria for more than 50 years.

Businessman Sir Erasmus Wilson put up a £10,000 bounty for anyone who could safely deliver the obelisk, and in 1877 John Dixon accepted the challenge. His engineer brother, Waynman Dixon, built an iron cylinder 'pontoon barge', the 'Cleopatra Iron Vessel', to carry the 193 tonnes of granite. Six men drowned trying to save the monument after Dixon's iron barge almost sunk in a storm. The needle was eventually recovered and erected on the London embankment in 1878. A tribute to the six men who lost their lives is attached to the stone.

51.508714, -0.120152

### Waterloo Bridge, Victoria Embankment

A work of art to admire. Five spans of concrete, clad in Portland stone. Monet painted 41 scenes from here between 1900 to 1904. Along with his contemporaries J.M.W. Turner and James Abbott McNeill Whistler, Monet was mesmerised by the 'atmospheric effects' of fog, smog and steam around Thames architecture – especially bridges.

51.509901, -0.117994

### Middle Temple Gardens, Holborn

Trees, roses and temples. The scene of Shakespeare's meeting between Richard Plantagenet and John Beaufort, which sparked the Wars of the Roses. The garden's real story is stranger than fiction. It was once part of the headquarters of the Knights Templar until the order was dissolved in 1312. The Knights Hospitallers took over the site until Henry VIII seized it in 1540. The gardens later passed to English barristers in 1608. The roses, flower beds and grounds remain the headquarters of the British legal profession.

➤ **Temple**, Victoria Embankment, is the nearest Underground station.

51.511186, -0.110313

### Statue of Isambard Kingdom Brunel, Victoria Embankment

The genius engineer who worked and learnt from nature, Brunel blended new ideas and inventions in engineering to solve problems that complemented surrounding nature.

51.510772, -0.115225

 ### Temple Pier, Victoria Embankment

Boat-hire services under a covered dock, directly opposite Temple station.

51.510560, -0.114964

 ### Gabriel's Pier, S Bank

A wooden deck pier over a low tide sandy beach.

51.508363, -0.109516

 ### Sir John Soane Museum, Holborn

One of most important museums in London is a series of townhouses once owned by this brilliant London architect. He was an almost obsessive collector of paintings, drawings and sculptures – most of which are still kept here.

51.515427, -0.115727

Victoria Tower Gardens

###  8 BLACKFRIARS BRIDGE, BLACKFRIARS

The bridge name commemorates a 13th-century Dominican monastery that was once here. The monks were known as black friars because of their dark cloaks. It's unclear why this site was so important to the ancients – but probably for the freshwater springs that have disappeared. Some pagan rituals are still carried out in and around the bridge at various annual festivals – but they tend to be random and infrequent.

51.510994, -0.104369

##  Rennie Garden, Southwark

Wooded garden down to a low tide beach, with plane trees, tulips and crocus blossoming in spring. Access the park from the bridge.

51.508242, -0.104115

###  9 MILLENNIUM BRIDGE, SOUTHWARK

Walk the steel that links Tate Modern with St Paul's, a remarkable connection between art and architecture.
The bridge was designed to form a viewing frame around both St Paul's and Tate Modern, from the opposite sides. The Tate Modern end is near the Globe Theatre and the Bankside Gallery. The northern end is next to the City of London School, below St Paul's Cathedral.

51.510173, -0.098438

Queenhithe Mosaic

### Queenhithe Dock and Wharf, London

The only remaining Celtic-Saxon dock in the world – this was a working dock for over a thousand years.

51.510328, -0.095099

### Queenhithe Mosiac, London

A 9m (30ft) mosaic on a wall depicts key moments in the city's last 2,000 years of history in a timeline – including the Battle of Hastings, the Great Fire, plagues and the Blitz.

51.510328, -0.095099

### River Walbrook, London

The Walbrook is a subterranean river in London.
The brook's name may come from weala broc, which means 'brook of the foreigners'. Foreigners were native Britons who were considered 'Welsh' by Saxons. Some historians believe it possible that the name references a 'Briton'-speaking quarter in London after the Saxon occupation of the E and London. The division of the city by the Walbrook was linked to Britons who lived on Cornhill to the E, while the Saxons lived on Ludgate Hill to the W.

51.509400, -0.092800

### Old London Bridge, London

It was always falling down... from 1825–1967. The Bridge was widened from 15–20m (52–65ft) in 1902. Unfortunately the extra weight was too much, so it's gone.

51.508132, -0.087800

### Public views terrace, London

A beautiful terrace overlooking the Thames with a view of London's skyline. Come here at night.

51.508984, -0.085677

### Church of Saint Magnus-the-Martyr, London

Designed by Sir Christopher Wren and built in 1671, this was where people crossing the Old London Bridge used to enter the City. The church sat on the approach Rd to the Old London Bridge (demolished in 1831) for 600 years.
The church is referenced in *Oliver Twist*, by Charles Dickens, and in the poem 'The Waste Land', by T.S. Eliot.

51.509389, -0.086108

### TOWER BRIDGE, LONDON

Palace, a fortress and a prison. One of London's top historic places. Built by Gundulf, bishop of Rochester, in 1078 for William the Conqueror.

51.507935, -0.078242

# 18. TOWER BRIDGE TO WOOLWICH FOOT TUNNEL, SOUTH BANK

## REBIRTH

E London s the UK's best rewilding programme. Not a 'rewilded' conservationist enclosure, but a natural and accessible ecology.

It's an access zone to the river, thanks to the 1980s-style Docklands redevelopment.

Bats hunt over low tide creeks. Shellfish filter-feed between reeds. Kingfishers fall into brackish pools of knotted hedge parsley. Saltmarsh grass and marsh dock grow in between tides.

And people... connecting with each other, touching nature, working and playing.

## 10 STEPPING STONES

St Mary the Virgin
Pageant Stairs Obelisk
Greenland Lock Marina
Deptford Creek
Greenwich Foot Tunnel S
Jetty Wharf
The Quantum Cloud
Greenwich Marsh
Thames Barrier
Woolwich Tunnel

**THE ANGEL**

A pub with well-priced ales. The best river views of Tower Bridge are upstairs.

101 Bermondsey Wall E, Rotherhithe, SE16 4NB

www.facebook.com/angelrotherhithe

02073 943214

## Tower Bridge, London

The Tower of London – palace, a fortress and a prison.

51.507935, -0.078242

## Shad Thames, London

A historic, cobbled street next to Tower Bridge in Bermondsey. This is where the largest warehouse complex in London was based in the 19th century.

51.502400, -0.070800

## ST MARY THE VIRGIN, ROTHERHITHE

Look for the maritime connections. Timber from the HMS *Temeraire* was used to make the communion table in the Lady Chapel when the warship was broken up in 1838. There are two bishop's chairs made from the same salvaged wood. Turner famously captured the ship's final journey to the breaker's yard at Deptford in his painting The Fighting Temeraire. The painting can be seen in the National Gallery.

51.501444, -0.053956

## Cobbles, St Mary the Virgin, Rotherhithe

Walk the cobbled streets that the Pilgrim Fathers trod before leaving for America.

The 18th-century church in St Marychurch Street has many links with the Pilgrim Fathers. The crew of the Mayflower ship worshipped here, and some were buried in the crypt. Captain Christopher Jones attended services here. There is a monument to Jones and the Pilgrims in the churchyard. Jones is buried somewhere in the churchyard, but no one seems to knows where. He wasn't famous when he died. The original church was Saxon, built on foundations of Roman bricks. The church would flood regularly as it was so close to the riverside.

51.501444, -0.053956

## Brunel Museum, Rotherhithe

A quirky museum about the world's first under-river tunnel. There are guided tours for exploring the tunnel shaft and the history of how the tunnel was built.

51.501574, -0.052856

## Thames Tunnel, Rotherhithe

Brunel described the tunnel as the 8th wonder of the world when it was built.

51.502021, -0.052773

## THE MAYFLOWER PUB

The oldest pub on the Thames, with a great story. A candlelit restaurant on the decked jetty beside the 1620 mooring point of the Pilgrim Fathers' Mayflower ship. Warm up by the open fire imagining who might have been sitting here more than 400 years ago.

117 Rotherhithe St, Rotherhithe, SE16 4NF

www.mayflowerpub.co.uk

02072 374088

Cumberland Wharf

## Cumberland Wharf, Rotherhithe

Touch the statue of a Bermondsey boy with his dog in 1920, beside the ghost of a Pilgrim Father. This is supposed to be where the pilgrims set sail from London.

The statue was commissioned in 1991 as part of a Docklands redevelopment scheme. Locals campaigned to have the statue upgraded in 2017. More than 50 locals went to the reopening. The event ended with everyone singing John Bunyan's pilgrim hymn, He Who Would Valiant Be. Locals celebrated The Mayflower's 400th anniversary at this site in 2020 too.

51.502374, -0.051729

## Rotherhithe Beach, Rotherhithe

Sit in the sand at sunset and look over the greatest city in the world. Feel the tide lapping your feet — more surreal than a night in the company of William Blake.

51.502903, -0.0515347

## Lavender Pond Park, Rotherhithe

A secret garden of wet meadows, native trees and a pond. It can get grubby and overgrown in between tidy ups.

51.506207, -0.037763

## ② PAGEANT STAIRS OBELISK, ROTHERHITHE

Erected during the redevelopment of the Pageant's Wharf and Surrey Docks in the 1980s, the monolith stands without an inscription.

The obelisk is square and pointed at the top. It's known as the Benben stone as it resembles the top stone on a pyramid.

In the Heliopolitan creation myth of Egypt, the Benben stone was the sacred mound that rose from the spring waters, giving birth to life. A representation of the same Benben stone sits on top of Cleopatra's Needle (see p344). The obelisk lines up with the main axis through Canary Wharf on the opposite bank. The same Benben stone symbol was built into the pointed tower of Canary Wharf.

51.506733, -0.035341

Rotherhithe Beach Reach

Lavender Wharf

### Pageant Wharf, Rotherhithe

Royal Navy ships were constructed here between 1741 and 1744. The yard fell into decline after becoming a ship-breaker. The steps are steep and lead down to a narrow section of foreshore of scattered stones and bricks.

➤ **Walking** along the side of the Thames only became possible thanks to the 1980s dockland redevelopment.

51.506718, -0.035329

### Cuckold's Point, Rotherhithe

It takes its name from a post with a pair of horns on top indicating a cuckold: a man whose wife had cheated on him. The post once commemorated the starting point of the Horn Fair, opposite to what is now the Canary Wharf Pier.

It's said that the fair was given as a concession by a former king who had seduced the wife of a miller after a hunting trip. The story is linked to old Welsh folklore about a pre-patriarchal age.

51.504452, -0.033812

### Surrey Docks City Farm, Rotherhithe

A working city farm that teaches visitors farming, animal care and horticulture. The farm produces crafts and other products for sale.

51.499722, -0.033080

Pageant Stairs Obelisk

###  **③ GREENLAND PIER, ROTHERHITHE**

Buzzing with nesting birds in spring and offering good views of the financial capital of London, Canary Wharf and the Shard. A ferry sometimes operates from the pier to Canary Wharf. Sitting by the dockside in sunshine is lovely.

51.494730, -0.032782

###  Greenland Lock Marina, Docklands

London's largest marina, 2½ miles downstream from Tower Bridge and 1½ miles upstream from Greenwich.

➤ **It's** an excellent base for cruising the Thames and the River Medway.

51.493585, -0.034703

###  Queen's Stairs (Drake's Steps), Foreshore

The steps named after Sir Francis Drake, who was knighted here aboard the *Golden Hinde* by Queen Elizabeth I.

51.489646, -0.030182

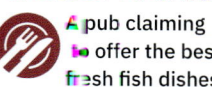

## Pepys Park Cannons, Deptford

With lots of blackberries and rosehips, this spot offers great views over the Thames and Canary Wharf. The Pepys Estate nearby was once one of London's largest council estates.

51.487916, -0.032388

## River Ravensbourne, Deptford

The river empties into the Thames at the tidal reach known as Deptford Creek. Deptford is named after a ford over River Ravensbourne. Deptford Dockyard, the first of the Royal Dockyards, was busiest from the mid-16th to late-19th centuries. The Ravensbourne Morris Men dance up the Beltaine Sunrise at Caesars Well, the source of the Ravensbourne River, every year on 1 May at 5.32am.

51.483500, -0.018500

## DEPTFORD CREEK, DEPTFORD

Find shellfish on the foreshore at low tide. One of the best places to get down to the waterside. Creekside Discovery Centre sometimes offers low-tide walks looking for plants.

51.482762, -0.018350

## Peter the Great Statue, Deptford Creek

A quirky statue commemorating The Tsar of Russia, Peter the Great, of all people.

He visited London in 1698 on a European Tour to learn how to modernise the Russian Navy. His plan was to study the English science of shipbuilding. Deptford was the Royal Naval Dockyard in 1698. Ships captained by Sir Walter Raleigh and Sir Francis Drake sailed from Deptford. The writer and diarist Samuel Pepys worked from Deptford. The monument to Peter the Great was opened in 2001 to commemorate the 300th anniversary of Peter's Great Embassy visit to England. The sculpture by Mikhail Shemyakin contains lots of strange symbols from various themes, ages and cultures.

51.482762, -0.018350

## GREENWICH FOOT TUNNEL S, GREENWICH

A unique experience... cross under the River Thames.

➤ **The** tunnel opened in 1902 between the Isle of Dogs and Greenwich – a feat of engineering. The light and sounds are spooky. Take the lift – and have fun.

51.4832445, -0.010241

## Cutty Sark, Greenwich

The entrance/exit to Greenwich is marked by the world's most famous tea clipper. The ship explores Britain's former role in empire and sea trade.

51.482832, -0.009767

##  Greenwich foreshore, Greenwich

Miles of sand and shingle beach.

51.484639, -0.004587

##  Crowleys Wharf, Greenwich

Steps down to the foreshore opposite a line of London plane trees. The steps are often closed, so take advantage when they're open. They're also known as Golden Anchor Stairs and take their name from the 19th-century public house that was here until 1902. The pub was demolished to make way for Greenwich Power Station.

51.486049, -0.001232

##  Greenwich Park, Greenwich

Look for red deer around the enclosed areas of the park. The gravel heaths of One Tree Hill and Crooms Hills have good views.

51.477083, 0.001464

## Greenwich Chestnuts, Greenwich

An avenue of trees where pipistrelle bats feed at dusk. The trees are more than 400 years old.

51.478839, 0.001322

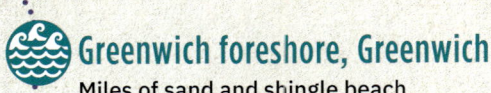

Royal Naval College, Greenwich

Jetty Wharf beach and trees

 ### Greenwich Reach, Greenwich

The Royal Naval College. The buildings once used by the Royal Hospital School in Greenwich were taken over by the National Maritime Museum in 1934.

51.481202, -0.005389

 ### JETTY WHARF, GREENWICH

Sit in the shade of derelict wharf and trees. Not a park, but a wild collective of willows and elder that periodically joins up with hardy invasive types, including staghorn sumac and others, to form a protective grove around a tiny camber of beach.

51.494442, 0.000929

 ### A slice of reality sculptor, Greenwich

A 'slice' of the sand dredger *Arco Trent*; getting very rusty now. The old cargo ship is mounted on a plinth. The ship's plumbing and pipe are visible.

➤ **The** riverside path that skirts around the giant O2 arena has a few other sculptures too.

51.504097, -0.000165

 ### N Greenwich Beach, Greenwich

A low-tide sand and views. Beach access can be difficult.

51.504682, 0.001608

London cable car

### 7 THE QUANTUM CLOUD

A 30m (98ft) sculpture of a human figure inside a cloud or dome. The piece, by Antony Gormley, represents the interconnectedness of all things. The art – created from steel tetrahedral units – was inspired by quantum physics and chaos theory. It was completed in 1999.

51.501491, 0.0083878

### 8 GREENWICH MARSH, GREENWICH

A rich habitat of freshwater lakes – best visited when meadows are in flower. Alive with dragonflies and bats. Bird hides offer great spots for nature watching.

51.495658, 0.016006

Greenwich reeds and foreshore

###  THAMES BARRIER, CHARLTON

A retractable barrier that protects London from the N Sea's tidal surges. London has suffered flooding for thousands of years – but it was the floods of 1953 that prompted action.

The Waverley Committee was established to investigate how to prevent another 1953 episode. The committee recommended a barrier as a better alternative to seawalls, which had been in place for hundreds of years. The barrier has been operational since 1982.

51.494890, 0.037176

###  The Thames Barrier Park, Charlton

Find the yew hedges that represent a green dock. Avenues of birch trees add something to the pioneering spirit of it all. The park is 34 acres.

51.494890, 0.037176

###  WOOLWICH TUNNEL, WOOLWICH

One of two subterranean foot tunnels under the Thames (see Greenwich Foot Tunnel, p355. Assume the lifts are out of order and you won't be disappointed. Takes about 10 minutes to walk or two minutes to cycle to Newham. More than 1,000 people use the tunnel each day.

> **Find** Waterfront Leisure Centre, Woolwich High St, London, SE18 6DL, and the entrance to the Woolwich Foot Tunnel where the TP meets the ECP.

51.494638, 0.062814

Woolwich Foot Tunnel

# 18. TOWER BRIDGE TO WOOLWICH FOOT TUNNEL, NORTH BANK

Pool of London

## 10 STEPPING STONES

St Katharine Docks Lock
Foreshore, Wapping
Limehouse Lock
Canary Wharf
Millwall Docks
Island Gardens/Greenwich Foot Tunnel
S Dock Lock
Settlers Memorial
Bow Creek Ecology Park
Woolwich Foot Tunnel

 **① ST KATHARINE DOCKS LOCK, WAPPING**

The docks opened in 1828, but they were redundant by 1968 because they were too shallow to take large ships. Now a marina, housing development and leisure site. There are also hotels, shops and restaurants.

51.506294, -0.071887

 ### Historic Cannon Bollard, Wapping

Bollards made from Napoleonic cannon in Wapping. England had a glut of French cannons following Napoleon's defeat. The muzzle half of the cannon had the cannon ball welded into the top with the other half sunk into the ground.

51.503646, -0.057489

## THE DICKENS INN

A pub with restaurants housed in an 18th-century warehouse in St Katharine Docks. Opened in 1976 by Cedric Charles Dickens, a great-grandson to the famous author.

The Dickens Inn, Wapping, E1W 1UH

www.dickensinn.co.uk

02074 82208

## Execution Dock, Wapping

King Henry's Stairs. Well, not anymore; the stairs are gone, replaced with a steel ladder.
> **Climb** down on the Thames shore at low tide.

51.503655, -0.057356

## FORESHORE, WAPPING

Foreshore is accessible at low tide by various stairs along the N bank of the Thames. The foreshore is a mixture of sand, mud and rock. Hire a kayak at Shadwell Basin. Wapping is the nearest Overground station.

51.507389, -0.050315

## LIMEHOUSE LOCK, LIMEHOUSE

Front door to the Thames. Beyond lie the Cotswolds, the Ridgeway, the Grand Union Canal, and the Severn.

51.509948, -0.036615

## → DETOUR - CYCLING 450M (1,475FT) – 5 MILES

### S Dock Marina, Limehouse

The marina connects the Thames with the Regent's Canal. S Dock Marina is London's largest marina, 2½ miles downstream of Tower Bridge.
> **Find** the FP that joins the TP (51.509672, -0.036974) and walk NE.

51.510774, -0.035218

### Limehouse Cut, Limehouse

Find the canal path to Stratford, the River Lee and on into N Essex and Essex Way to Harwich.

51.511776, -0.032220

### St Anne's Church, Limehouse

A churchyard full of giant London plane trees – tall, leafy. Touch the bark. The strange camouflage-patterned flakes, like the skin of a snake.

The Rod of Asclepius takes its name from the Greek god Asclepius, who was associated with medicinal arts. Land is medicine. The Tree of Hippocrates is the plane tree under which, according to legend, Hippocrates of Kos (father of medicine) taught his pupils the art of medicine. Two immigrant plane trees from the USA and Greece were blended together to produce the species known as London plane. It's one of England's greatest exports. China has more London plane in its cities than any other tree. Shanghai is full of London plane. The reason they're so popular? They clean the air (of pollution) better than any other plant.

51.511654, -0.030343

### BREAD STREET KITCHEN & BAR

A riverside FP alongside a restaurant with toilet access.

44 Narrow Street, Limehouse, E14 8DJ

www.gordonramsay
restaurants.com/the-
narrow

02075 927950

### SMITH'S OF WAPPING

Food service under the motto 'Famous for fish'. Close to Wapping Overground station and Tower Bridge Underground station, featuring floor-to-ceiling windows with river views.

22 Wapping High St, London E1W 1NJ

www.smithsrestaurants.
com/smiths-wapping

02074 883456

### THE PROSPECT OF WHITBY

One of London's oldest pubs, next to the Shadwell Basin. Spectacular views over the Thames, including from the beer garden and first-floor balcony and terrace.

57 Wapping Wall, Wapping, E1W 3SH

www.greeneking.co.uk/
pubs/greater-london/
prospect-of-whitby

02074 811095

Limehouse Cut from Rectory Gardens

## St Anne's Church Pyramid, Limehouse

There is a mysterious pyramid in the churchyard of the London plane, designed by the architect and freemason Nicholas Hawksmoor.

The pyramid is inscribed with a carving of a unicorn and the words 'wisdom of Solomon' in both English and Hebrew. Made out of Portland stone, the pyramid would have been nearly white when it was built. The churchyard also features a two-sided gravestone from the 1760s. One side is inscribed normally, while the other is upside down.

51.511654, -0.030343

## Regents Canal, Limehouse

A canal towpath and navigable access to Regents Canal – all the way to the Grand Union Canal. Travel via Regents Park. Kings Cross and Islington are ahead.

➤ **The** canal provides a link from the Paddington arm of the Grand Union Canal, 500m (1,640ft) NW of Paddington Basin in the W to the Limehouse Basin and the Thames in the E.

51.512993, -0.036139

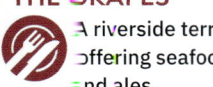

**THE GRAPES**

A riverside terrace offering seafood and ales.

76 Narrow Street,
Limehouse E14 8BP

www.thegrapes.co.uk

02079 374396

## Hertford Union Canal, Limehouse

Find the Regents Canal and take the R fork at S Hackney along the Hertford Union Canal cycle path.

➤ **Follow** the River Lee into the River Stort of N Essex via Epping Forest, Bishops Stortford and Saffron Walden to eventually connect to the Icknield Way.

51.509731, -0.036928

## London Museum Docklands, Canary Wharf

A museum covering the history of the River Thames over 500 years, built in warehouses on the Isle of Dogs, not far from Canary Wharf. Entry is free.

51.507582, -0.024036

## ④ CANARY WHARF, ISLE OF DOGS

At 235m (770ft), this was the UK's tallest building when it was completed in 1991.

➤ **Find** the brass strip on the Canary Wharf Estate that runs along West India Avenue and crosses Westferry Circus. The Canary Wharf Estate was developed around a symmetrical axis that runs through Canary Wharf Tower and Westferry Circus. The brass strip line extends W, across the Thames, through the stone obelisk at Pageant Stairs on the S bank.

51.505577, -0.026833

St Anne's Church, Limehouse

Canary Wharf from Olympian Way, North Greenwich

 ## Pyramid Roof, Canary Wharf

Look for the 40m (130ft) high pyramid on top of the Canary Wharf skyscraper.

The skyscraper architect César Pelli described the pyramid design as strengthening the 'axis bundi' – the vertical line with which ancient stone masons connected buildings to heaven and earth.

51.505577, -0.026833

 ## Canary Wharf Pier, Canary Wharf

The marshes from Canary Wharf to Isle of Dogs were once peppered in smock windmills. Those mills – pyramid-shaped money-machines of the first part of the 18th century – were replaced by something even more profitable and pyramidical in nature.

Deregulated money markets… and the tower on Canary Wharf.

51.505144, -0.027969

## THE GUN PUB

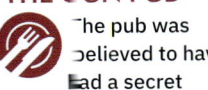

The pub was believed to have had a secret passage connected to a horse owned by Nelson. Rumoured to be where Nelson and Lady Hamilton met. A room above the bar is called the Lady Hamilton Room. The pub is reputed to be haunted by her ghost.

27 Coldharbour, Docklands, London E14 9N

www.thegundocklands.com

02075 90075

## ⑤ MILLWALL DOCKS, ISLE OF DOGS

A giant ramp into the Thames. An area for open-water swimming, kayaking, paddleboarding and sailing. The Royal Yachting Association offers sailing courses.

51.493987, -0.024841

## Masthouse Terrace Pier, Isle of Dogs

Constructed in 1857 for the sideways launch of Brunel's SS *Great Eastern* into the Thames.

The launch site is a tight meander on the Thames, between the Isle of Dogs and Deptford. At the time of its launch in 1858, the SS *Great Eastern* was the largest ship the world had ever seen. She was also the first ship to be constructed almost entirely of metal. She was built to carry passengers and cargo between England and Australia. Cost restraints meant building a new dock to accommodate the largest ship was not affordable. So Brunel and his partner Russell chose 'Napier Yard', next to Millwall Dock. Millwall was at the centre of 19th-century shipbuilding.

51.487584, -0.021758

## ⑥ ISLAND GARDENS/GREENWICH FOOT TUNNEL, ISLE OF DOGS

The Greenwich foot tunnel N entrance is in the park. Island Gardens is the view of Greenwich featured in Canaletto's famous 18th century painting, A View of Greenwich from the River.

➤ **Find** Mudchute DLR station, Spindrift Ave, E14 9ZT. Exit on the E Ferry Rd and walk R ⅓ mile to Manchester Rd. Turn L another 220m (720ft) before turning R again on to Douglas Path down to the Thames, the tunnel and the gardens. The café in the park is open most days.

51.486510, -0.009433

## ⑦ S DOCK LOCK, DOCKLANDS

Watch the blue bridge rise over the home of the Canal and River Trust. Some of the best views of old Docklands and the financial centre Canary Wharf.

51.501377, -0.008721

## ⑧ SETTLERS MEMORIAL, BLACKWALL

The First Settlers Memorial was unveiled in 1928 by the American ambassador. Dedicated to the first settlers of America who sailed from Blackwall in 1606 in three small merchant ships.
It was unveiled again in 1951 with the addition of a bronze mermaid by Harold Brown on top.
Barratts developers restored it in 1999 and added an astrolabe to replace the mermaid.

51.507894, 0.000358

## E India Dock Basin, Blackwall

Look for warblers in the reeds around the flooded basin. The dock today is like a millpond, but 200 years ago it was one of London's busiest ports delivering spices from the Far East.

51.509151, 0.004076

## River Lea, Leamouth

The furthest E of all Thames main tributaries. It's known as Bow Creek as it empties into the Thames.

51.507100, 0.009200

## Lee Navigation, Leamouth

A canalised river that incorporates the River Lea. It flows from Hertford Castle Weir to the Thames at Bow Creek.

51.507100, 0.009200

## River Lea, Bow Creek

Look for sand martins that nest and feed around Royal Dock and Lower Lee.

➤ **Pass** under the A13 walkway to Wharfside Rd for the park. The DLR service runs R through the middle of the park.

51.512876, 0.002948

## BOW CREEK ECOLOGY PARK, BLACKWALL, TOWER HAMLETS

A little island of woodland close to the E bank of Bow Creek. It's actually a bend in the river made up of streams, ponds and meadows. It's best in summer when the wildflowers are out (formerly Limmo Peninsula Ecological Park).

51.511543, 0.003195

## Bargehouse Causeway, Blackwall

➤ **Find** the launch site on the N bank of Bugsby's Reach.

51.508248, 0.002886

## WOOLWICH FOOT TUNNEL, N WOOLWICH

The TP starts/ends at the entrance to a tunnel on the other side of the river. Surrounded by the sounds of industry and river traffic, and E of the Thames flood barrier. It's as far from the Thames source as it's possible to get on the trail. From the calm surrounding of a bubbling underground spring, to the chaos of a tunnel beside a flood barrier.

➤ **The** ECP joins the TP from here, where everything and anything is still possible. Even cheating time.

51.498638, 0.061837

CONWAY
Bloomsbury Publishing Plc
50 Bedford Square, London, WC1B 3DP, UK
Bloomsbury Publishing Ireland Limited
29 Earlsfort Terrace, Dublin 2, D02 AY28, Ireland

BLOOMSBURY, CONWAY and the Conway logo are trademarks of Bloomsbury Publishing Plc

First published in Great Britain 2026

This book is a guide for when you spend time outdoors. Undertaking any activity outdoors carries with it some risks that cannot be entirely eliminated. For example, you might get lost on a route or caught in bad weather. Before you spend time outdoors, we therefore advise that you always take the necessary precautions, such as checking weather forecasts and ensuring that you have all the equipment you need. Any walking routes that are described in this book should not be relied upon as a sole means of navigation, so we recommend that you refer to an Ordnance Survey map or authoritative equivalent.

This book may also reference businesses and venues. Whilst every effort is made by the author and the publisher to ensure the accuracy of the business and venue information contained in our books before they go to print, changes to such information can occur during the production and lifetime of a publication. Therefore, we also advise that you check with businesses or venues for the latest information before setting out.

All internet addresses given in this book were correct at the time of going to press. Bloomsbury Publishing Plc does not have any control over, or responsibility for, any third-party websites referred to or in this book. The author and the publisher regret any inconvenience caused if some facts have changed or sites have ceased to exist, but can accept no responsibility for any such changes.

A catalogue record for this book is available from the British Library

Library of Congress Cataloguing-in-Publication data has been applied for

ISBN: PB: 978-1-8448-6676-2; ePub: 978-1-8448-6677-9; ePDF: 978-1-8448-6678-6

2 4 6 8 10 9 7 5 3 1

Typeset in IBM Plex Sans by Nick Avery Design
Printed and bound in China by RR Donnelley Asia Printing Solutions Ltd

MIX
Paper | Supporting
responsible forestry
FSC
www.fsc.org FSC® C144853

To find out more about our authors and books visit www.bloomsbury.com and sign up for our newsletters
For product safety related questions contact productsafety@bloomsbury.com